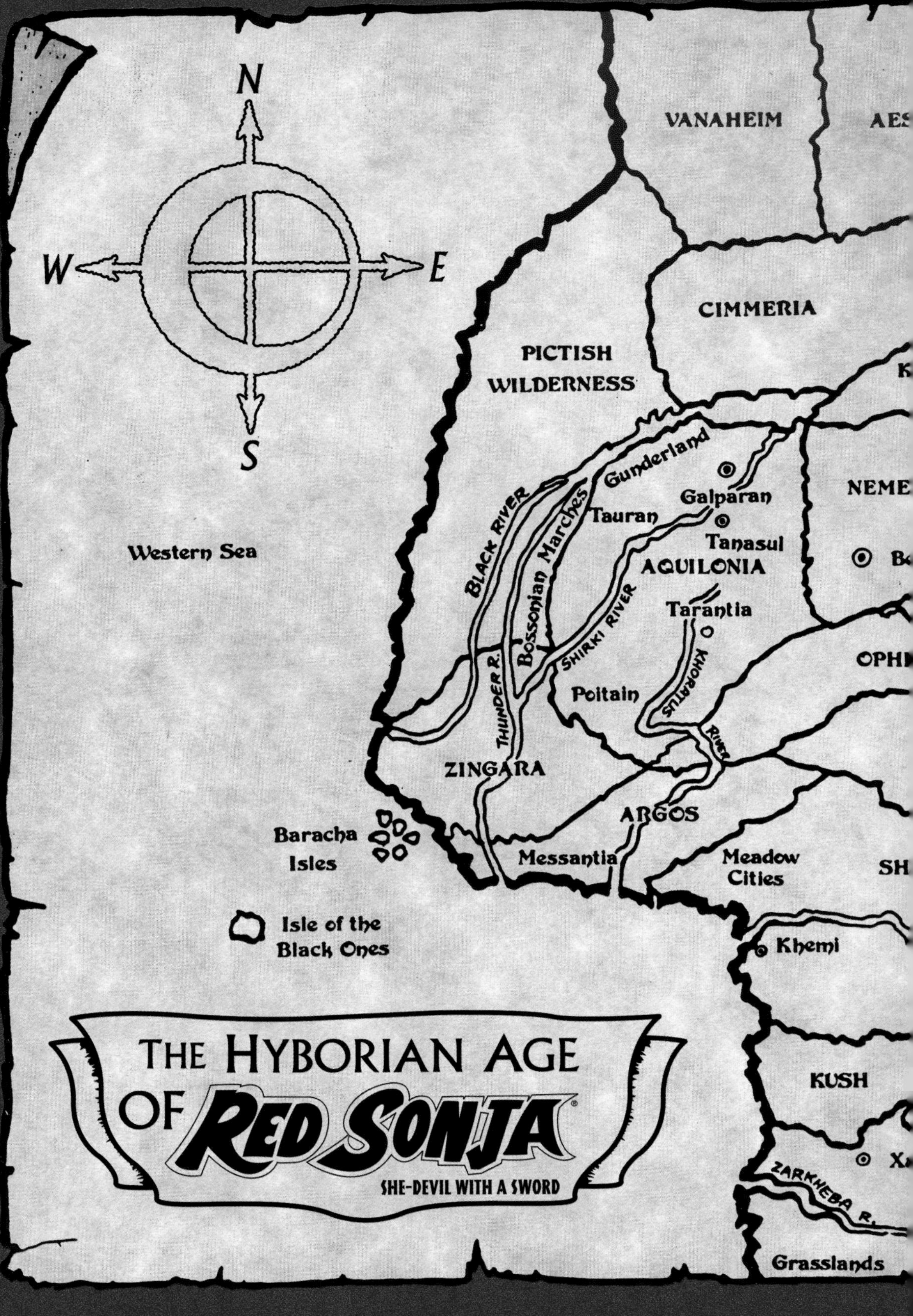
N
W
E
S
VANAHEIM
AES
CIMMERIA
PICTISH WILDERNESS
K
Gunderland
Galparan
NEME
Tauran
Tanasul
Western Sea
AQUILONIA
BLACK RIVER
Bossonian Marches
SHIRKI RIVER
Tarantia
OPH
THUNDER R.
KHORATUS
RIVER
Poitain
ZINGARA
ARGOS
Baracha Isles
Messantia
Meadow Cities
SH
Isle of the Black Ones
Khemi
KUSH
ZARKHEBA R.
Grasslands
THE HYBORIAN AGE OF RED SONJA
SHE-DEVIL WITH A SWORD

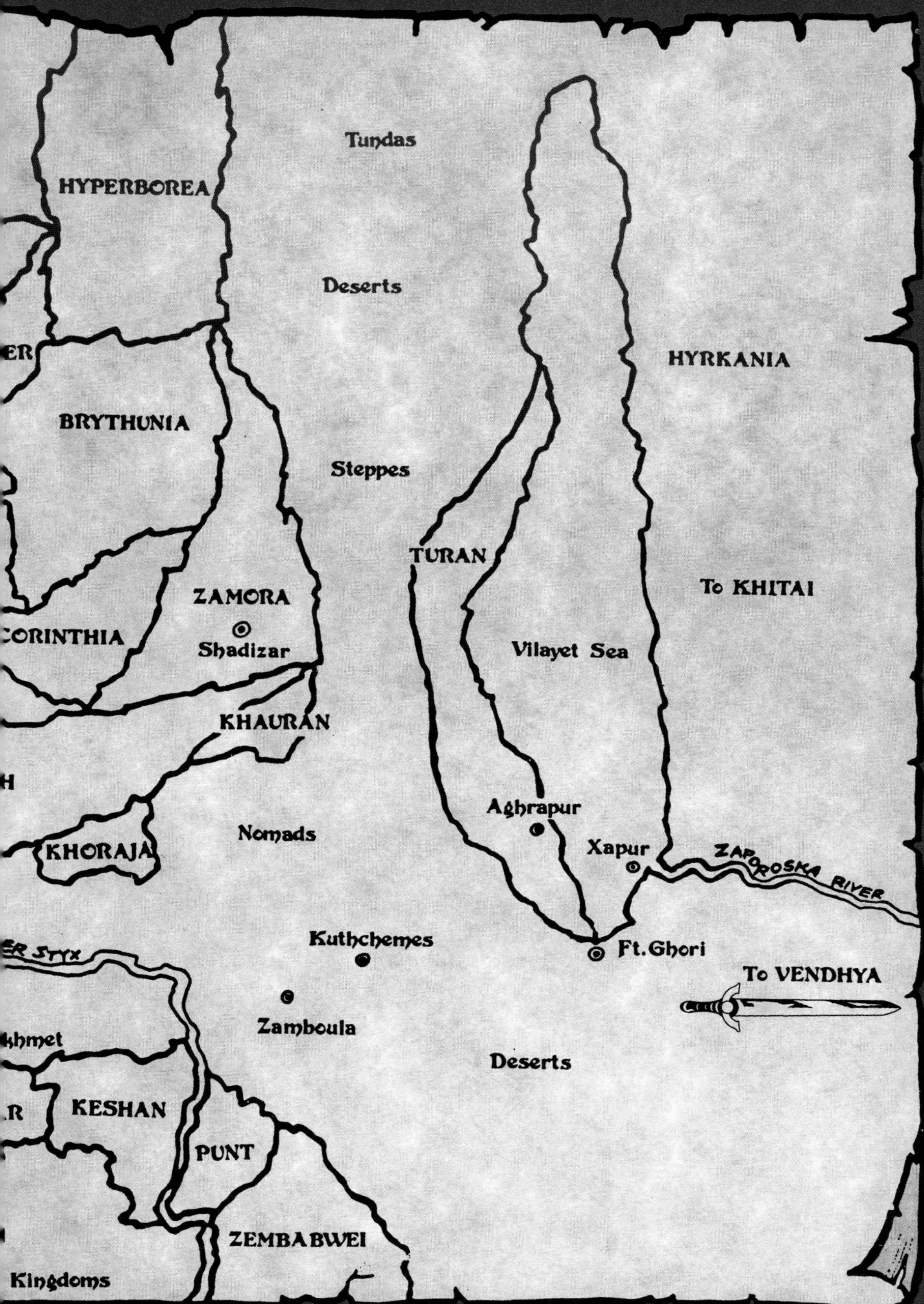
Tundas
HYPERBOREA
Deserts
HYRKANIA
BRYTHUNIA
Steppes
TURAN
To KHITAI
ZAMORA
Shadizar
Vilayet Sea
KHAURAN
Aghrapur
Nomads
Xapur
KHORAJA
ZAPOROSKA RIVER
Kuthchemes
Ft. Ghori
To VENDHYA
Zamboula
Deserts
KESHAN
PUNT
ZEMBABWEI
Kingdoms

Dynamite Entertainment Presents

RED SONJA®

WRATH OF THE GODS

Dedicated to **Robert E. Howard**

plot **Luke Lieberman** & **Ethan Ryker**

script **Luke Lieberman**

art **Walter Geovani**

colors **Vinicius Andrade**

cover **Lucio Parrillo**

letters **Simon Bowland**

based on the heroine created by **Robert E. Howard**

This volume collects Red Sonja: Wrath of the Gods issues one through five by Dynamite Entertainment.

Executive Editor - Red Sonja **Luke Lieberman**

Special thanks to **Arthur Lieberman** *at Red Sonja llc.*

DYNAMITE ENTERTAINMENT
www.dynamiteentertainment.com

DYNAMITE ENTERTAINMENT
NICK BARRUCCI — PRESIDENT
JUAN COLLADO — CHIEF OPERATING OFFICER
JOSEPH RYBANDT — EDITOR
JOSH JOHNSON — CREATIVE DIRECTOR
RICH YOUNG — DIR. BUSINESS DEVELOPMENT
JASON ULLMEYER — GRAPHIC DESIGNER

First Edition   ISBN-10: 1-60690-144-3   ISBN-13: 978-1-60690-144-1   10 9 8 7 6 5 4 3 2 1

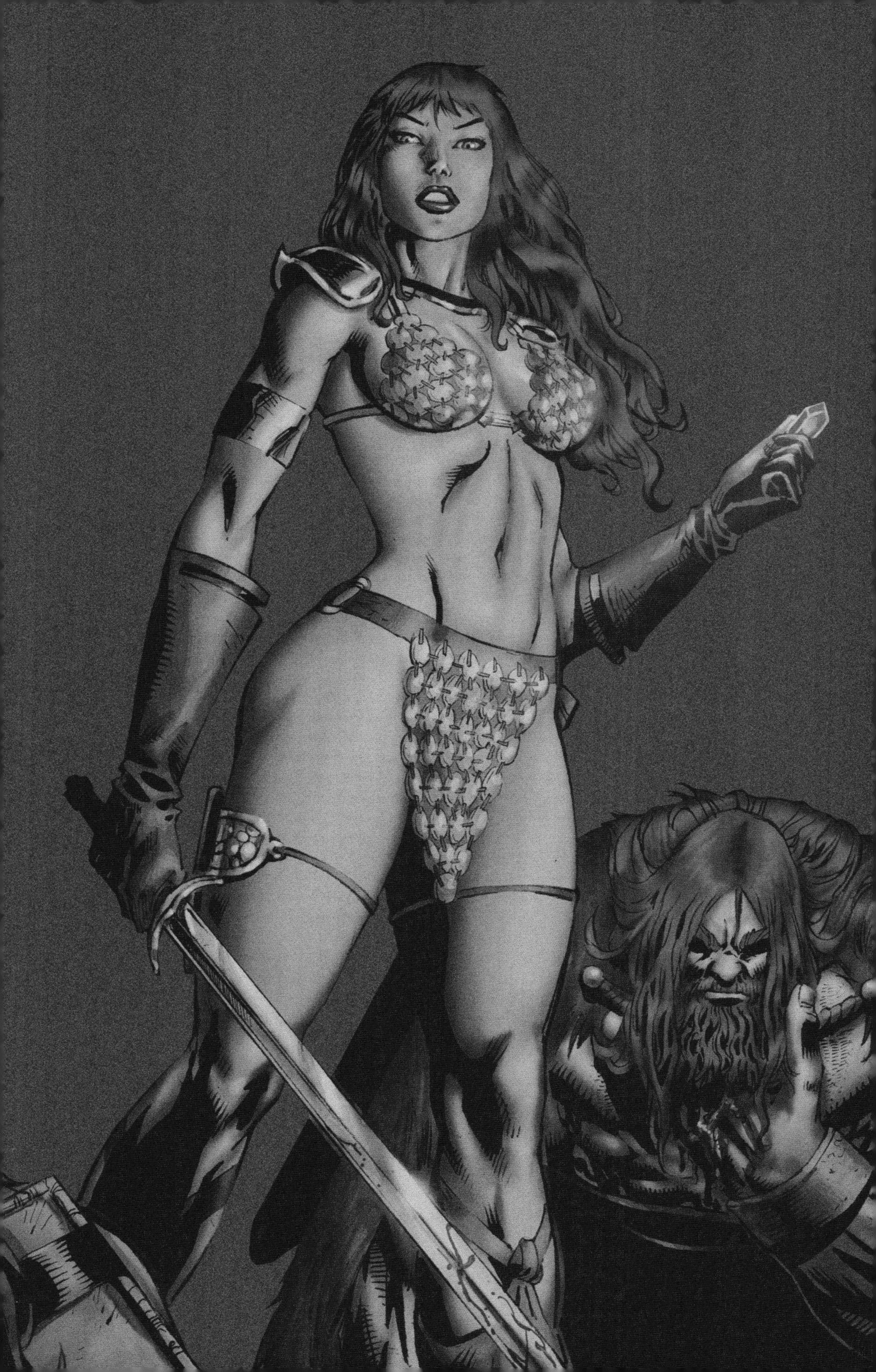

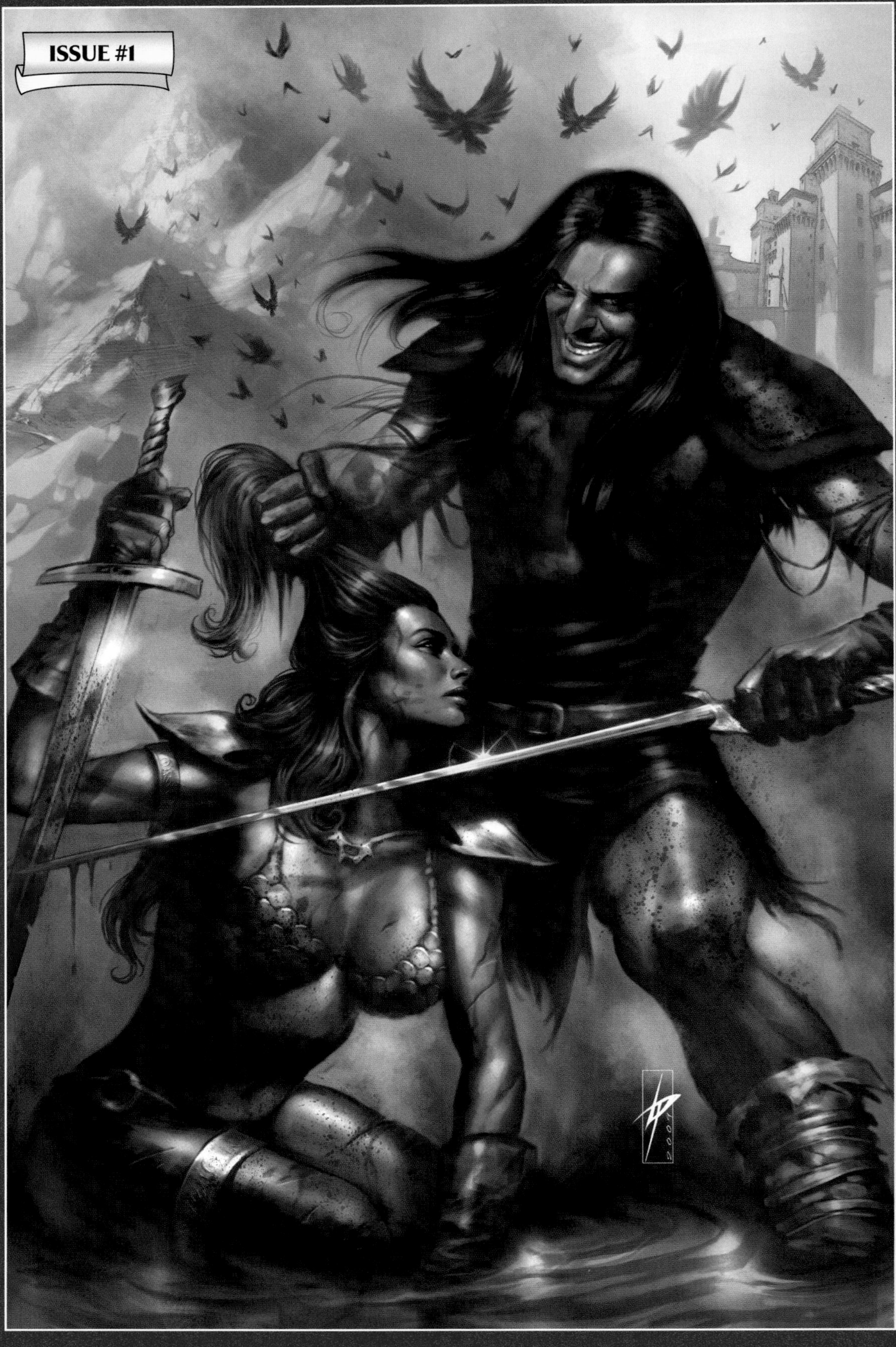
ISSUE #1

ISSUE #1 COVER BY LUCIO PARRILLO

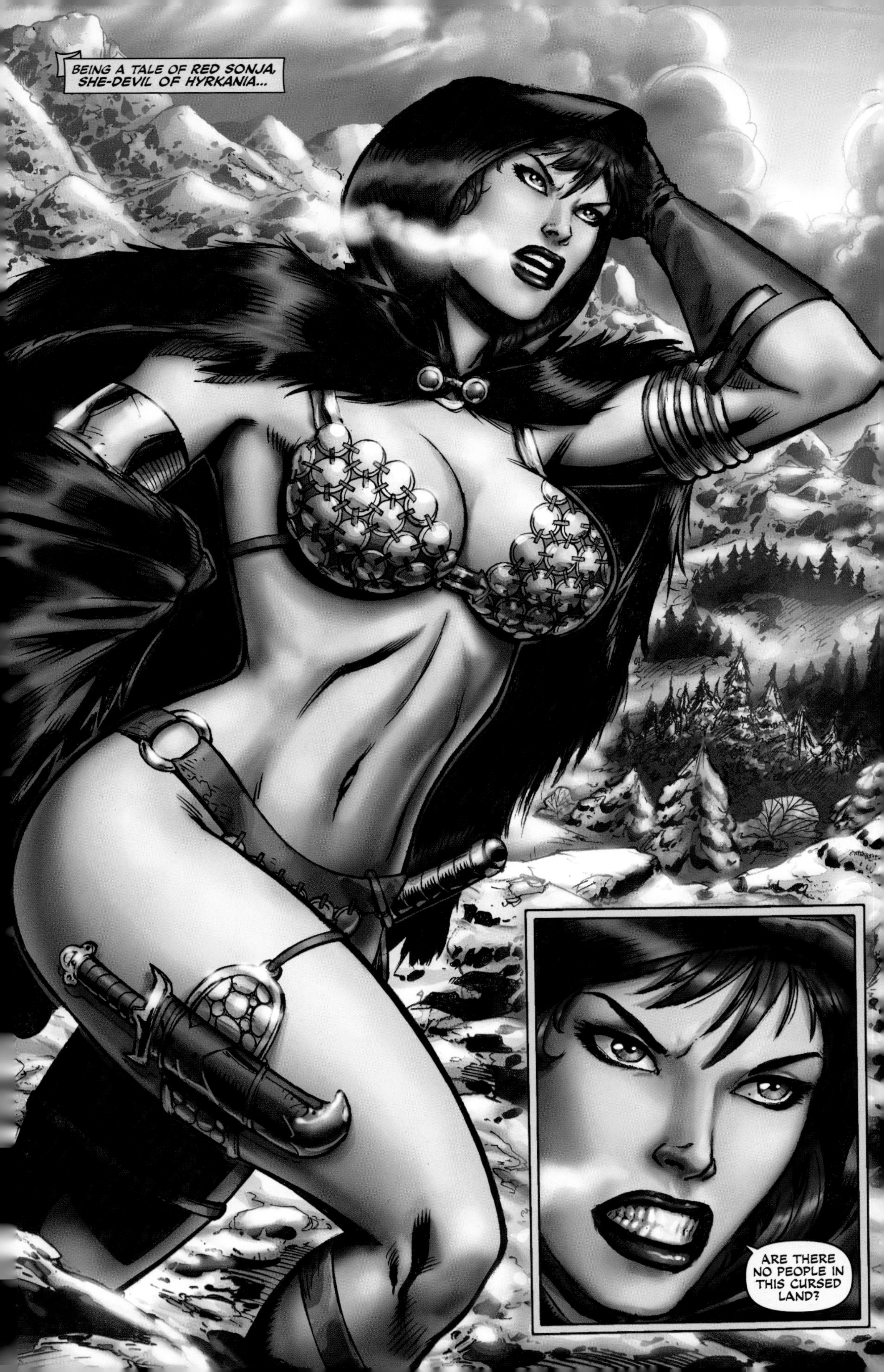
BEING A TALE OF RED SONJA, SHE-DEVIL OF HYRKANIA...
ARE THERE NO PEOPLE IN THIS CURSED LAND?

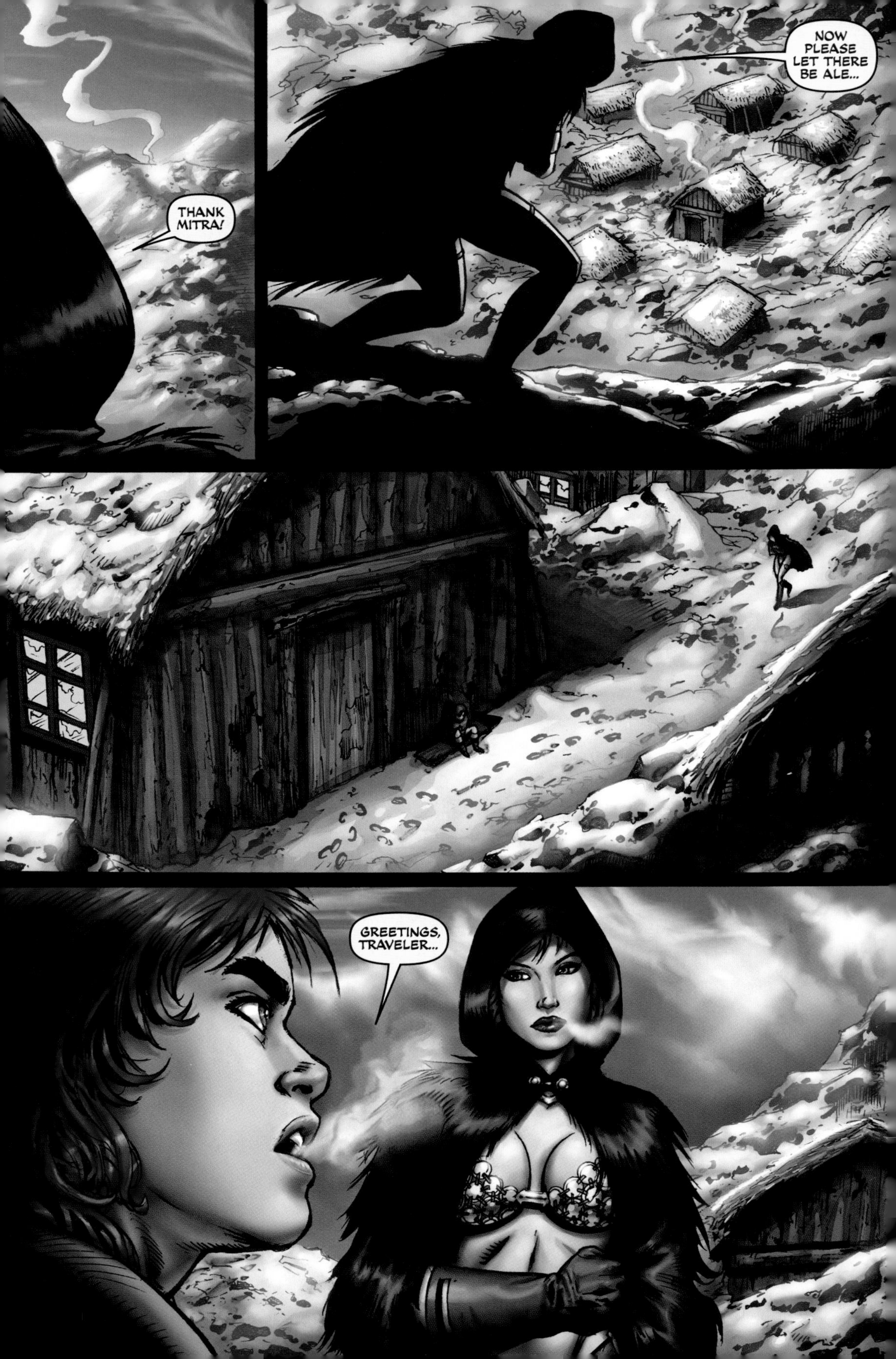
THANK MITRA!
NOW PLEASE LET THERE BE ALE...
GREETINGS, TRAVELER...

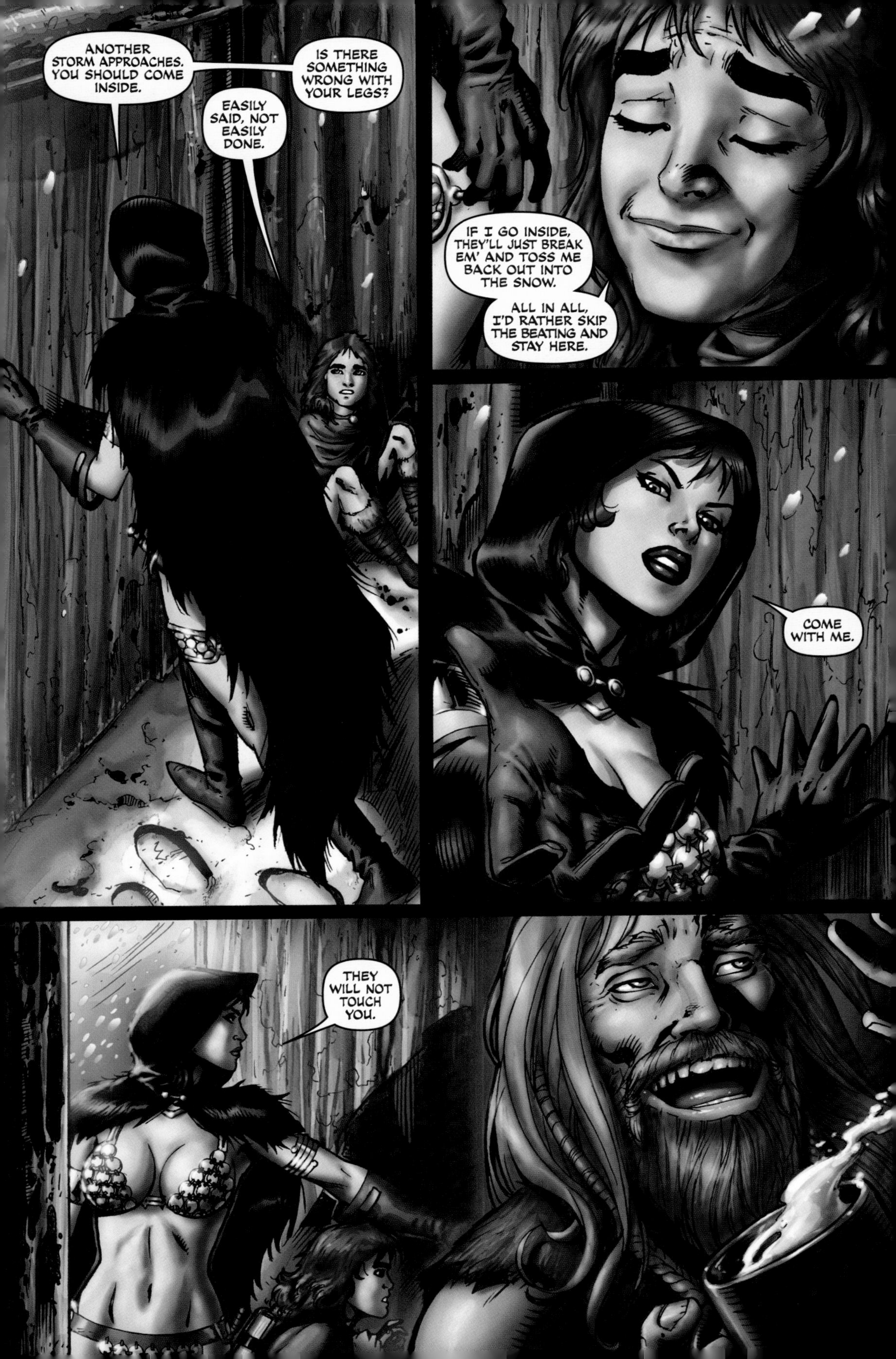
ANOTHER STORM APPROACHES. YOU SHOULD COME INSIDE.
IS THERE SOMETHING WRONG WITH YOUR LEGS?
EASILY SAID, NOT EASILY DONE.
IF I GO INSIDE, THEY'LL JUST BREAK EM' AND TOSS ME BACK OUT INTO THE SNOW.
ALL IN ALL, I'D RATHER SKIP THE BEATING AND STAY HERE.
COME WITH ME.
THEY WILL NOT TOUCH YOU.

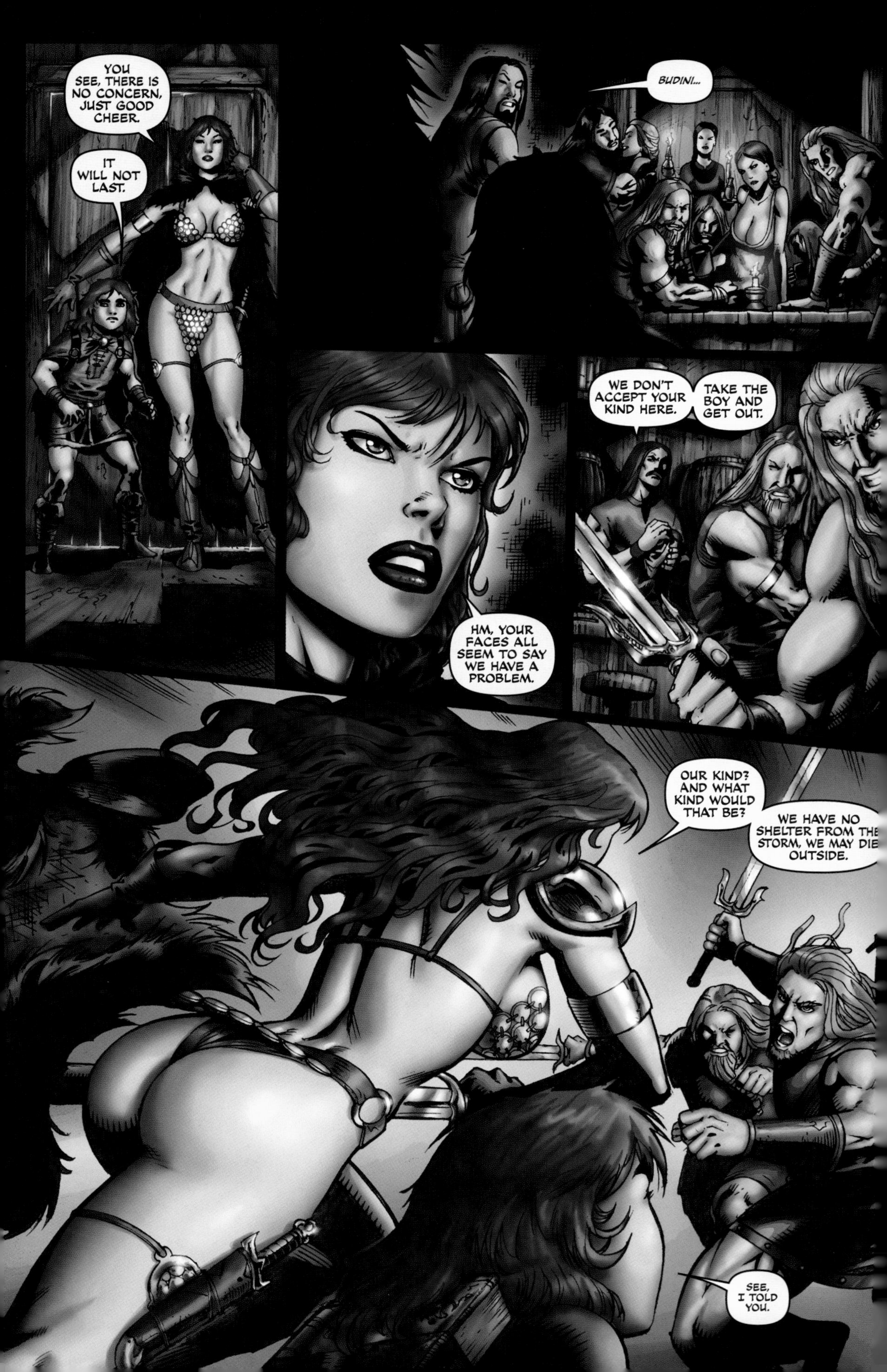
YOU SEE, THERE IS NO CONCERN, JUST GOOD CHEER.
IT WILL NOT LAST.
BUDINI...
HM, YOUR FACES ALL SEEM TO SAY WE HAVE A PROBLEM.
WE DON'T ACCEPT YOUR KIND HERE.
TAKE THE BOY AND GET OUT.
OUR KIND? AND WHAT KIND WOULD THAT BE?
WE HAVE NO SHELTER FROM THE STORM, WE MAY DIE OUTSIDE.
SEE, I TOLD YOU.

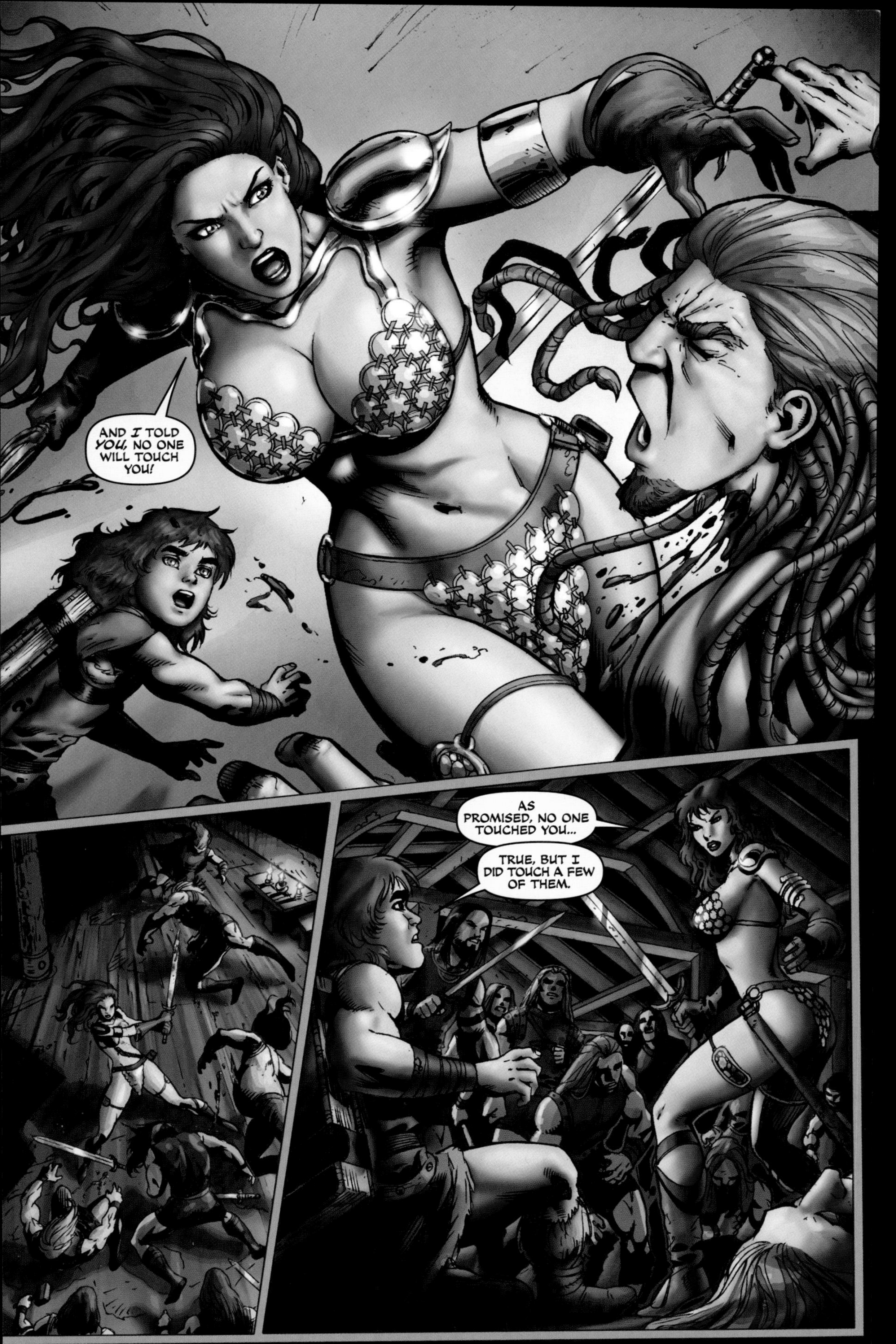
AND I TOLD YOU, NO ONE WILL TOUCH YOU!
AS PROMISED, NO ONE TOUCHED YOU...
TRUE, BUT I DID TOUCH A FEW OF THEM.

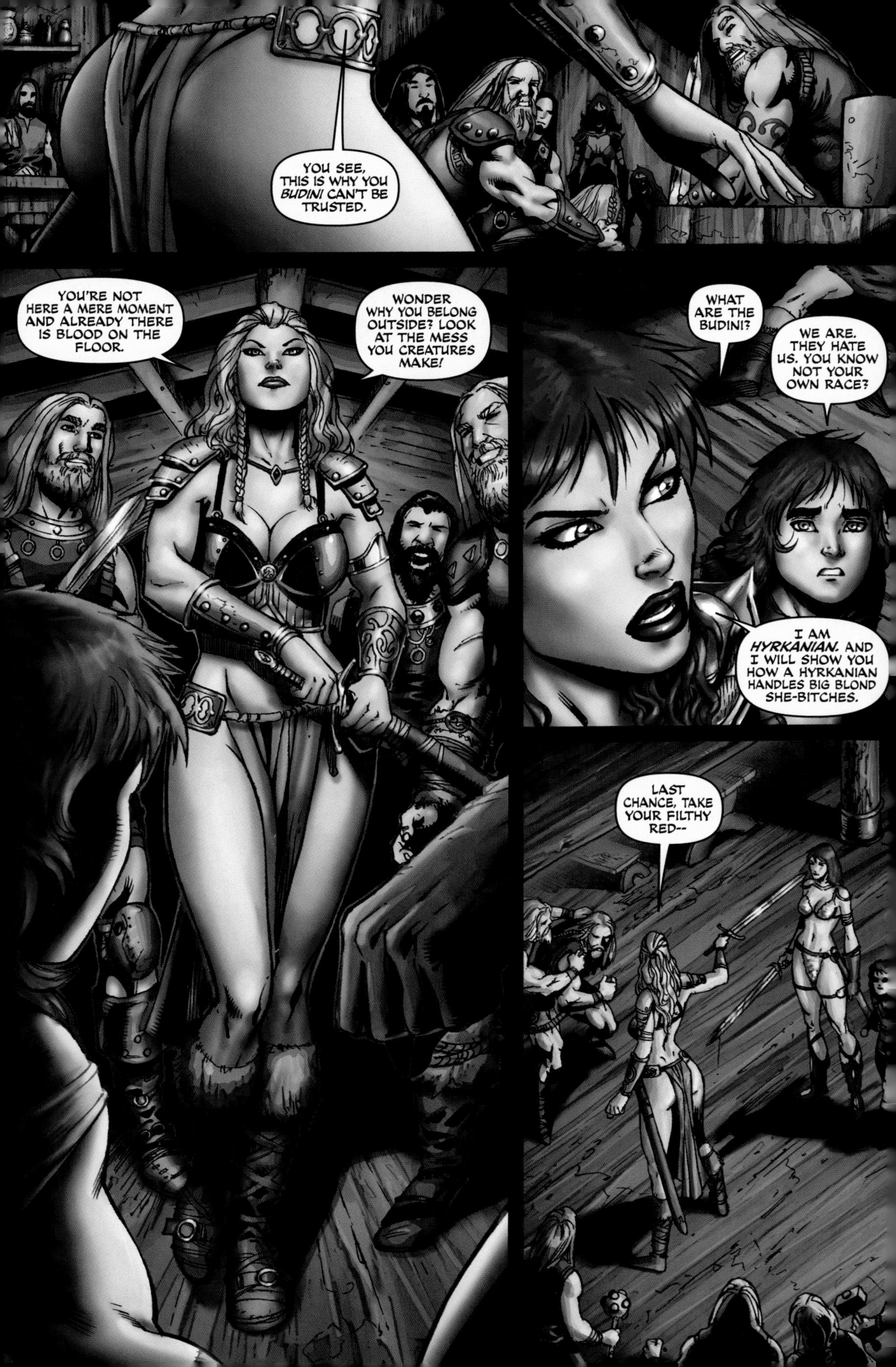
YOU SEE, THIS IS WHY YOU *BUDINI* CAN'T BE TRUSTED.
YOU'RE NOT HERE A MERE MOMENT AND ALREADY THERE IS BLOOD ON THE FLOOR.
WONDER WHY YOU BELONG OUTSIDE? LOOK AT THE MESS YOU CREATURES MAKE!
WHAT ARE THE BUDINI?
WE ARE. THEY HATE US. YOU KNOW NOT YOUR OWN RACE?
I AM *HYRKANIAN.* AND I WILL SHOW YOU HOW A HYRKANIAN HANDLES BIG BLOND SHE-BITCHES.
LAST CHANCE, TAKE YOUR FILTHY RED--

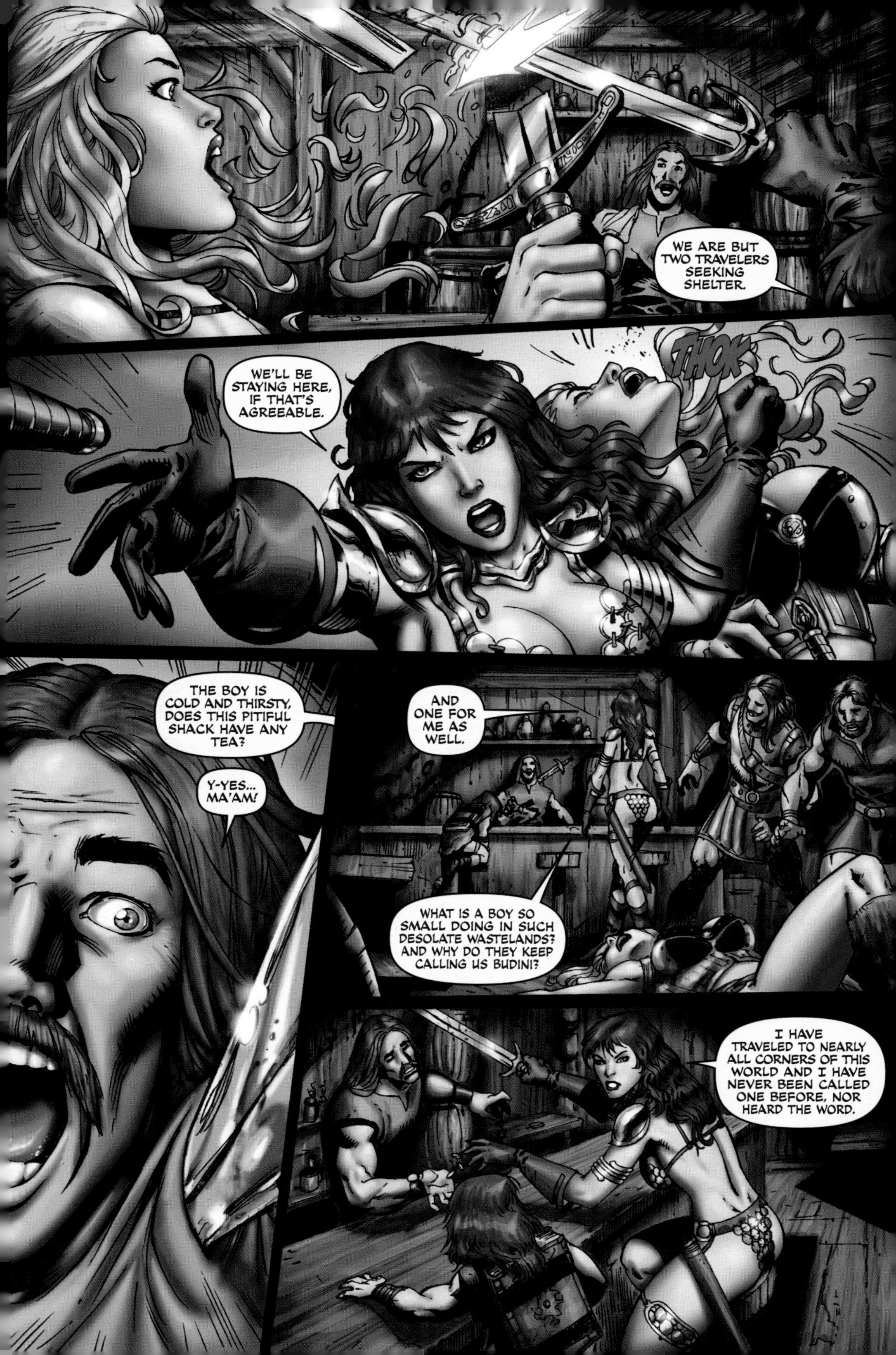
WE ARE BUT TWO TRAVELERS SEEKING SHELTER.
WE'LL BE STAYING HERE, IF THAT'S AGREEABLE.
THOK
THE BOY IS COLD AND THIRSTY, DOES THIS PITIFUL SHACK HAVE ANY TEA?
Y-YES... MA'AM!
AND ONE FOR ME AS WELL.
WHAT IS A BOY SO SMALL DOING IN SUCH DESOLATE WASTELANDS? AND WHY DO THEY KEEP CALLING US BUDINI?
I HAVE TRAVELED TO NEARLY ALL CORNERS OF THIS WORLD AND I HAVE NEVER BEEN CALLED ONE BEFORE, NOR HEARD THE WORD.

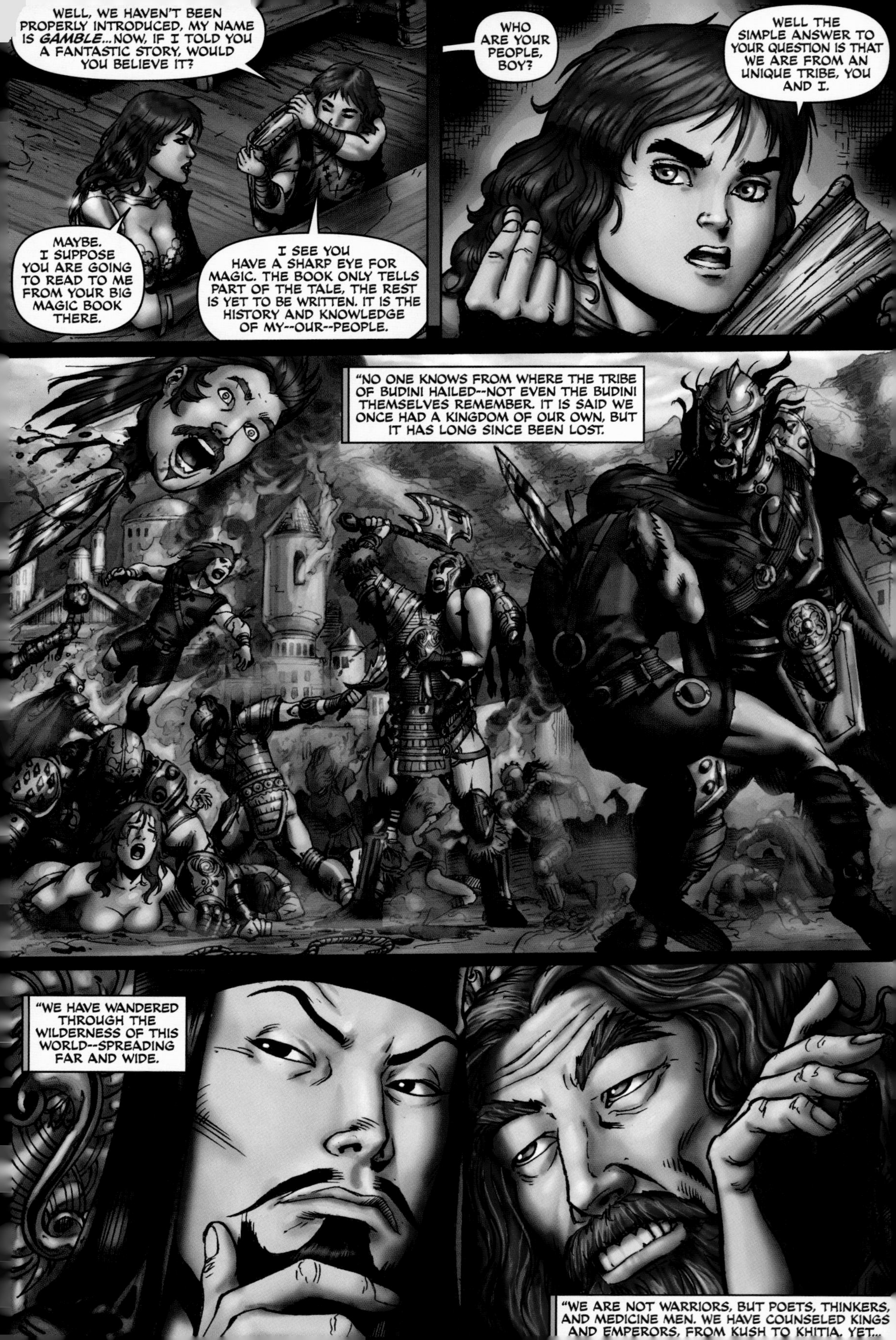
WELL, WE HAVEN'T BEEN PROPERLY INTRODUCED, MY NAME IS *GAMBLE*...NOW, IF I TOLD YOU A FANTASTIC STORY, WOULD YOU BELIEVE IT?
MAYBE. I SUPPOSE YOU ARE GOING TO READ TO ME FROM YOUR BIG MAGIC BOOK THERE.
I SEE YOU HAVE A SHARP EYE FOR MAGIC. THE BOOK ONLY TELLS PART OF THE TALE, THE REST IS YET TO BE WRITTEN. IT IS THE HISTORY AND KNOWLEDGE OF MY--OUR--PEOPLE.
WHO ARE YOUR PEOPLE, BOY?
WELL THE SIMPLE ANSWER TO YOUR QUESTION IS THAT WE ARE FROM AN UNIQUE TRIBE, YOU AND I.
"NO ONE KNOWS FROM WHERE THE TRIBE OF BUDINI HAILED--NOT EVEN THE BUDINI THEMSELVES REMEMBER. IT IS SAID WE ONCE HAD A KINGDOM OF OUR OWN, BUT IT HAS LONG SINCE BEEN LOST.
"WE HAVE WANDERED THROUGH THE WILDERNESS OF THIS WORLD--SPREADING FAR AND WIDE.
"WE ARE NOT WARRIORS, BUT POETS, THINKERS, AND MEDICINE MEN. WE HAVE COUNSELED KINGS AND EMPERORS, FROM KUSH TO KHITIA. YET...

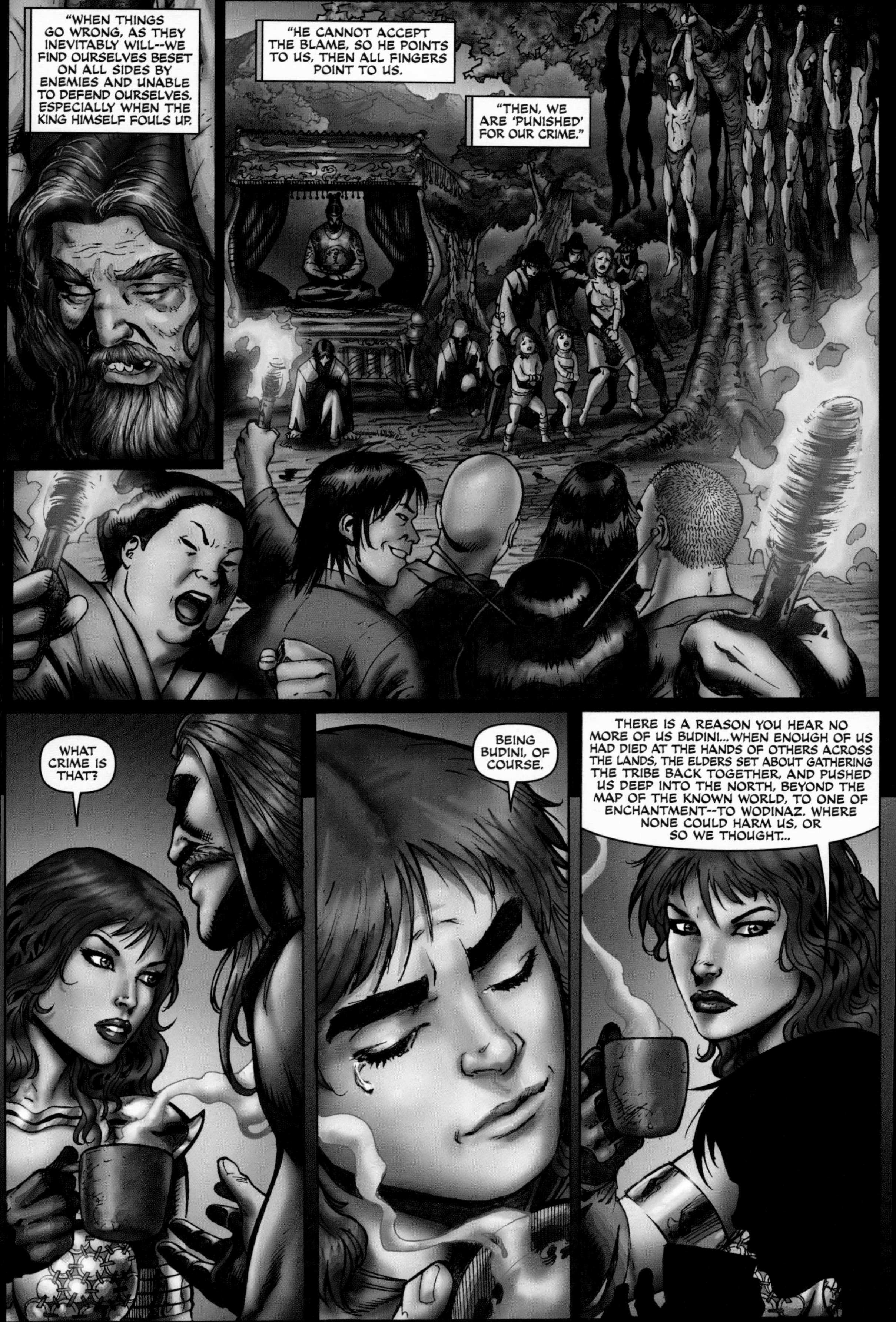
"WHEN THINGS GO WRONG, AS THEY INEVITABLY WILL--WE FIND OURSELVES BESET ON ALL SIDES BY ENEMIES AND UNABLE TO DEFEND OURSELVES. ESPECIALLY WHEN THE KING HIMSELF FOULS UP.
"HE CANNOT ACCEPT THE BLAME, SO HE POINTS TO US, THEN ALL FINGERS POINT TO US.
"THEN, WE ARE 'PUNISHED' FOR OUR CRIME."
WHAT CRIME IS THAT?
BEING BUDINI, OF COURSE.
THERE IS A REASON YOU HEAR NO MORE OF US BUDINI...WHEN ENOUGH OF US HAD DIED AT THE HANDS OF OTHERS ACROSS THE LANDS, THE ELDERS SET ABOUT GATHERING THE TRIBE BACK TOGETHER, AND PUSHED US DEEP INTO THE NORTH, BEYOND THE MAP OF THE KNOWN WORLD, TO ONE OF ENCHANTMENT--TO WODINAZ. WHERE NONE COULD HARM US, OR SO WE THOUGHT...

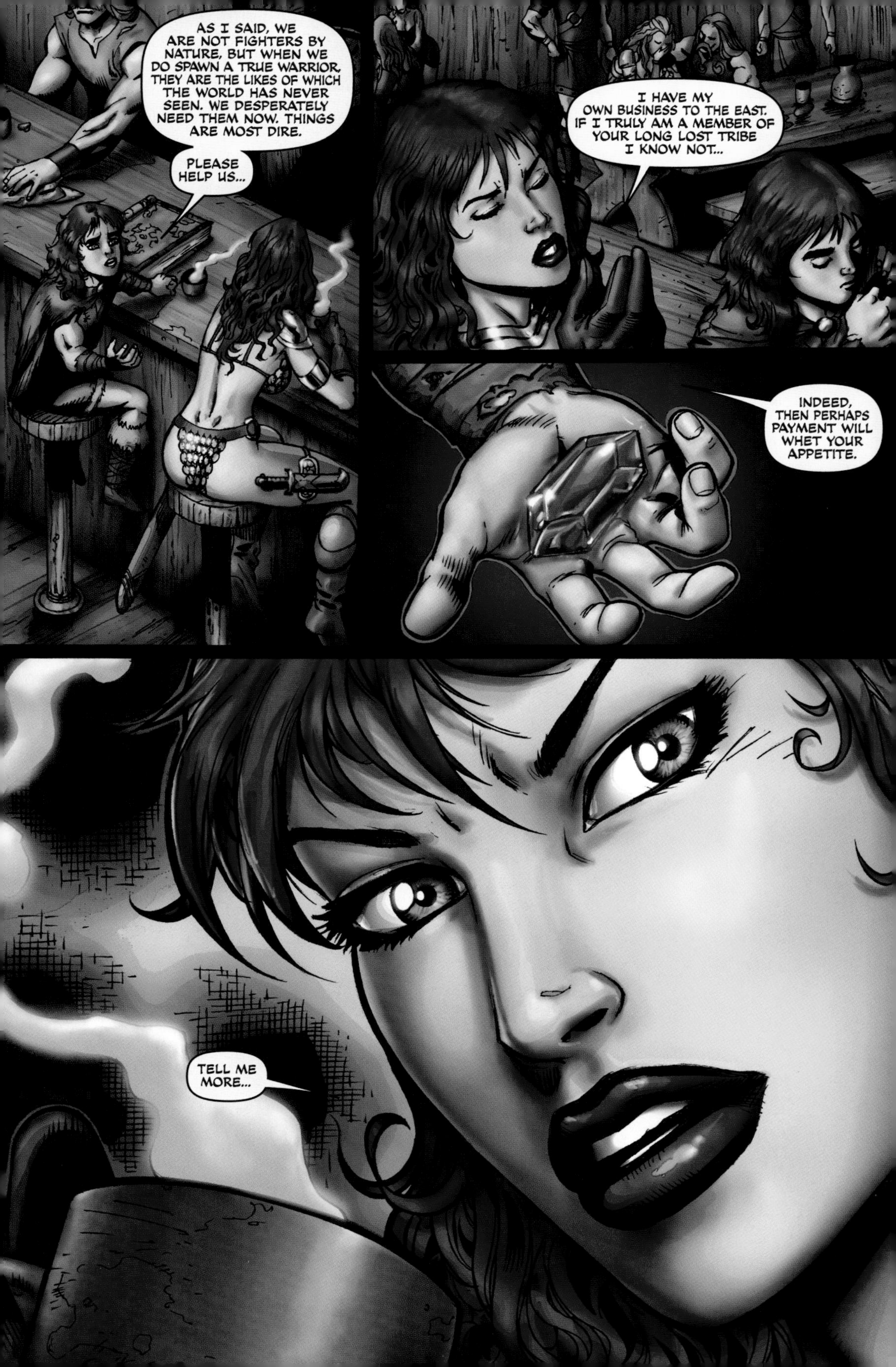
AS I SAID, WE ARE NOT FIGHTERS BY NATURE, BUT WHEN WE DO SPAWN A TRUE WARRIOR, THEY ARE THE LIKES OF WHICH THE WORLD HAS NEVER SEEN. WE DESPERATELY NEED THEM NOW. THINGS ARE MOST DIRE.
PLEASE HELP US...
I HAVE MY OWN BUSINESS TO THE EAST. IF I TRULY AM A MEMBER OF YOUR LONG LOST TRIBE I KNOW NOT...
INDEED, THEN PERHAPS PAYMENT WILL WHET YOUR APPETITE.
TELL ME MORE...

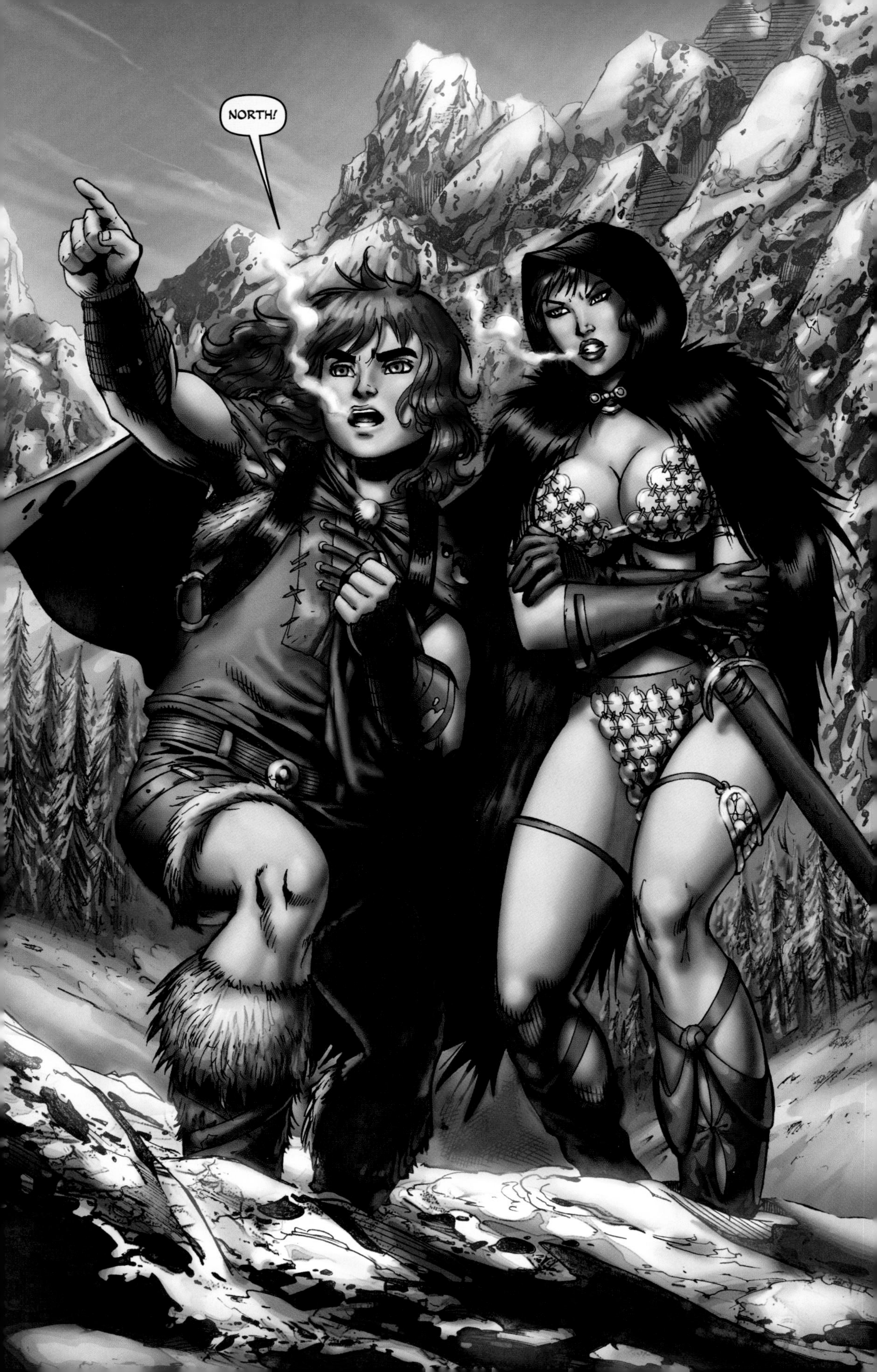
NORTH!

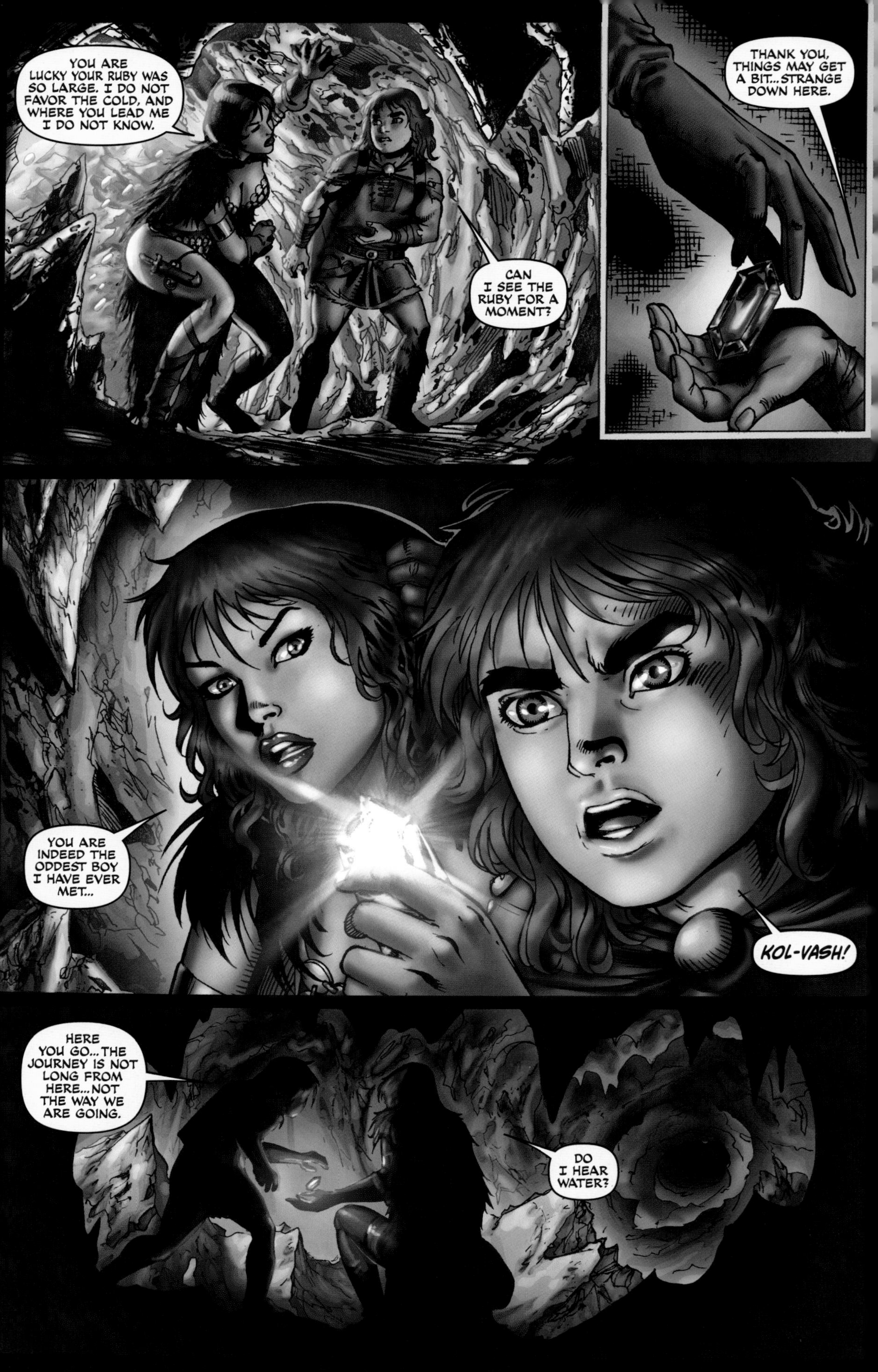
YOU ARE LUCKY YOUR RUBY WAS SO LARGE. I DO NOT FAVOR THE COLD, AND WHERE YOU LEAD ME I DO NOT KNOW.
CAN I SEE THE RUBY FOR A MOMENT?
THANK YOU, THINGS MAY GET A BIT...STRANGE DOWN HERE.
YOU ARE INDEED THE ODDEST BOY I HAVE EVER MET...
KOL-VASH!
HERE YOU GO...THE JOURNEY IS NOT LONG FROM HERE...NOT THE WAY WE ARE GOING.
DO I HEAR WATER?

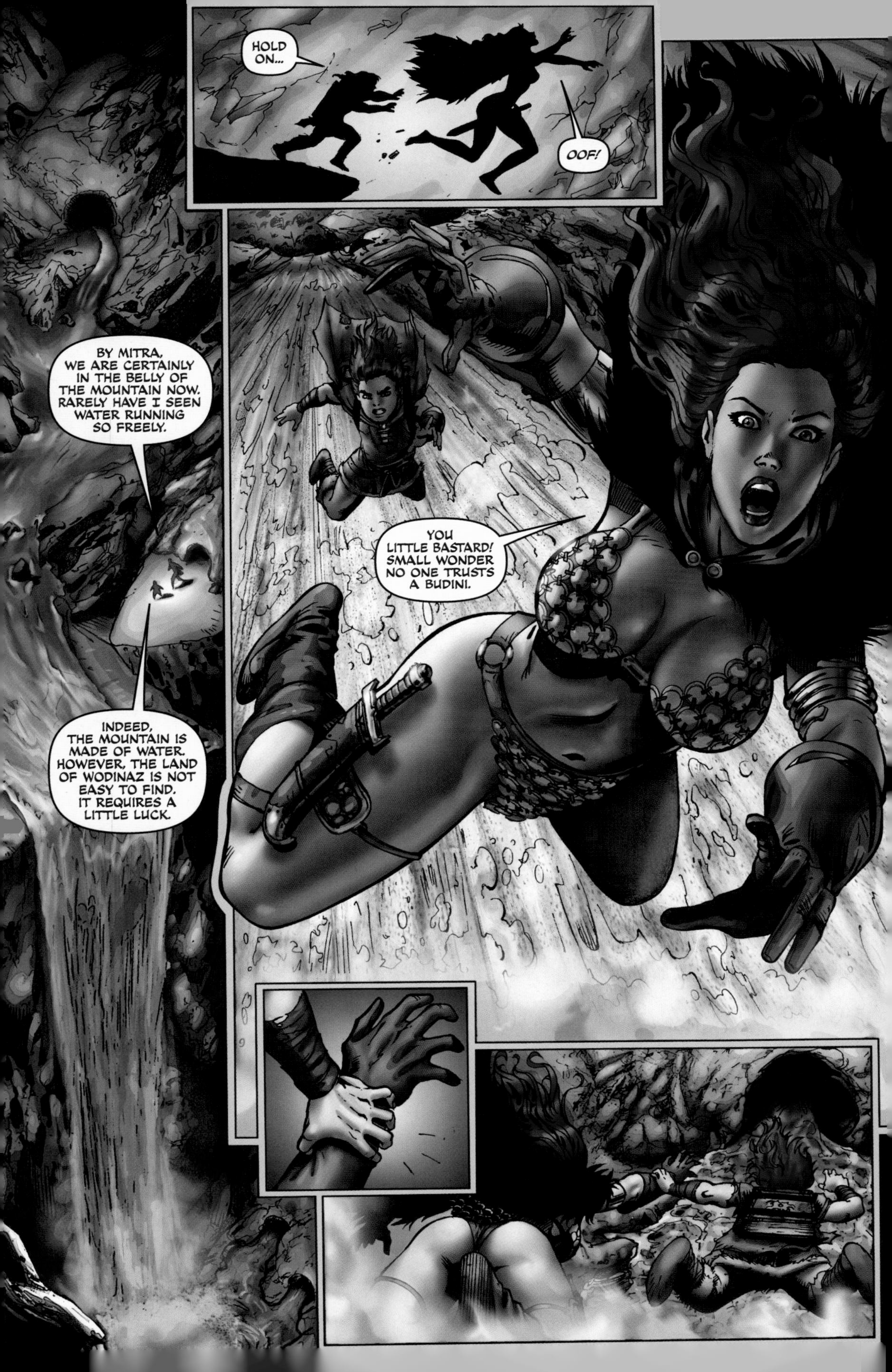

HOLD ON...
OOF!
BY MITRA, WE ARE CERTAINLY IN THE BELLY OF THE MOUNTAIN NOW. RARELY HAVE I SEEN WATER RUNNING SO FREELY.
INDEED, THE MOUNTAIN IS MADE OF WATER. HOWEVER, THE LAND OF WODINAZ IS NOT EASY TO FIND. IT REQUIRES A LITTLE LUCK.
YOU LITTLE BASTARD! SMALL WONDER NO ONE TRUSTS A BUDINI.

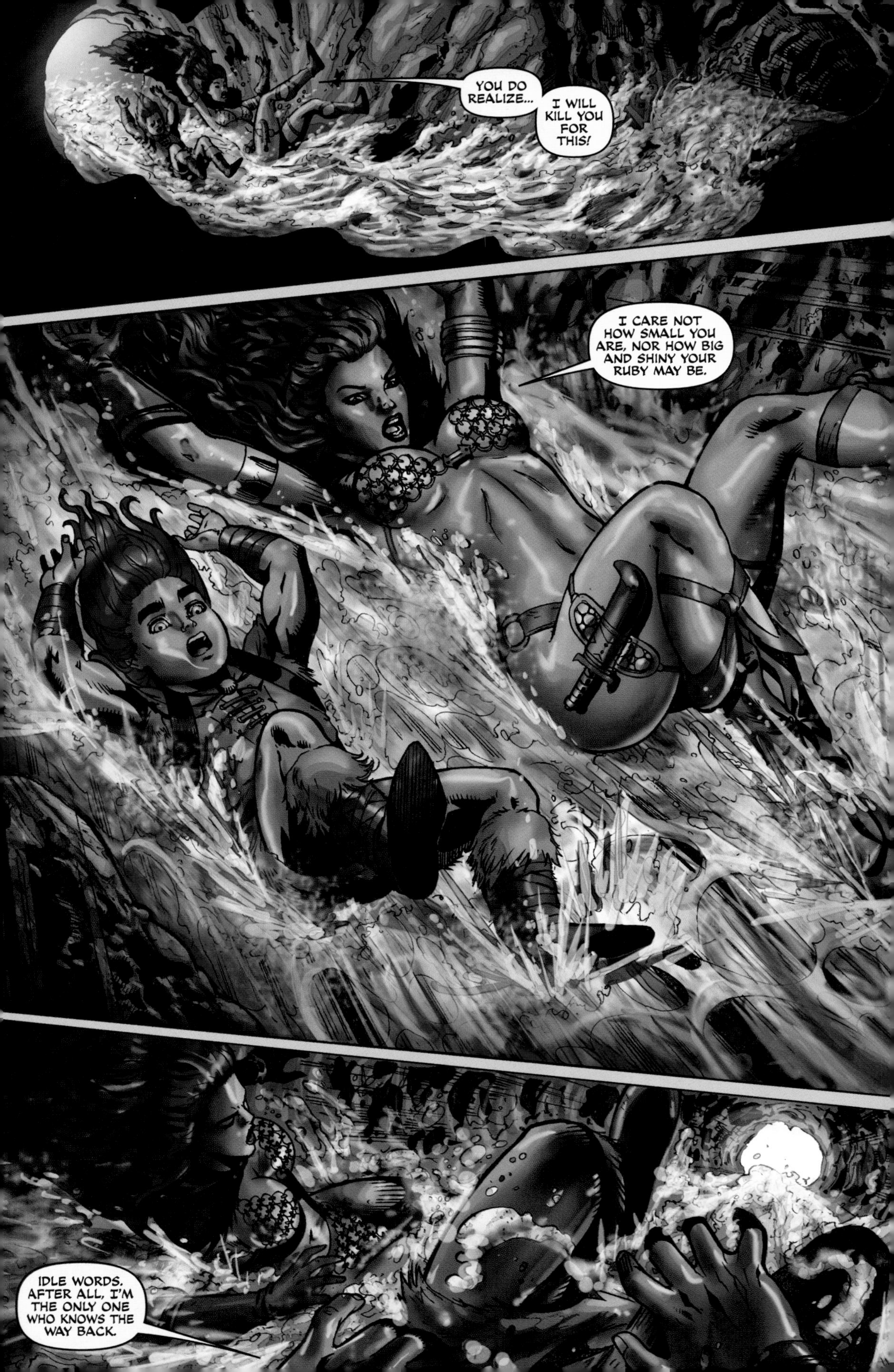

YOU DO REALIZE...
I WILL KILL YOU FOR THIS!
I CARE NOT HOW SMALL YOU ARE, NOR HOW BIG AND SHINY YOUR RUBY MAY BE.
IDLE WORDS. AFTER ALL, I'M THE ONLY ONE WHO KNOWS THE WAY BACK.

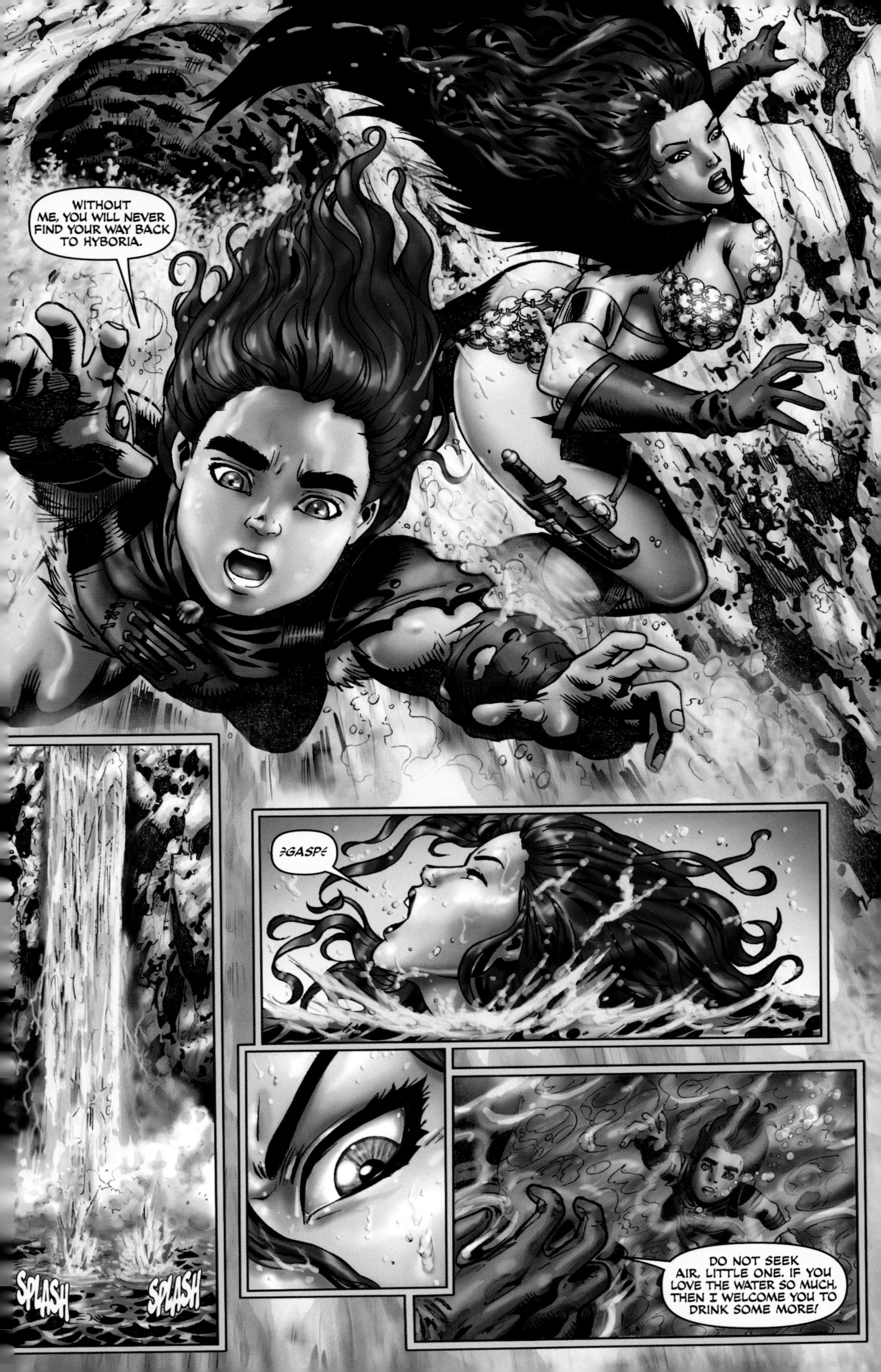
WITHOUT ME, YOU WILL NEVER FIND YOUR WAY BACK TO HYBORIA.
GASP
SPLASH
SPLASH
DO NOT SEEK AIR, LITTLE ONE. IF YOU LOVE THE WATER SO MUCH, THEN I WELCOME YOU TO DRINK SOME MORE!

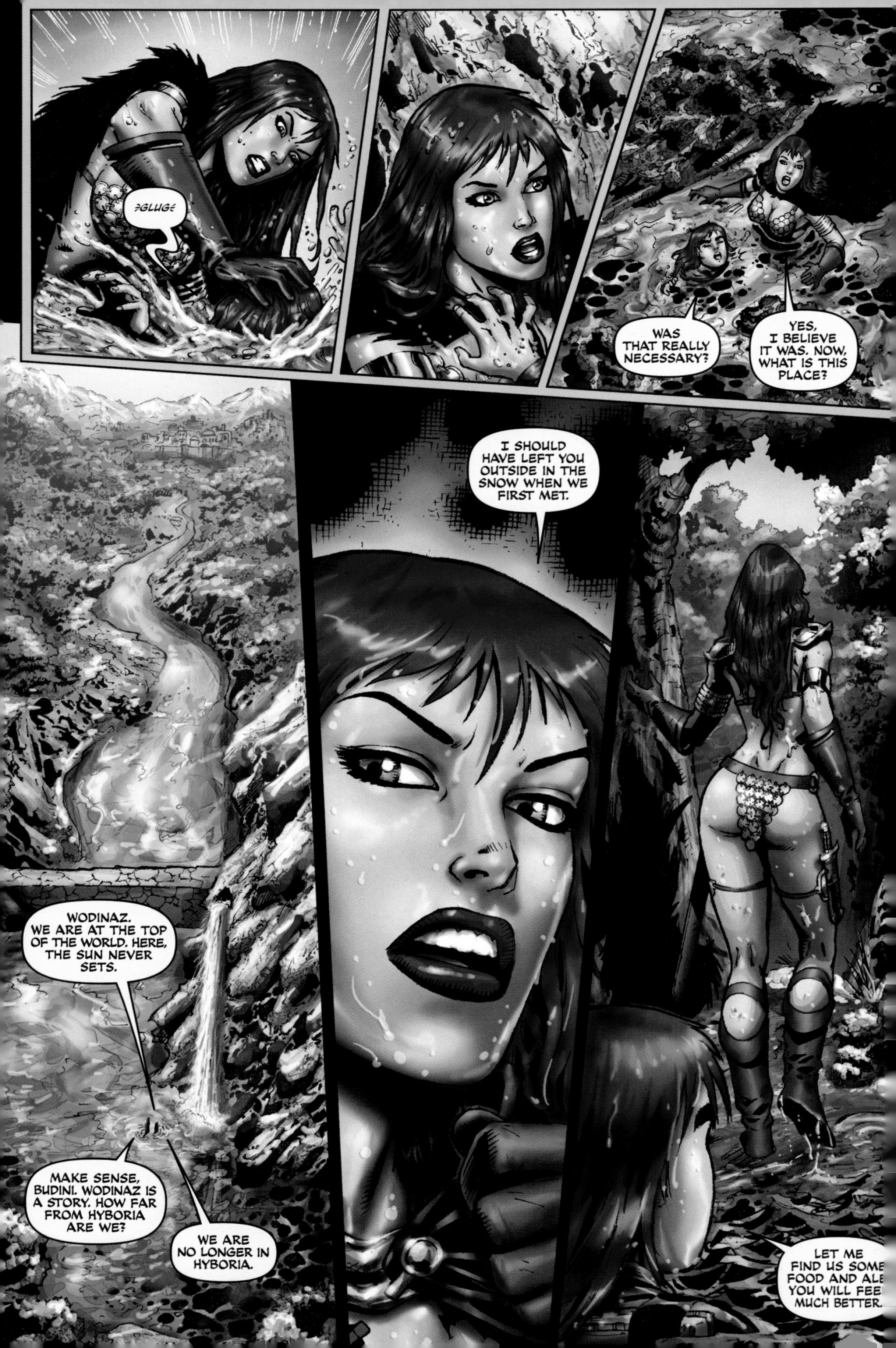

GLUG
WAS THAT REALLY NECESSARY?
YES, I BELIEVE IT WAS. NOW, WHAT IS THIS PLACE?
I SHOULD HAVE LEFT YOU OUTSIDE IN THE SNOW WHEN WE FIRST MET.
WODINAZ. WE ARE AT THE TOP OF THE WORLD. HERE, THE SUN NEVER SETS.
MAKE SENSE, BUDINI. WODINAZ IS A STORY. HOW FAR FROM HYBORIA ARE WE?
WE ARE NO LONGER IN HYBORIA.
LET ME FIND US SOME FOOD AND ALE. YOU WILL FEEL MUCH BETTER.

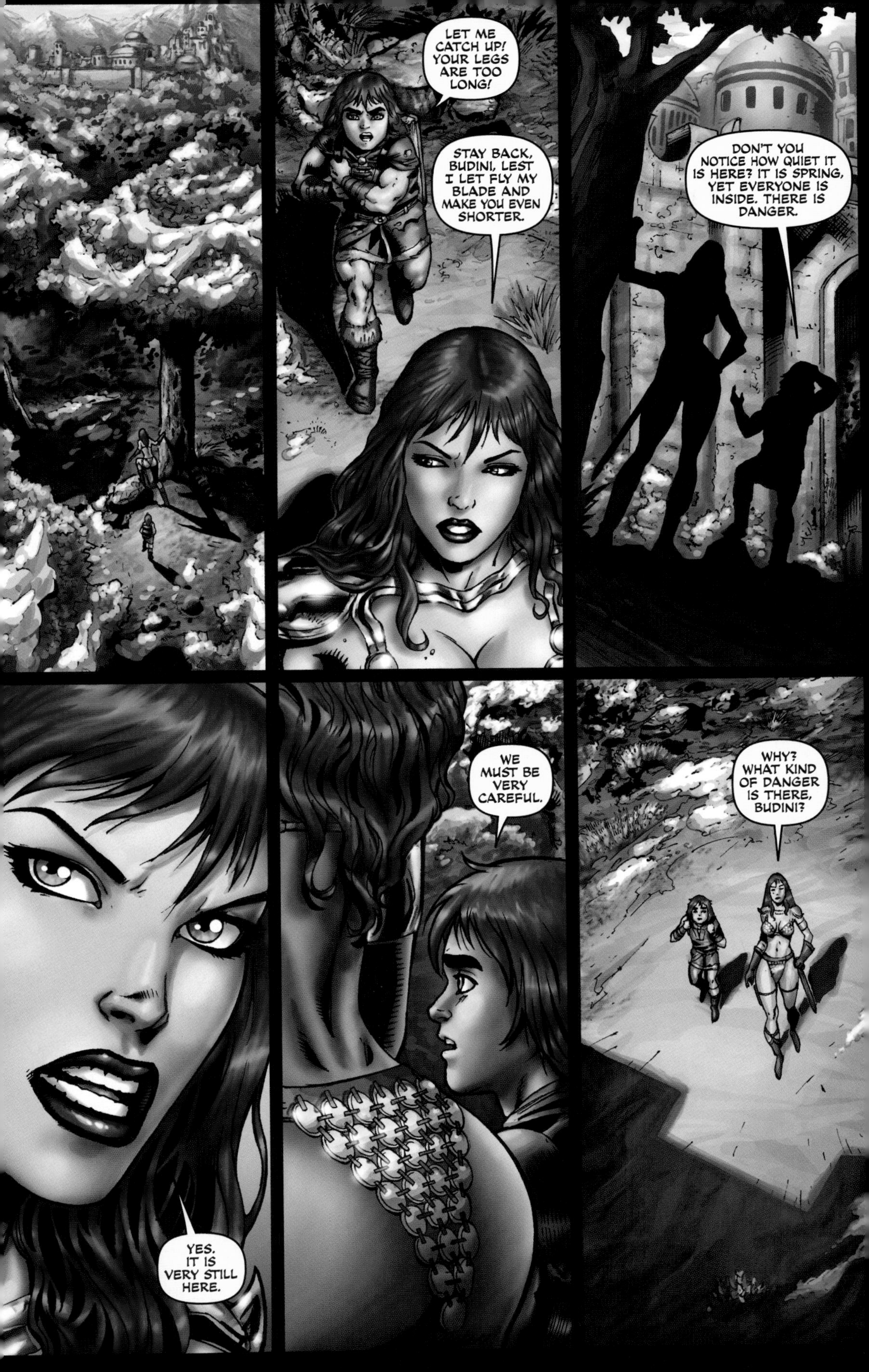
LET ME CATCH UP! YOUR LEGS ARE TOO LONG!
STAY BACK, BUDINI, LEST I LET FLY MY BLADE AND MAKE YOU EVEN SHORTER.
DON'T YOU NOTICE HOW QUIET IT IS HERE? IT IS SPRING, YET EVERYONE IS INSIDE. THERE IS DANGER.
YES. IT IS VERY STILL HERE.
WE MUST BE VERY CAREFUL.
WHY? WHAT KIND OF DANGER IS THERE, BUDINI?

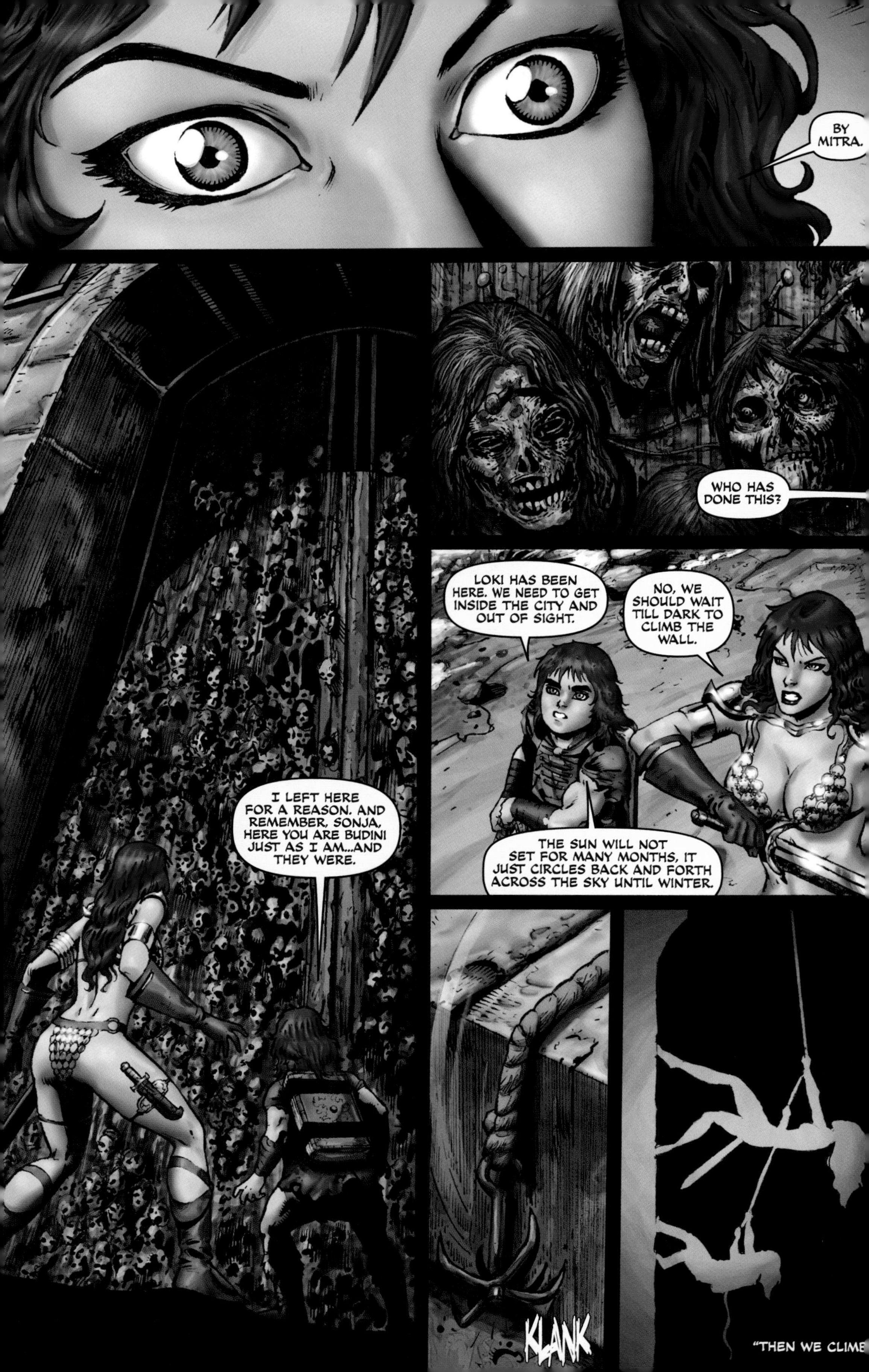
BY MITRA.
WHO HAS DONE THIS?
I LEFT HERE FOR A REASON. AND REMEMBER, SONJA, HERE YOU ARE BUDINI JUST AS I AM...AND THEY WERE.
LOKI HAS BEEN HERE. WE NEED TO GET INSIDE THE CITY AND OUT OF SIGHT.
NO, WE SHOULD WAIT TILL DARK TO CLIMB THE WALL.
THE SUN WILL NOT SET FOR MANY MONTHS, IT JUST CIRCLES BACK AND FORTH ACROSS THE SKY UNTIL WINTER.
KLANK
"THEN WE CLIMB

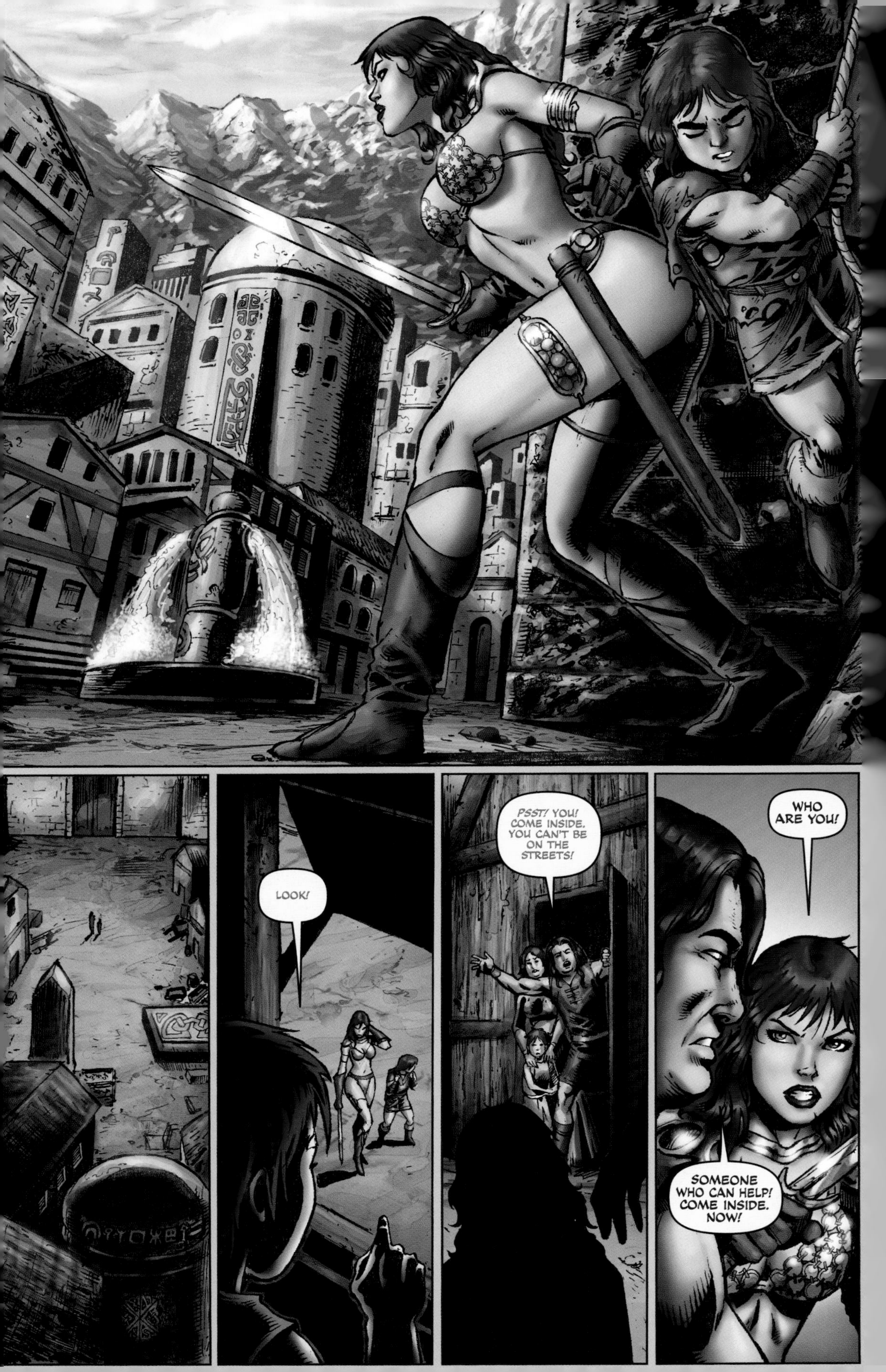

LOOK!
PSST! YOU! COME INSIDE. YOU CAN'T BE ON THE STREETS!
WHO ARE YOU!
SOMEONE WHO CAN HELP! COME INSIDE. NOW!

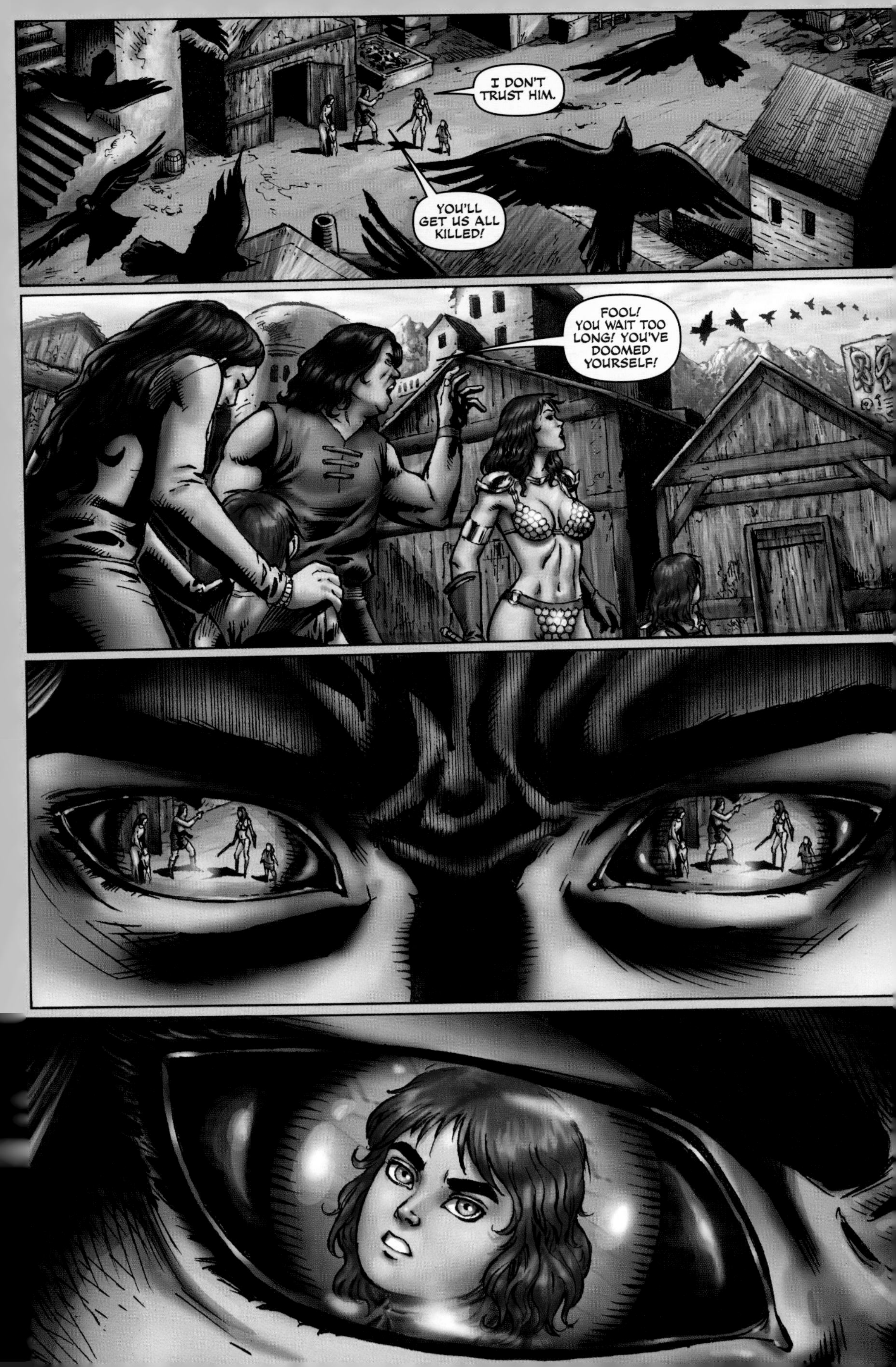
I DON'T TRUST HIM.
YOU'LL GET US ALL KILLED!
FOOL! YOU WAIT TOO LONG! YOU'VE DOOMED YOURSELF!

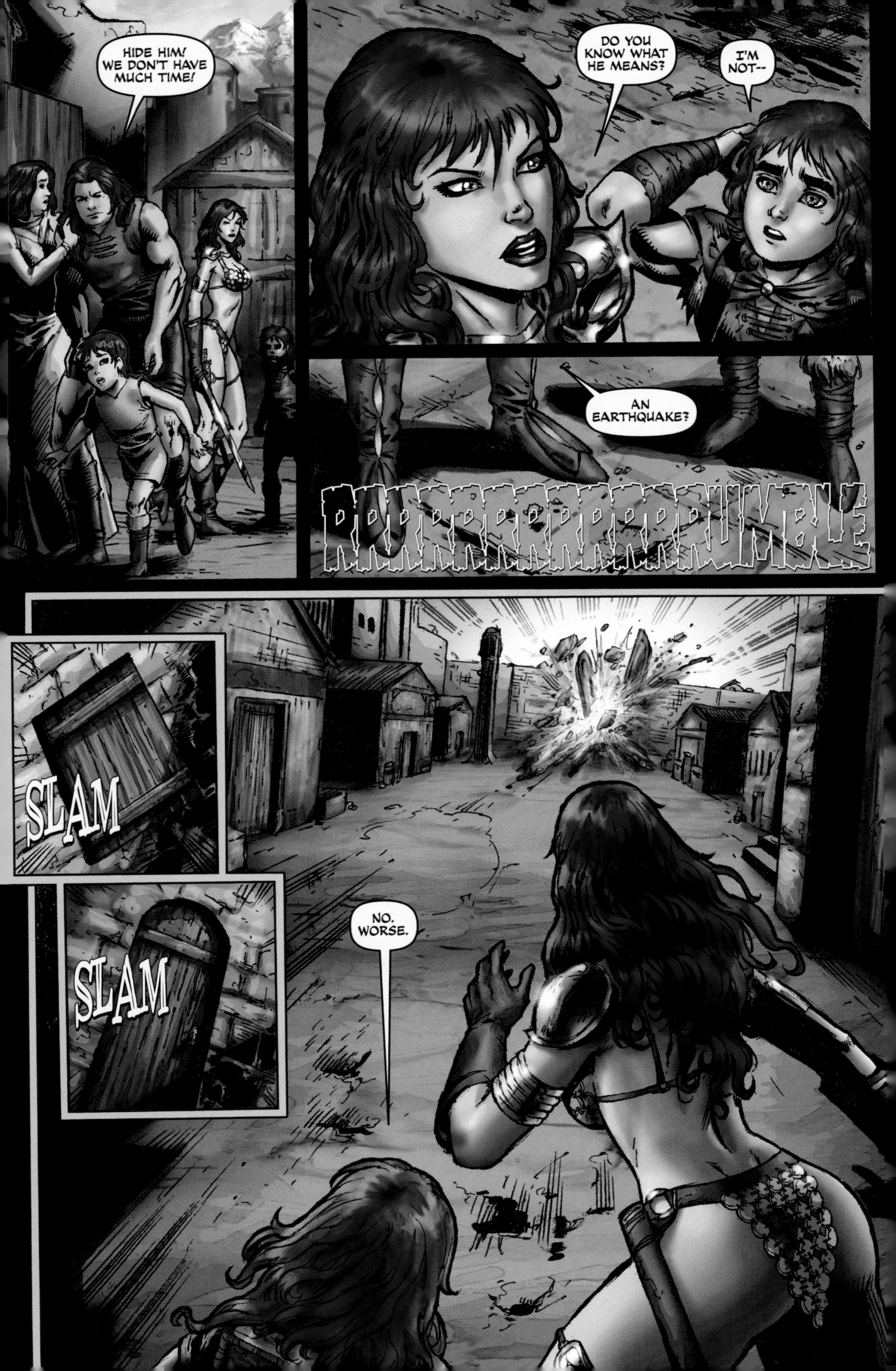
HIDE HIM! WE DON'T HAVE MUCH TIME!
DO YOU KNOW WHAT HE MEANS?
I'M NOT--
AN EARTHQUAKE?
RRRRRRRRRRRUMBLE
SLAM
SLAM
NO. WORSE.

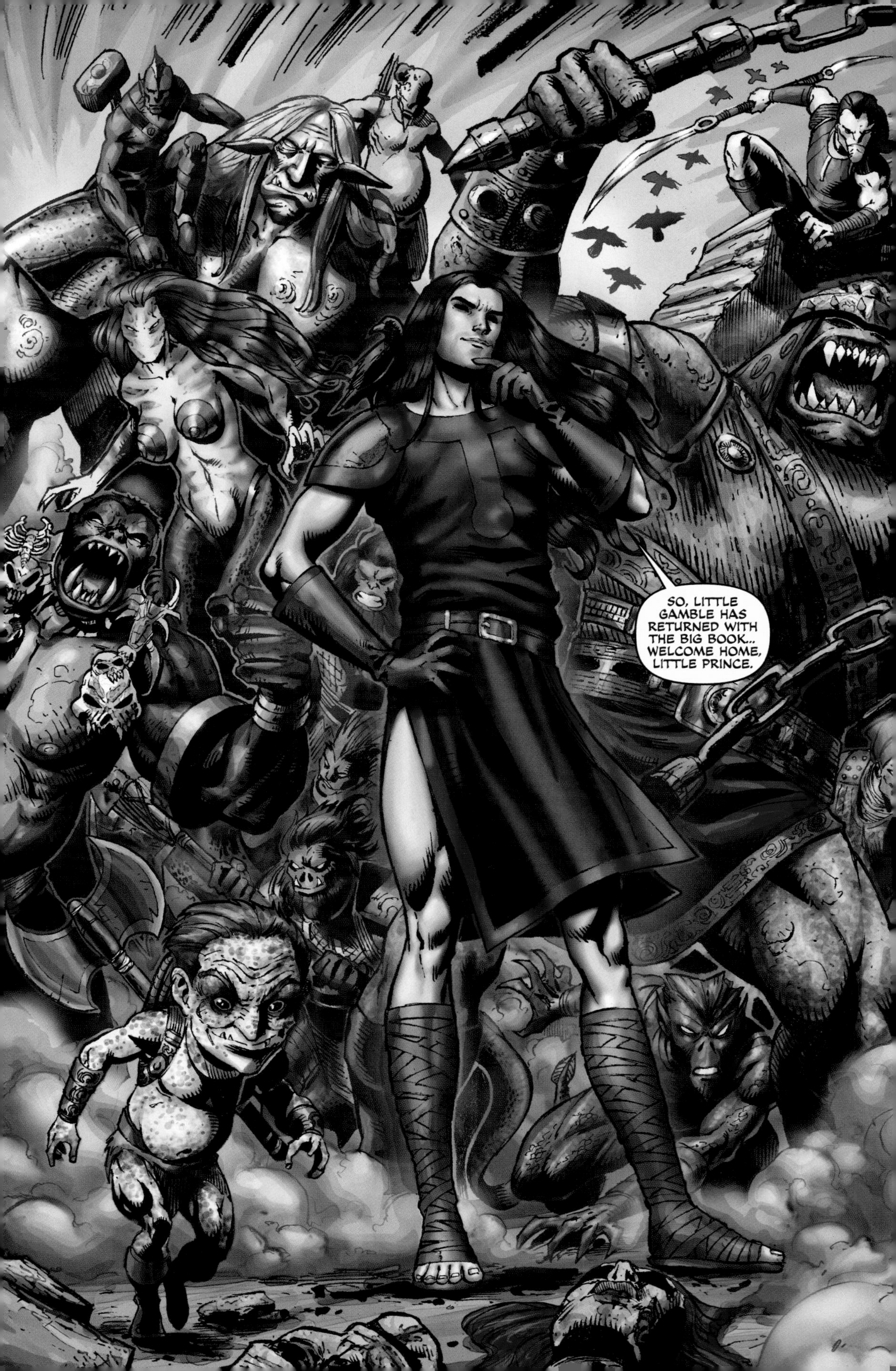
SO, LITTLE GAMBLE HAS RETURNED WITH THE BIG BOOK... WELCOME HOME, LITTLE PRINCE.

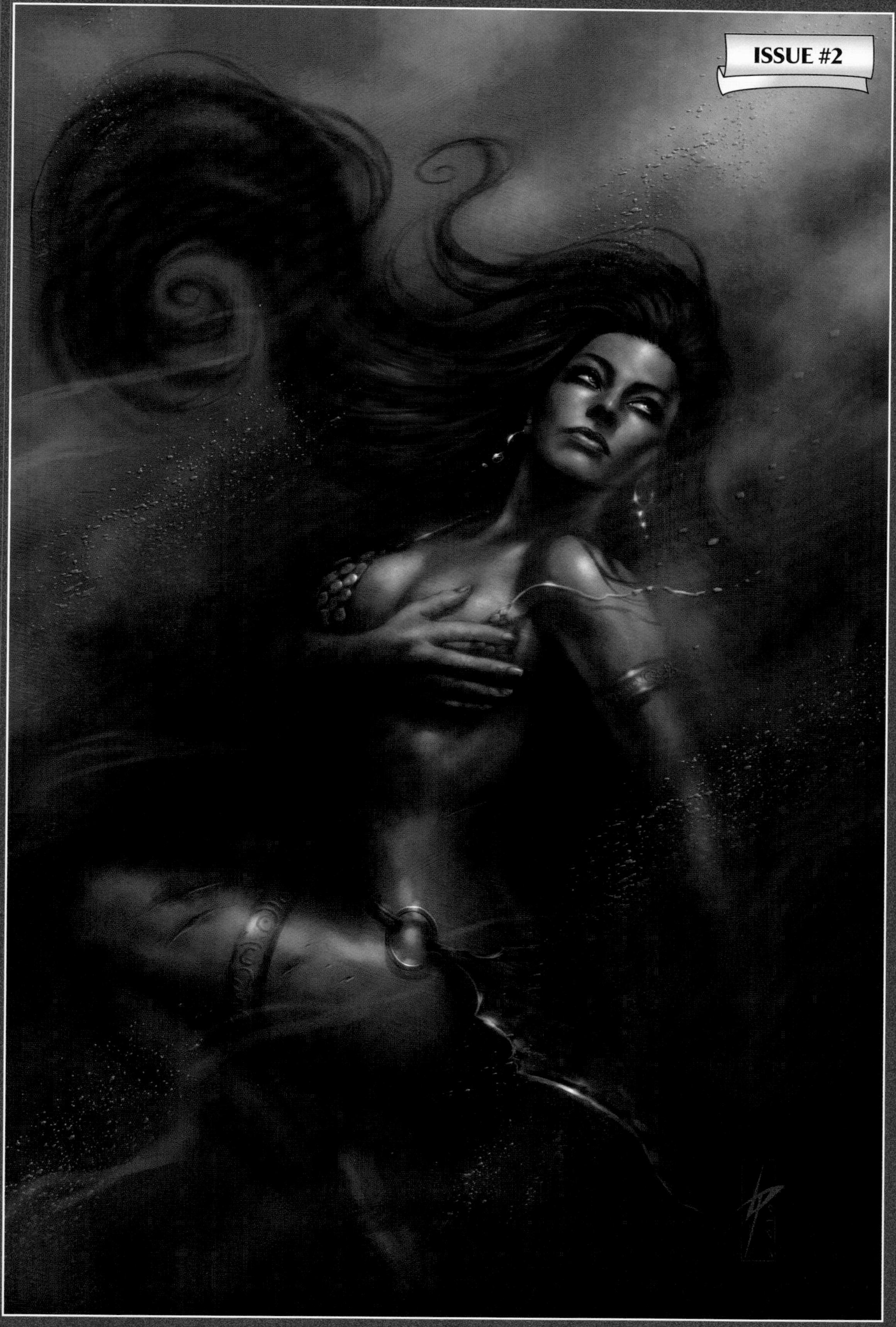
ISSUE #2

ISSUE #2 COVER BY LUCIO PARRILLO

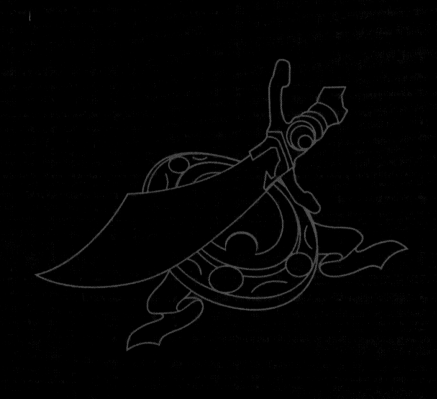

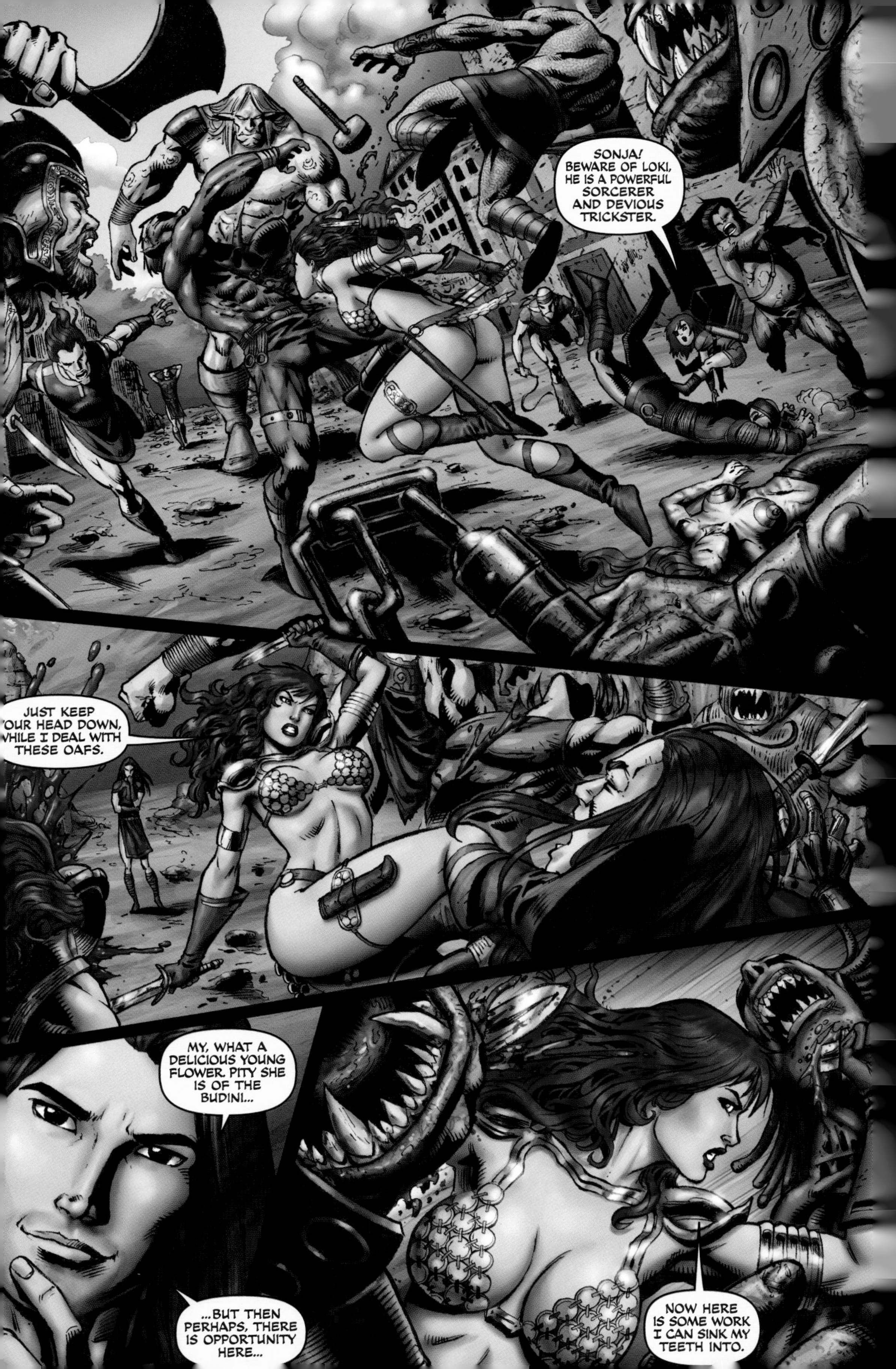
SONJA! BEWARE OF LOKI, HE IS A POWERFUL SORCERER AND DEVIOUS TRICKSTER.
JUST KEEP YOUR HEAD DOWN, WHILE I DEAL WITH THESE OAFS.
MY, WHAT A DELICIOUS YOUNG FLOWER. PITY SHE IS OF THE BUDINI...
...BUT THEN PERHAPS, THERE IS OPPORTUNITY HERE...
NOW HERE IS SOME WORK I CAN SINK MY TEETH INTO.

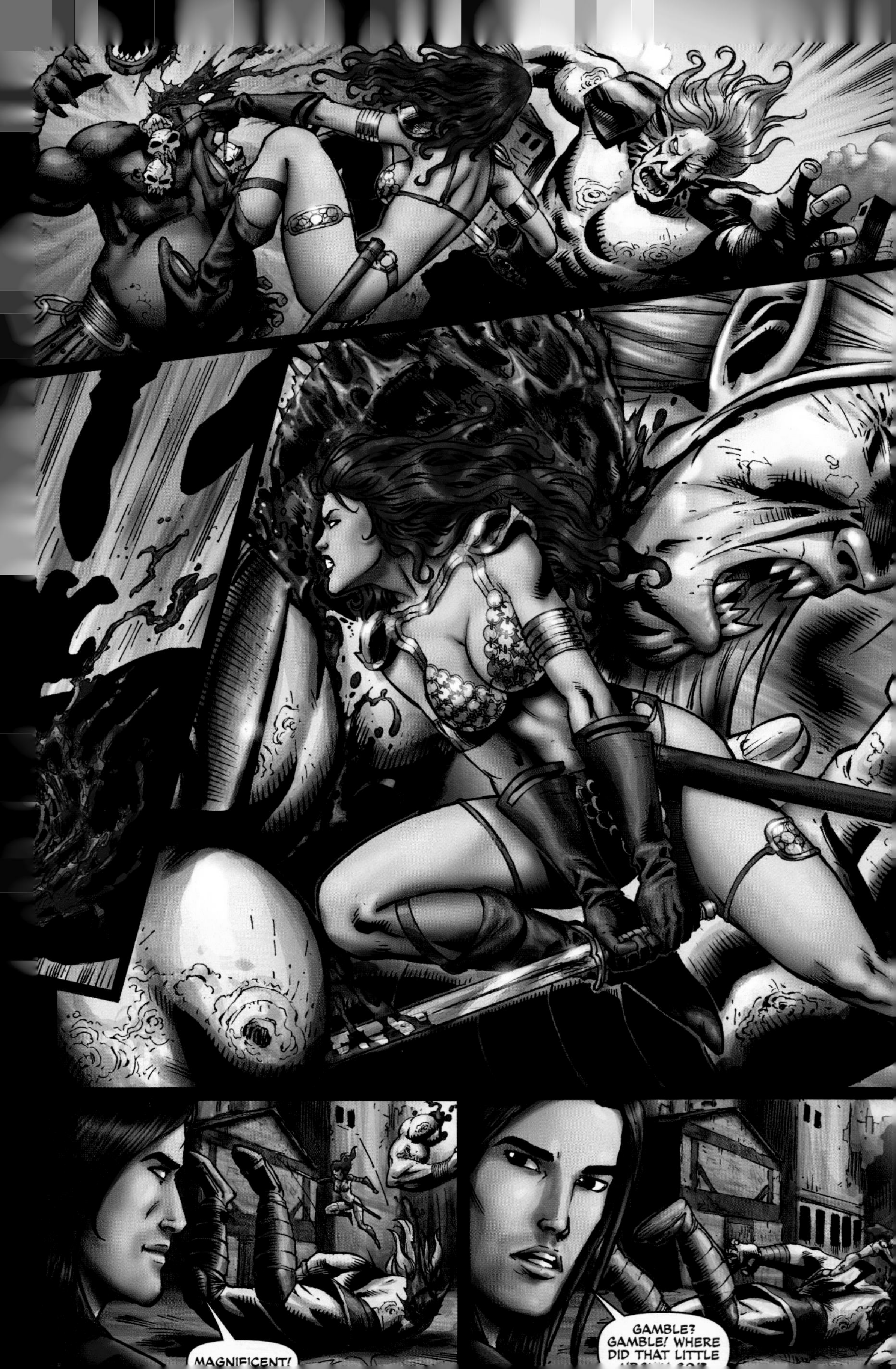
MAGNIFICENT!
GAMBLE? GAMBLE! WHERE DID THAT LITTLE

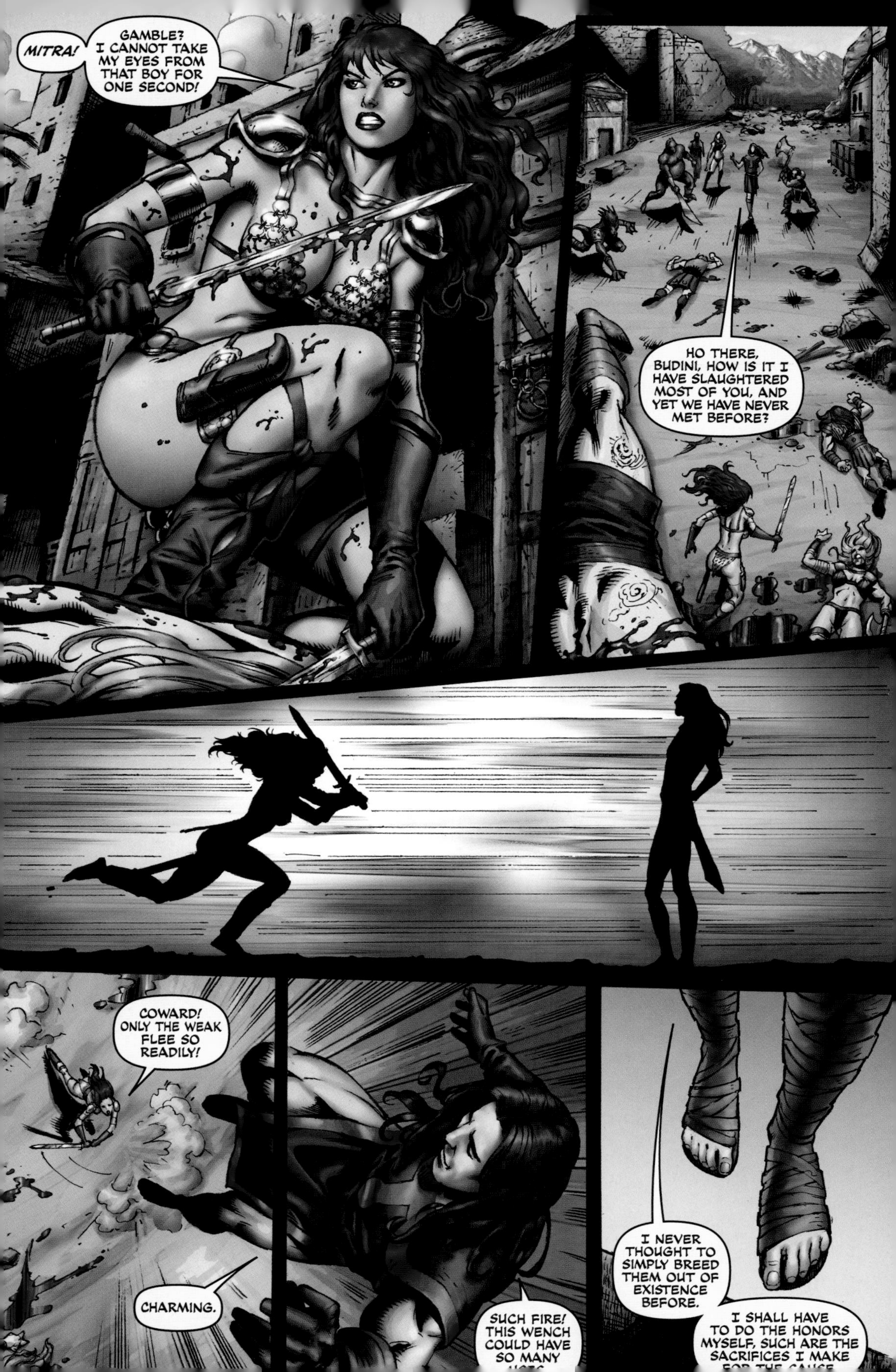
MITRA!
GAMBLE? I CANNOT TAKE MY EYES FROM THAT BOY FOR ONE SECOND!
HO THERE, BUDINI, HOW IS IT I HAVE SLAUGHTERED MOST OF YOU, AND YET WE HAVE NEVER MET BEFORE?
COWARD! ONLY THE WEAK FLEE SO READILY!
CHARMING.
SUCH FIRE! THIS WENCH COULD HAVE SO MANY
I NEVER THOUGHT TO SIMPLY BREED THEM OUT OF EXISTENCE BEFORE.
I SHALL HAVE TO DO THE HONORS MYSELF, SUCH ARE THE SACRIFICES I MAKE

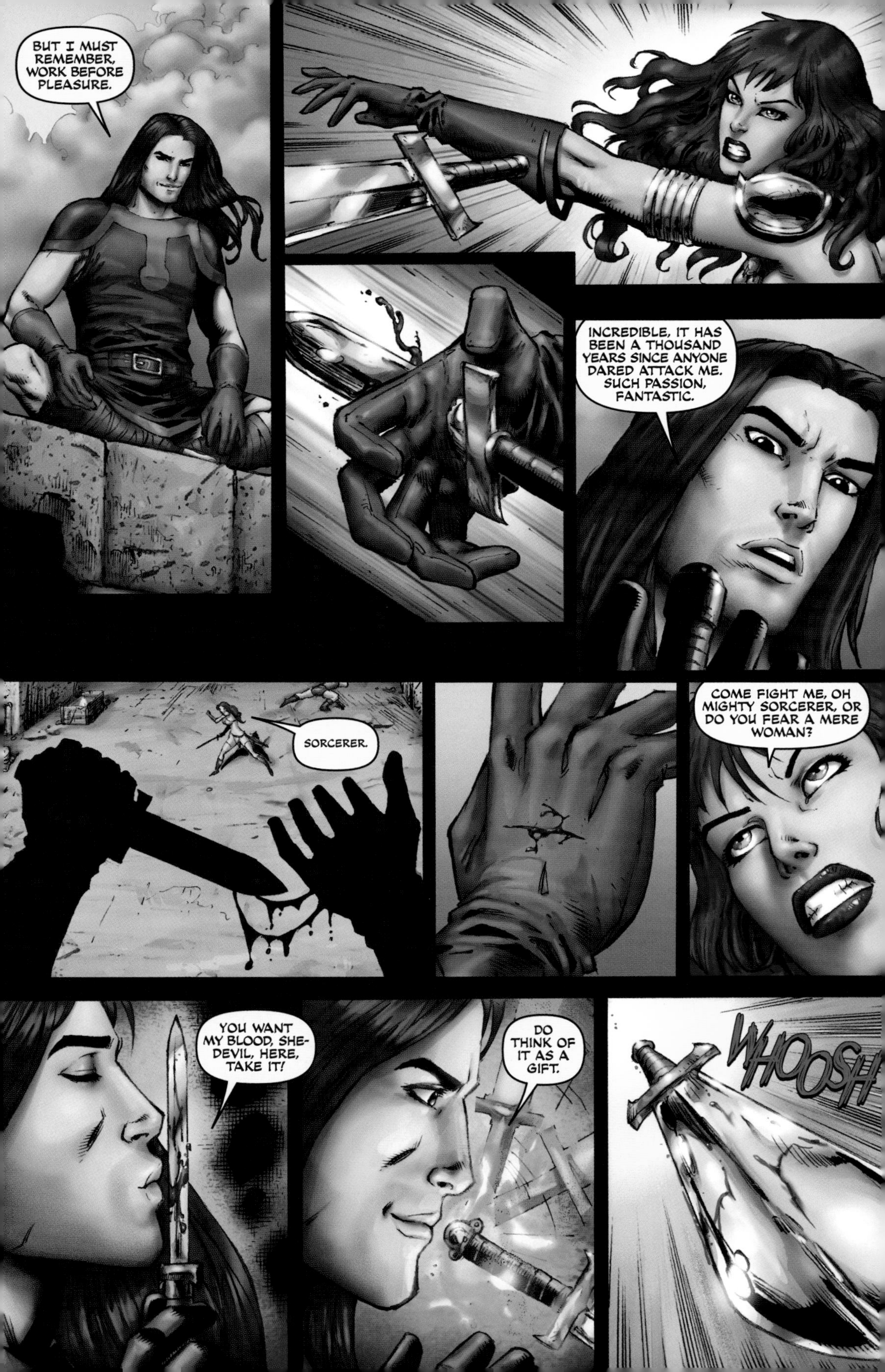
BUT I MUST REMEMBER, WORK BEFORE PLEASURE.
INCREDIBLE, IT HAS BEEN A THOUSAND YEARS SINCE ANYONE DARED ATTACK ME. SUCH PASSION, FANTASTIC.
SORCERER.
COME FIGHT ME, OH MIGHTY SORCERER, OR DO YOU FEAR A MERE WOMAN?
YOU WANT MY BLOOD, SHE-DEVIL, HERE, TAKE IT!
DO THINK OF IT AS A GIFT.
WHOOSH

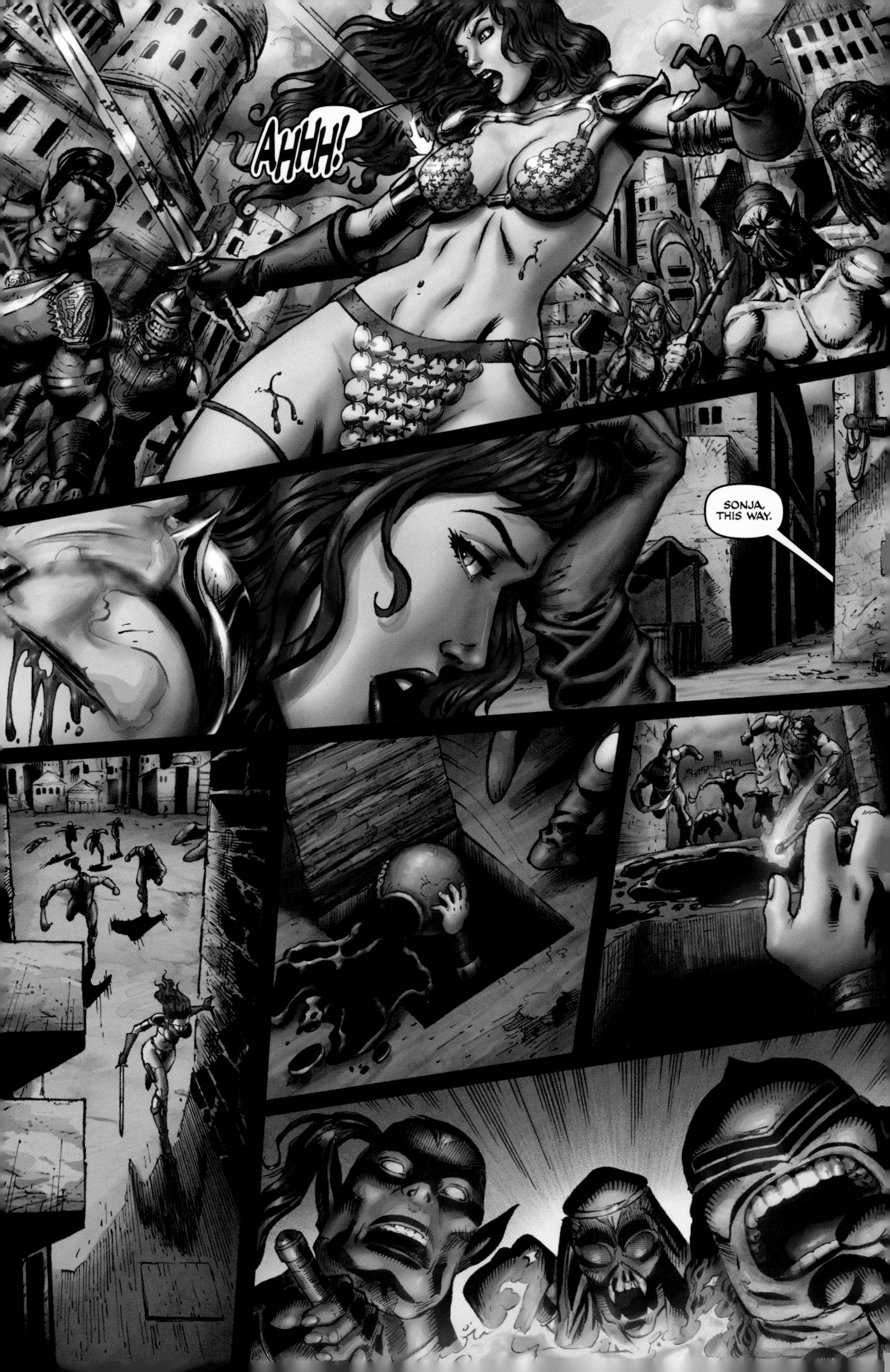
AHHH!
SONJA, THIS WAY.

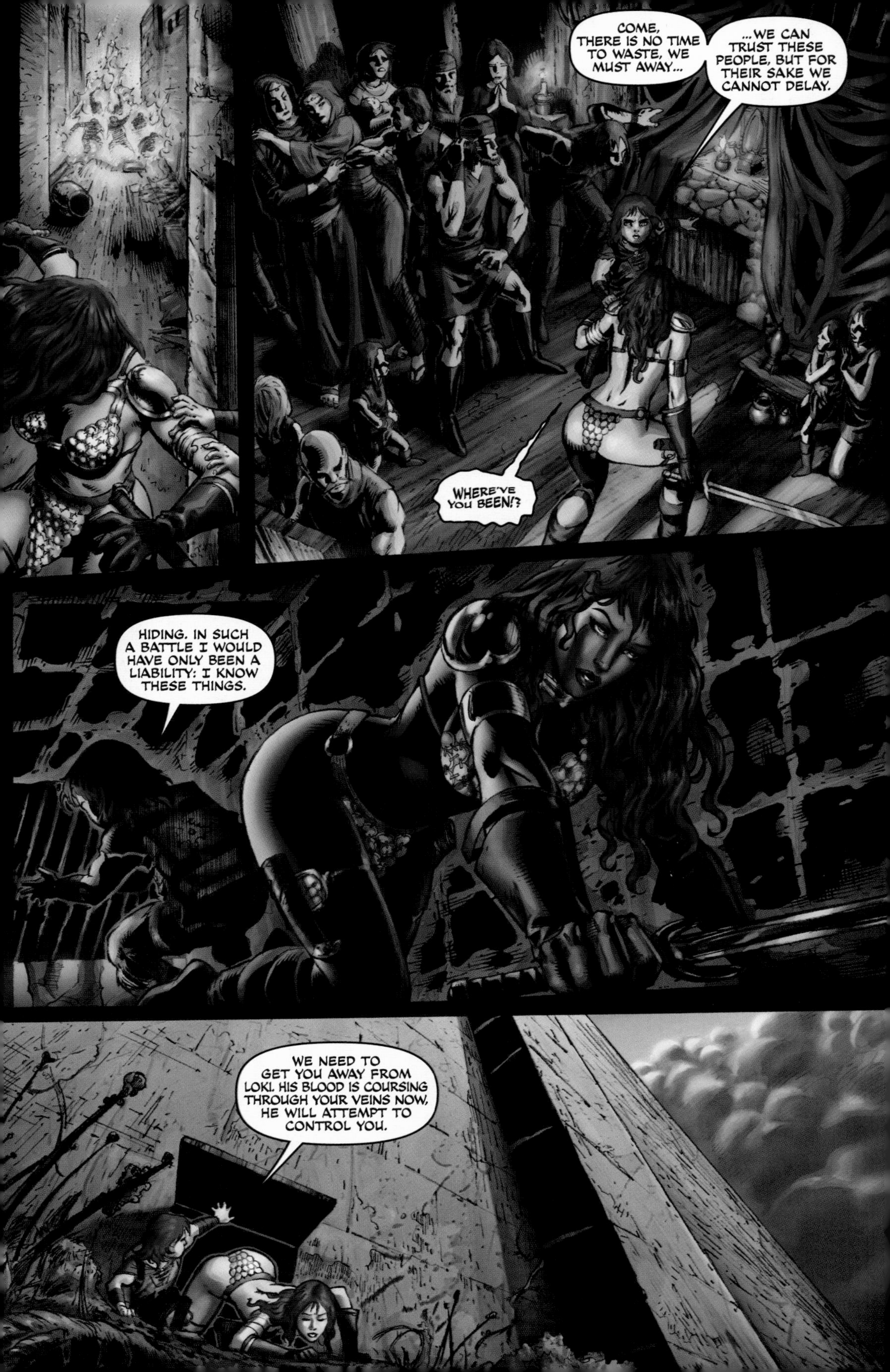
COME, THERE IS NO TIME TO WASTE, WE MUST AWAY...
...WE CAN TRUST THESE PEOPLE, BUT FOR THEIR SAKE WE CANNOT DELAY.
WHERE'VE YOU BEEN!?
HIDING. IN SUCH A BATTLE I WOULD HAVE ONLY BEEN A LIABILITY: I KNOW THESE THINGS.
WE NEED TO GET YOU AWAY FROM LOKI. HIS BLOOD IS COURSING THROUGH YOUR VEINS NOW, HE WILL ATTEMPT TO CONTROL YOU.

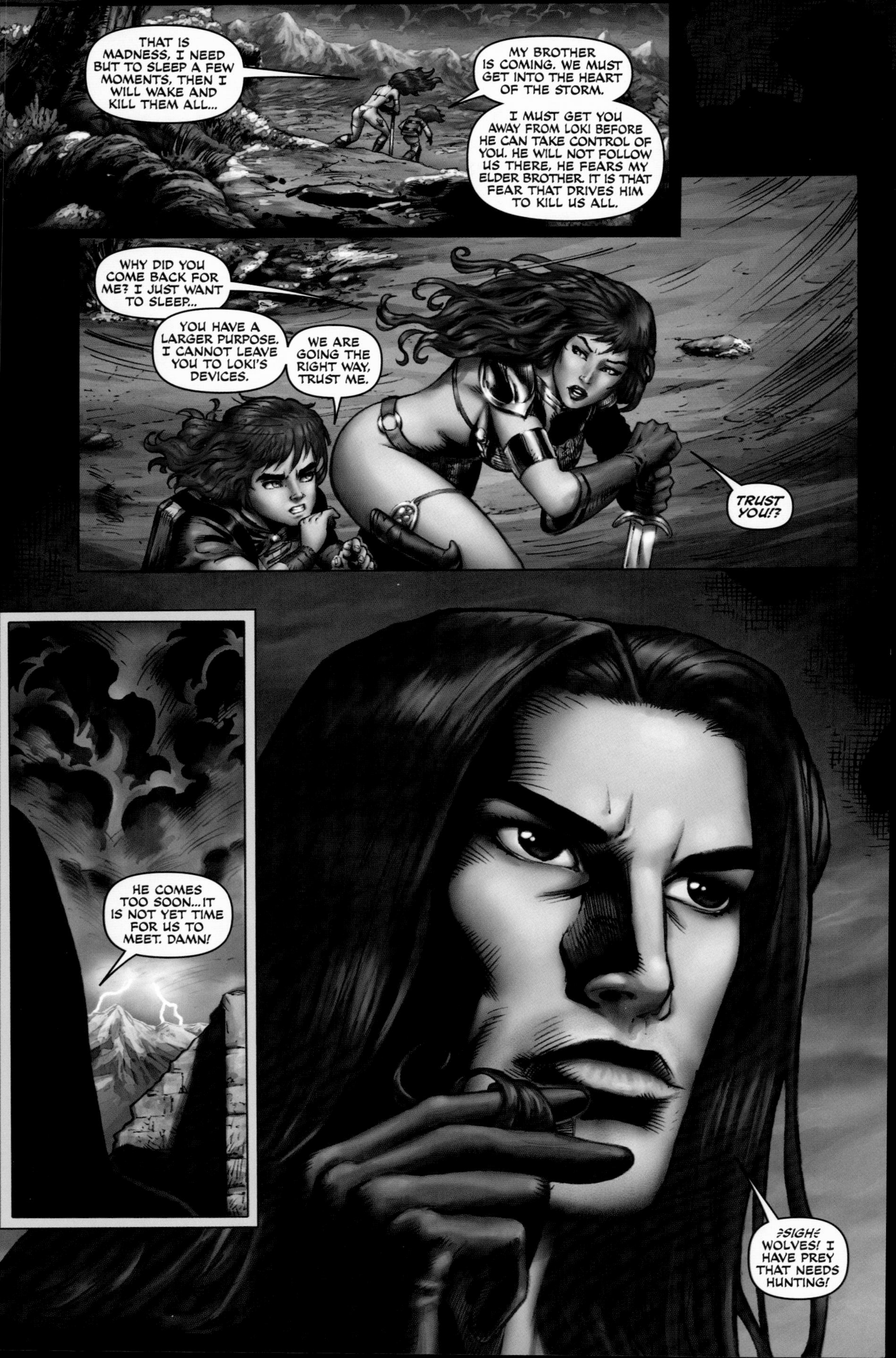

THAT IS MADNESS, I NEED BUT TO SLEEP A FEW MOMENTS, THEN I WILL WAKE AND KILL THEM ALL...
MY BROTHER IS COMING. WE MUST GET INTO THE HEART OF THE STORM.
I MUST GET YOU AWAY FROM LOKI BEFORE HE CAN TAKE CONTROL OF YOU. HE WILL NOT FOLLOW US THERE, HE FEARS MY ELDER BROTHER. IT IS THAT FEAR THAT DRIVES HIM TO KILL US ALL.
WHY DID YOU COME BACK FOR ME? I JUST WANT TO SLEEP...
YOU HAVE A LARGER PURPOSE. I CANNOT LEAVE YOU TO LOKI'S DEVICES.
WE ARE GOING THE RIGHT WAY, TRUST ME.
TRUST YOU!?
HE COMES TOO SOON...IT IS NOT YET TIME FOR US TO MEET. DAMN!
SIGH WOLVES! I HAVE PREY THAT NEEDS HUNTING!

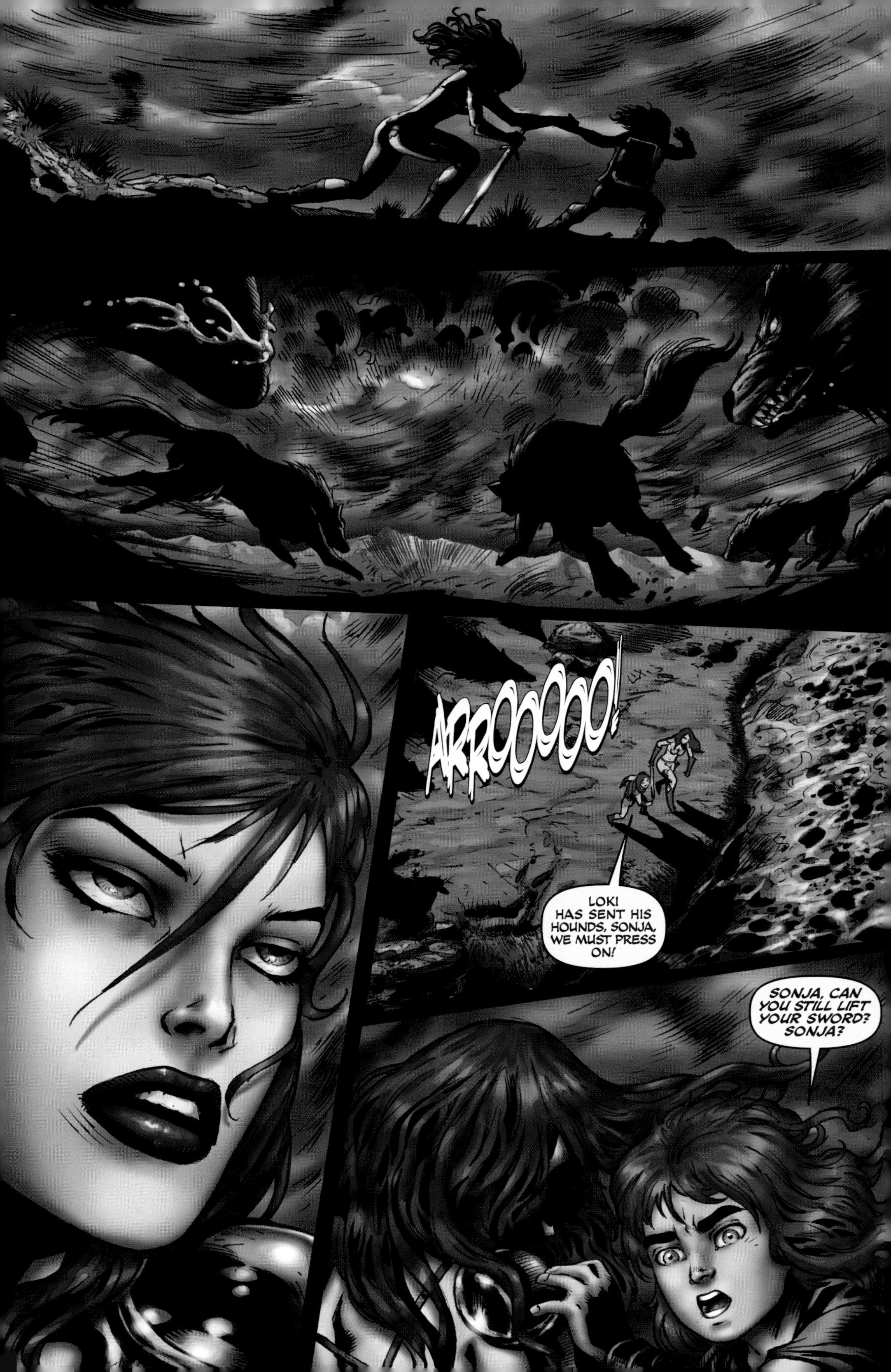
ARROOOOO!
LOKI HAS SENT HIS HOUNDS, SONJA, WE MUST PRESS ON!
SONJA, CAN YOU STILL LIFT YOUR SWORD? SONJA?

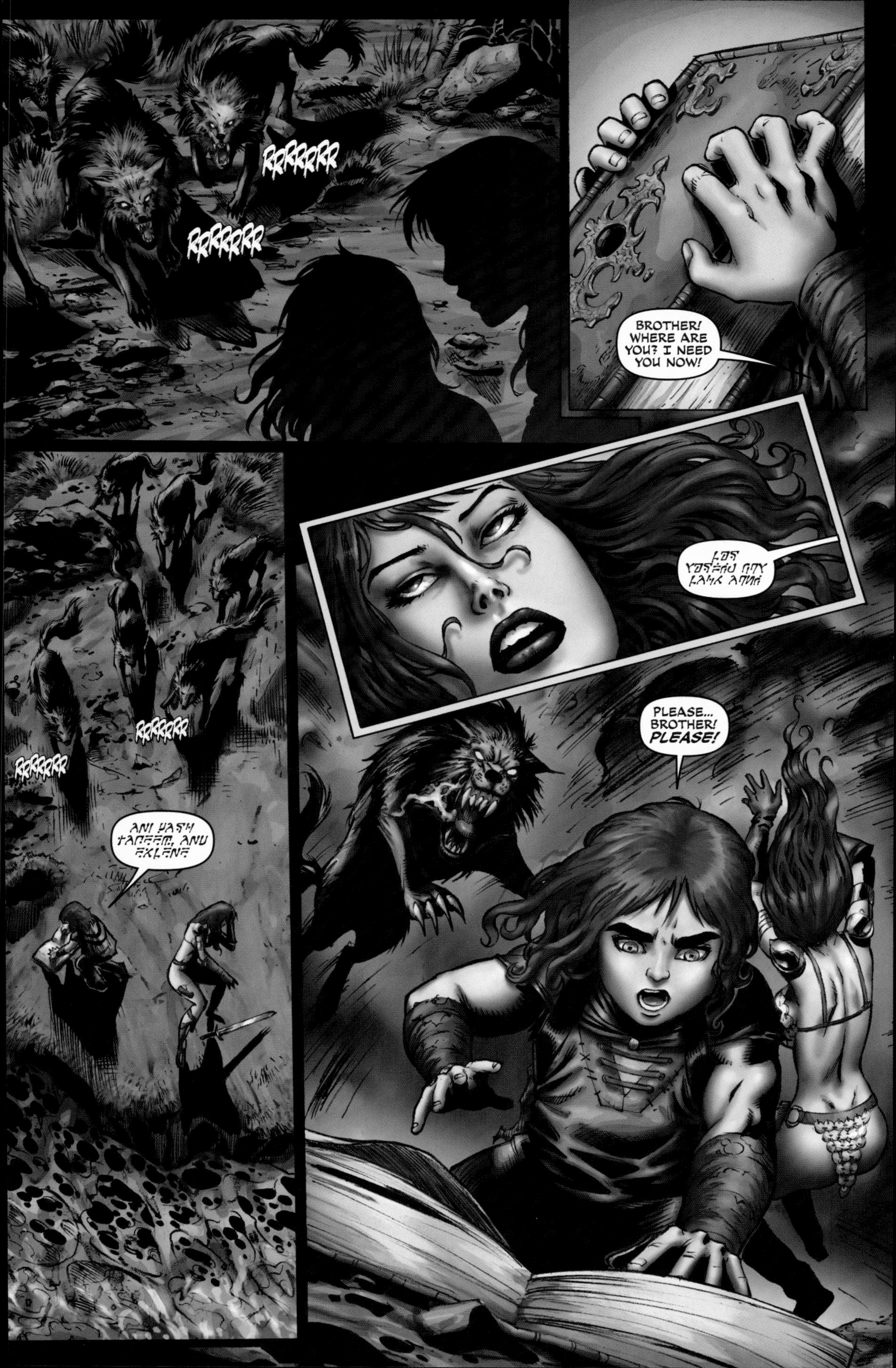
RRRRRRR
RRRRRRR
BROTHER! WHERE ARE YOU? I NEED YOU NOW!
RRRRRRR
RRRRRRR
PLEASE... BROTHER! *PLEASE!*

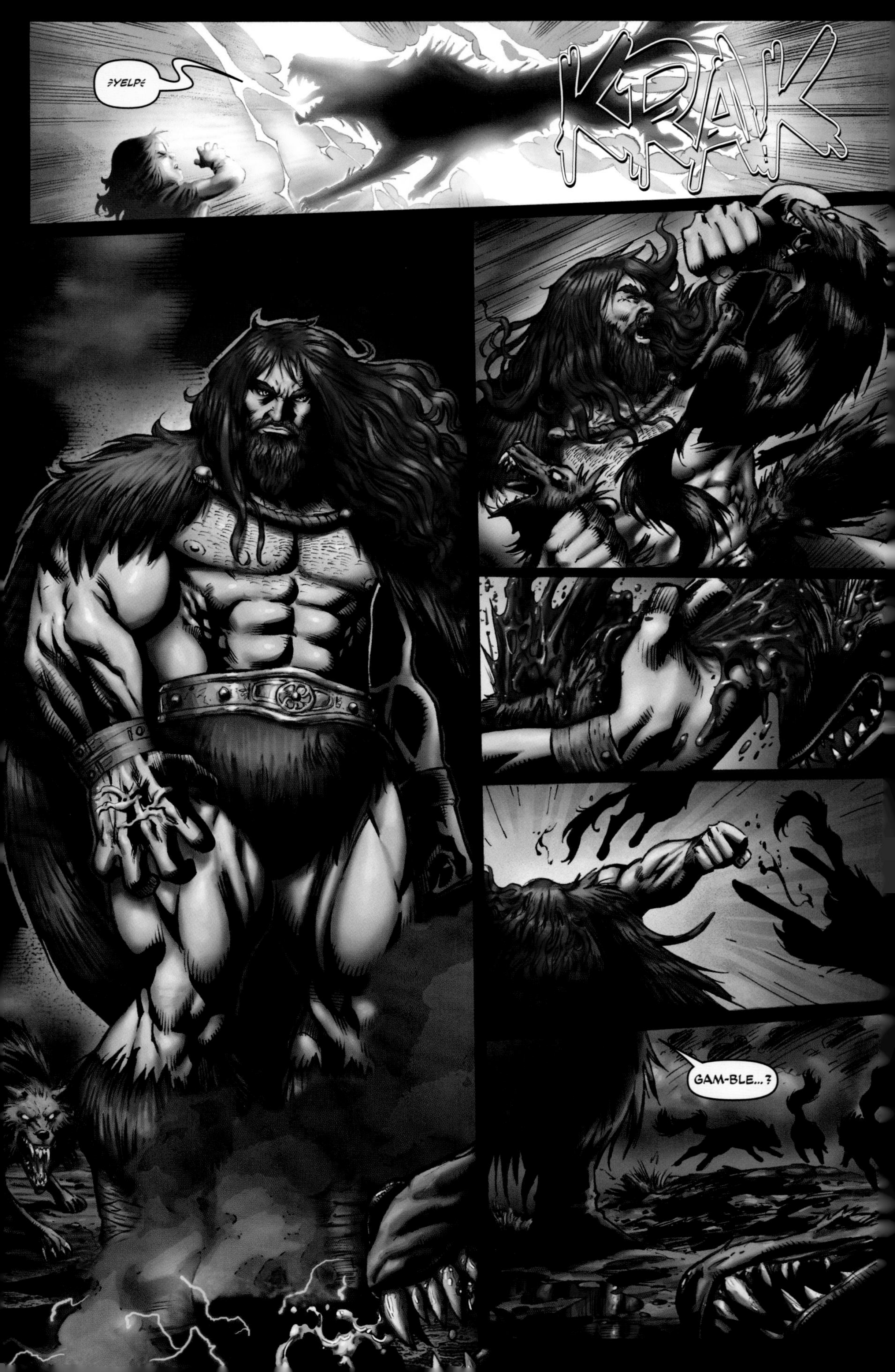

YELP
KRAK
GAM-BLE...?

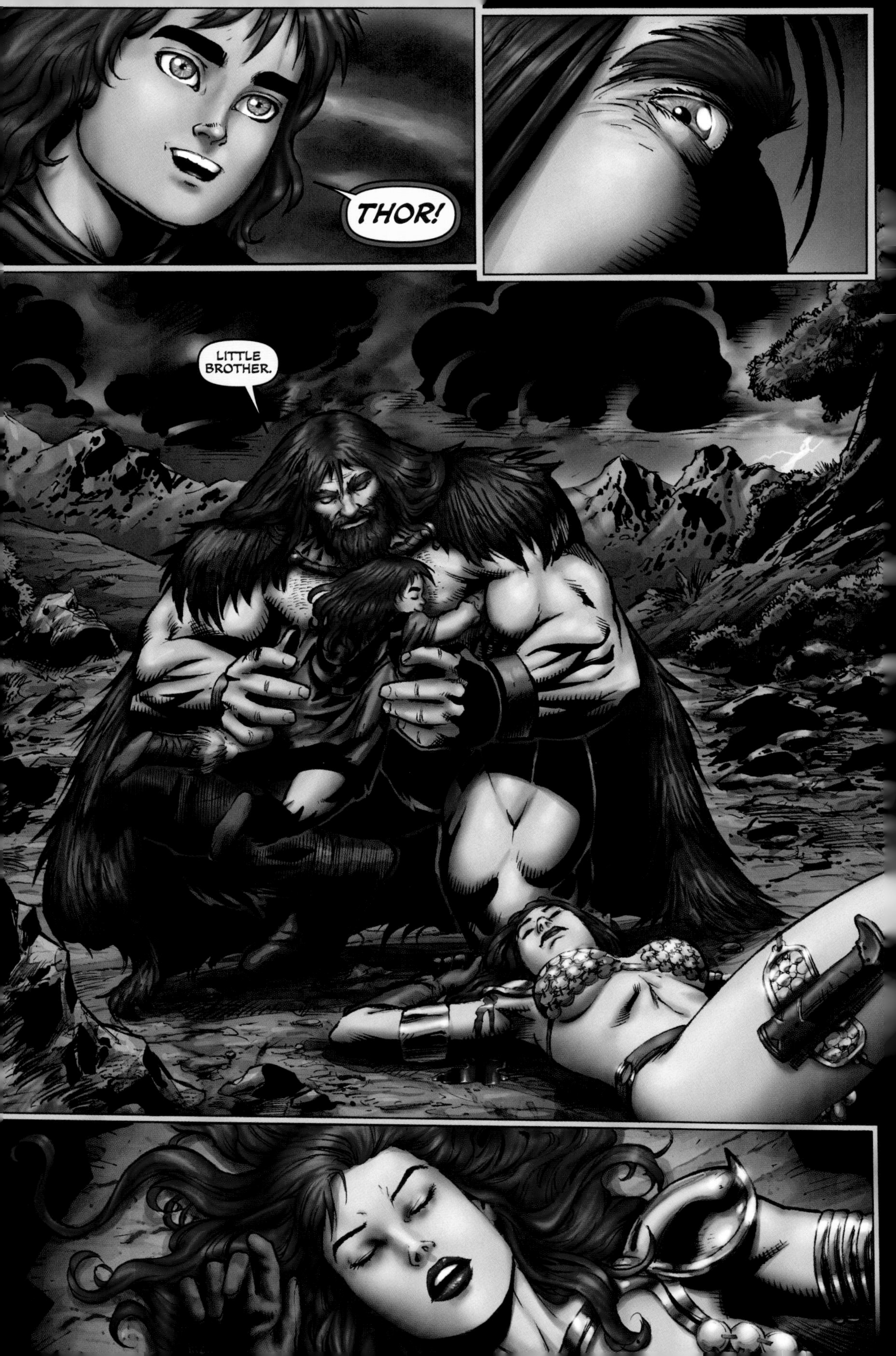
THOR!
LITTLE BROTHER.

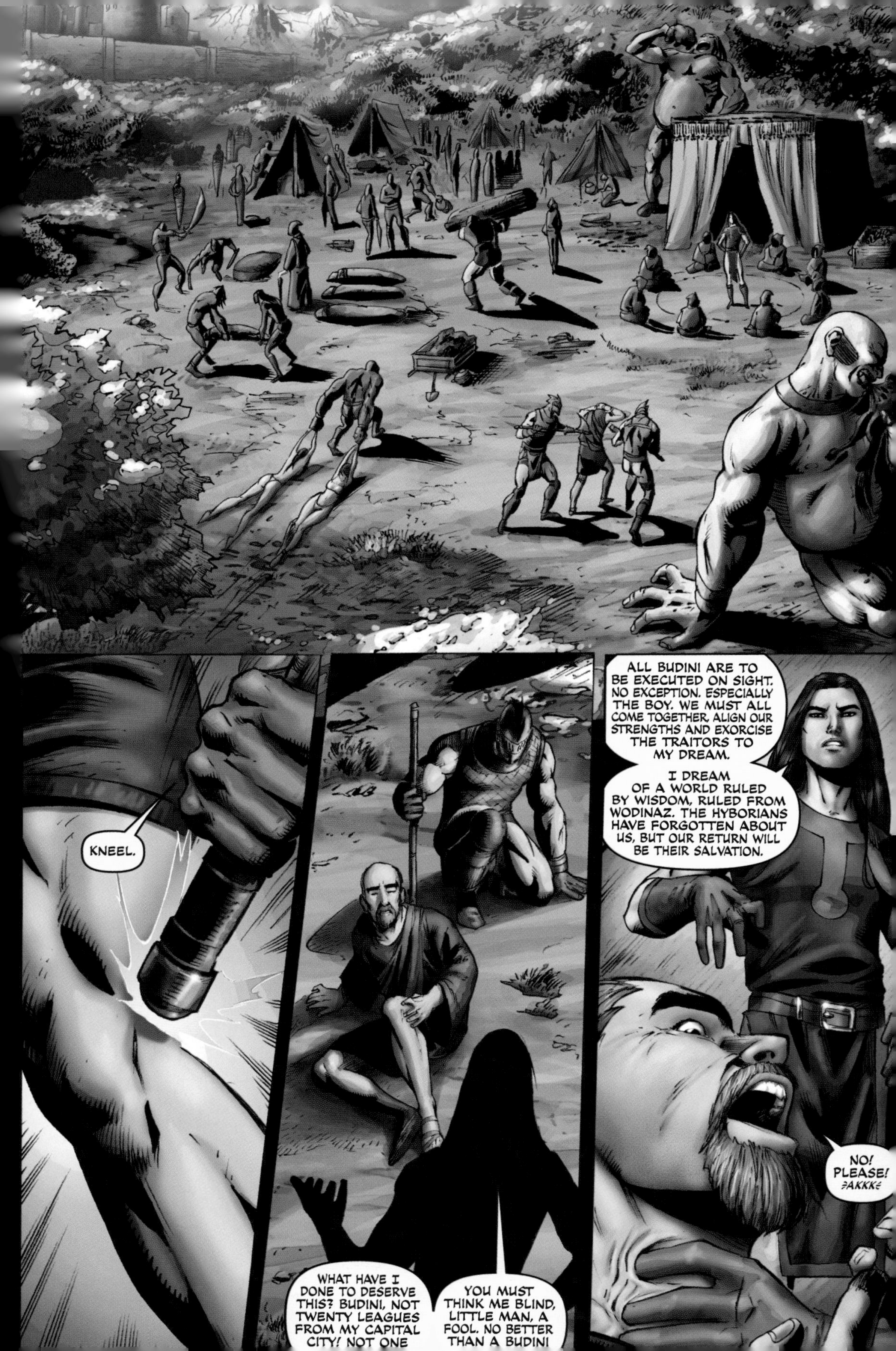
KNEEL.
ALL BUDINI ARE TO BE EXECUTED ON SIGHT. NO EXCEPTION. ESPECIALLY THE BOY. WE MUST ALL COME TOGETHER, ALIGN OUR STRENGTHS AND EXORCISE THE TRAITORS TO MY DREAM.
I DREAM OF A WORLD RULED BY WISDOM, RULED FROM WODINAZ. THE HYBORIANS HAVE FORGOTTEN ABOUT US, BUT OUR RETURN WILL BE THEIR SALVATION.
WHAT HAVE I DONE TO DESERVE THIS? BUDINI, NOT TWENTY LEAGUES FROM MY CAPITAL CITY! NOT ONE
YOU MUST THINK ME BLIND, LITTLE MAN, A FOOL. NO BETTER THAN A BUDINI
NO! PLEASE! AKKK

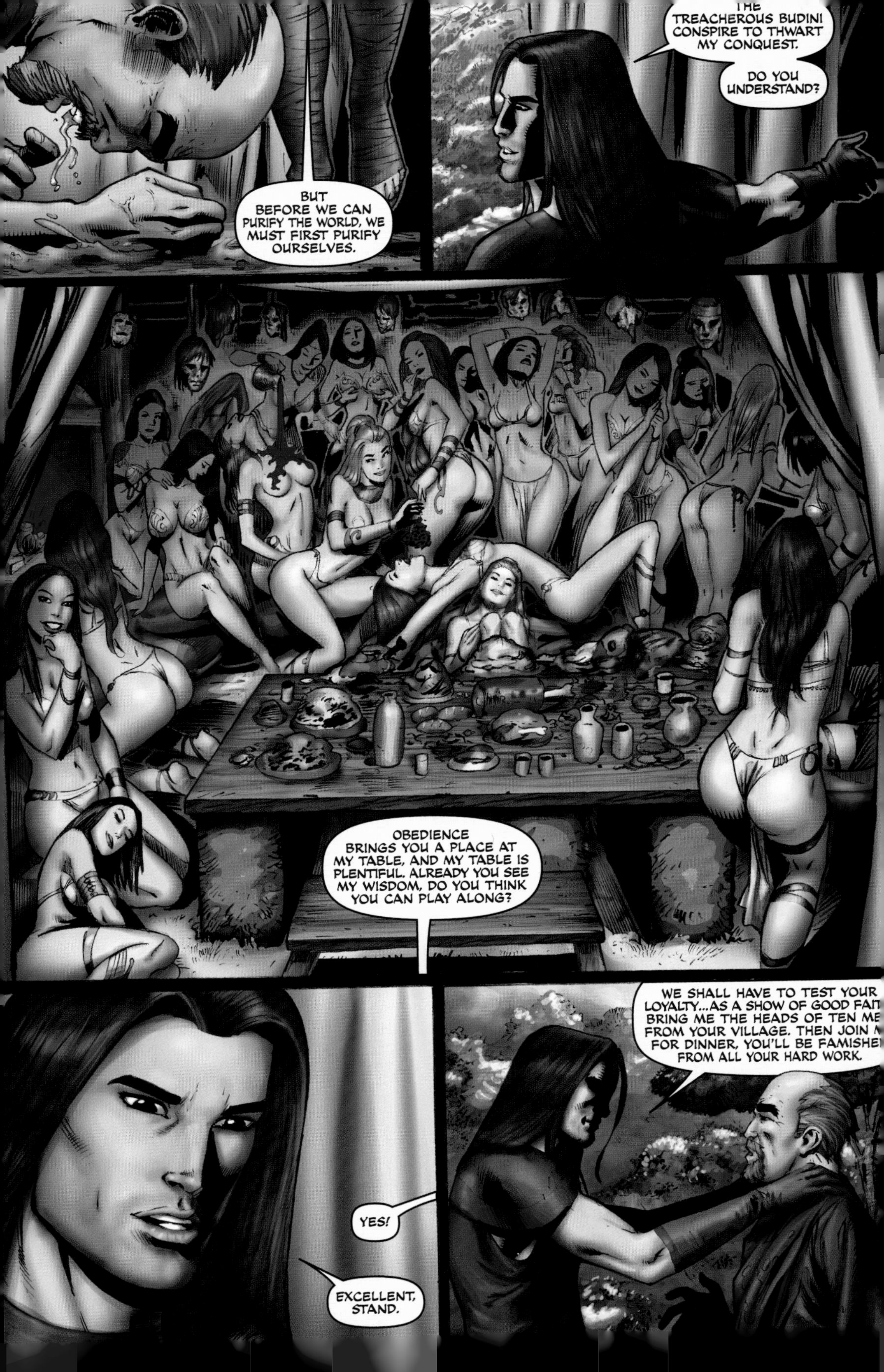
BUT BEFORE WE CAN PURIFY THE WORLD, WE MUST FIRST PURIFY OURSELVES.
THE TREACHEROUS BUDINI CONSPIRE TO THWART MY CONQUEST.
DO YOU UNDERSTAND?
OBEDIENCE BRINGS YOU A PLACE AT MY TABLE, AND MY TABLE IS PLENTIFUL. ALREADY YOU SEE MY WISDOM, DO YOU THINK YOU CAN PLAY ALONG?
YES!
EXCELLENT, STAND.
WE SHALL HAVE TO TEST YOUR LOYALTY...AS A SHOW OF GOOD FAIT BRING ME THE HEADS OF TEN ME FROM YOUR VILLAGE. THEN JOIN M FOR DINNER, YOU'LL BE FAMISHE FROM ALL YOUR HARD WORK.

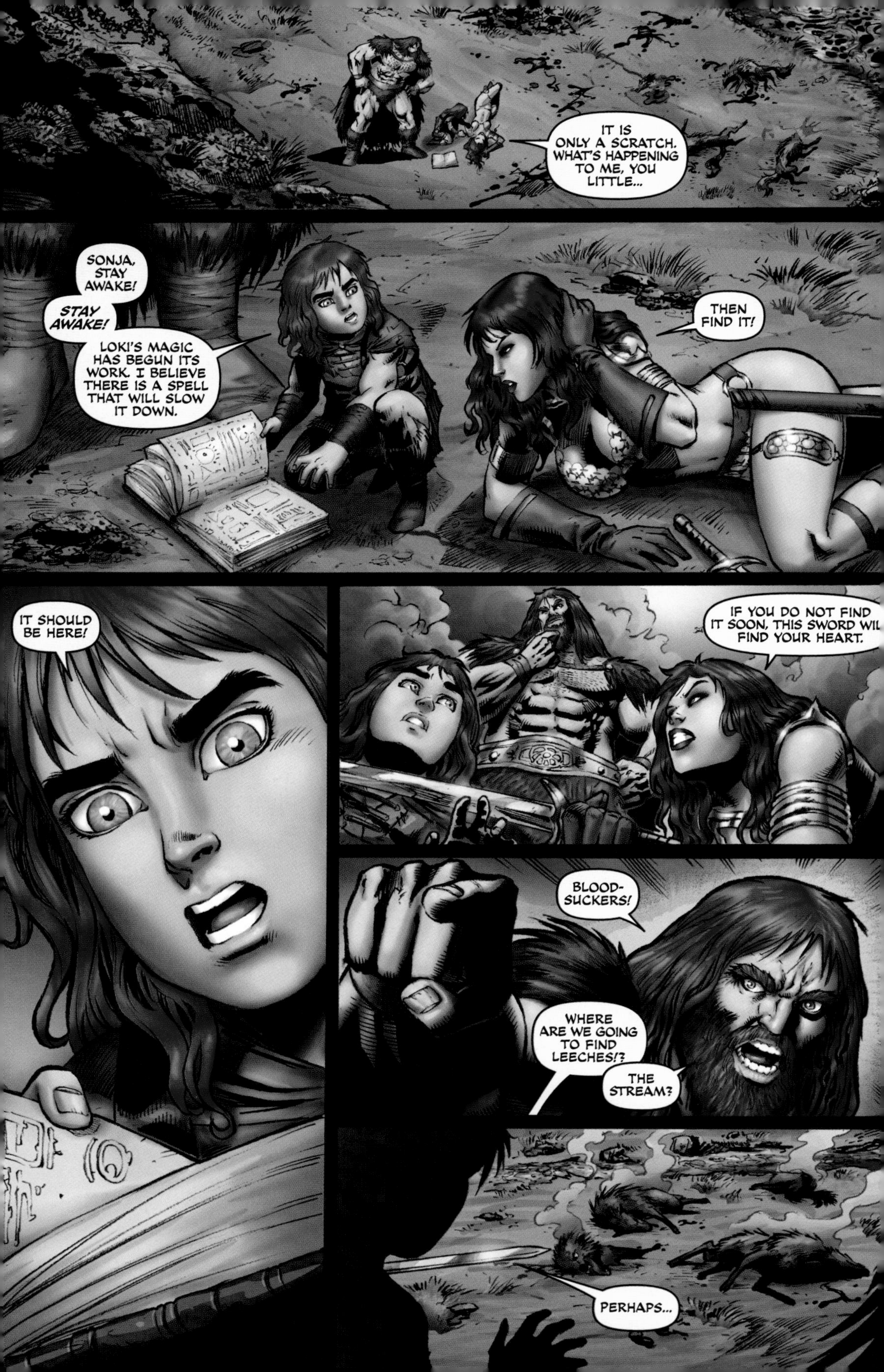
IT IS ONLY A SCRATCH. WHAT'S HAPPENING TO ME, YOU LITTLE...
SONJA, STAY AWAKE!
STAY AWAKE!
LOKI'S MAGIC HAS BEGUN ITS WORK. I BELIEVE THERE IS A SPELL THAT WILL SLOW IT DOWN.
THEN FIND IT!
IT SHOULD BE HERE!
IF YOU DO NOT FIND IT SOON, THIS SWORD WIL FIND YOUR HEART.
BLOOD-SUCKERS!
WHERE ARE WE GOING TO FIND LEECHES!?
THE STREAM?
PERHAPS...

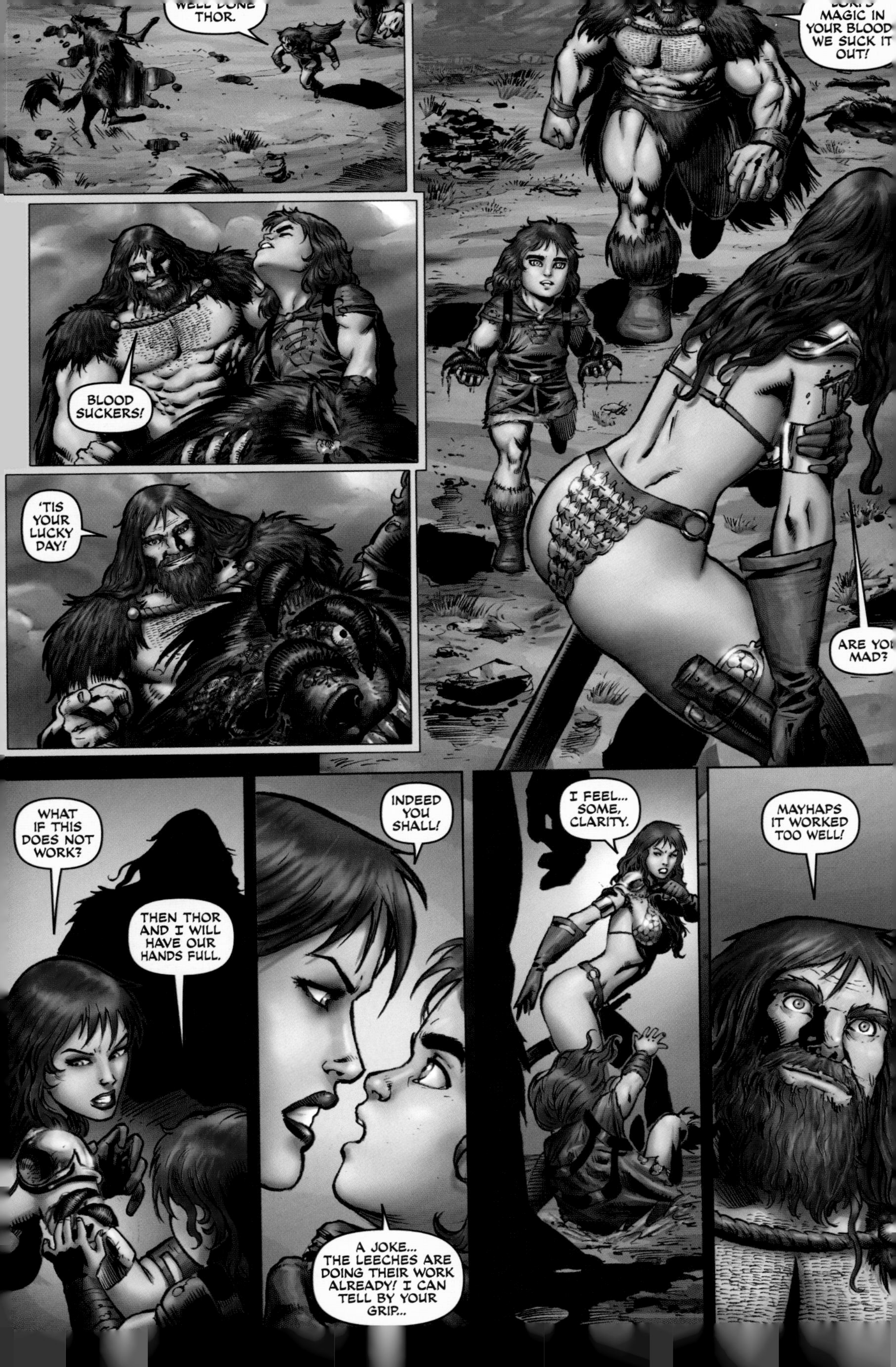
WELL DONE THOR.
MAGIC IN YOUR BLOOD WE SUCK IT OUT!
BLOOD SUCKERS!
'TIS YOUR LUCKY DAY!
MAD?
WHAT IF THIS DOES NOT WORK?
THEN THOR AND I WILL HAVE OUR HANDS FULL.
INDEED YOU SHALL!
A JOKE... THE LEECHES ARE DOING THEIR WORK ALREADY! I CAN TELL BY YOUR GRIP...
I FEEL... SOME, CLARITY.
MAYHAPS IT WORKED TOO WELL!

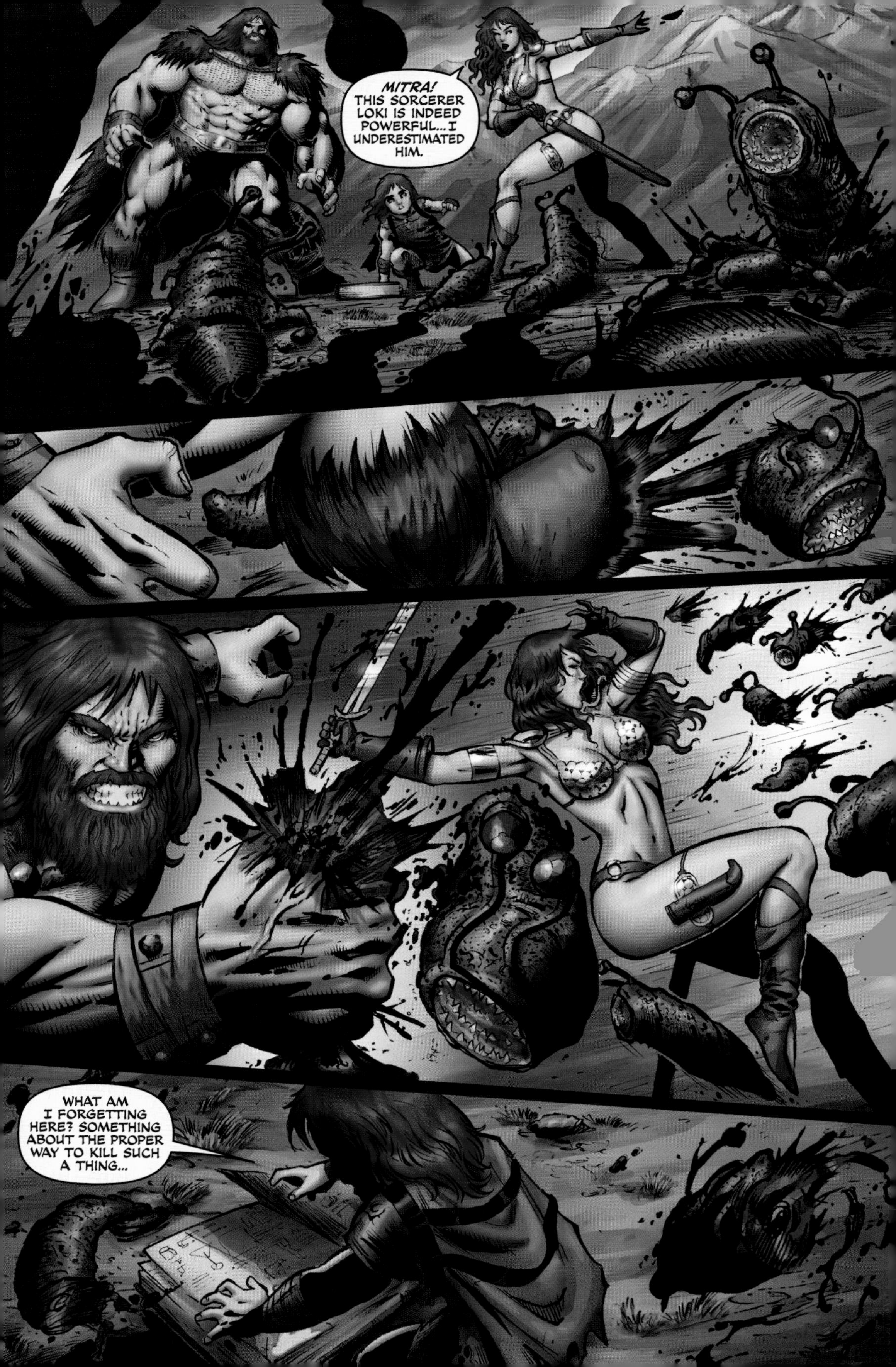
MITRA! THIS SORCERER LOKI IS INDEED POWERFUL... I UNDERESTIMATED HIM.
WHAT AM I FORGETTING HERE? SOMETHING ABOUT THE PROPER WAY TO KILL SUCH A THING...

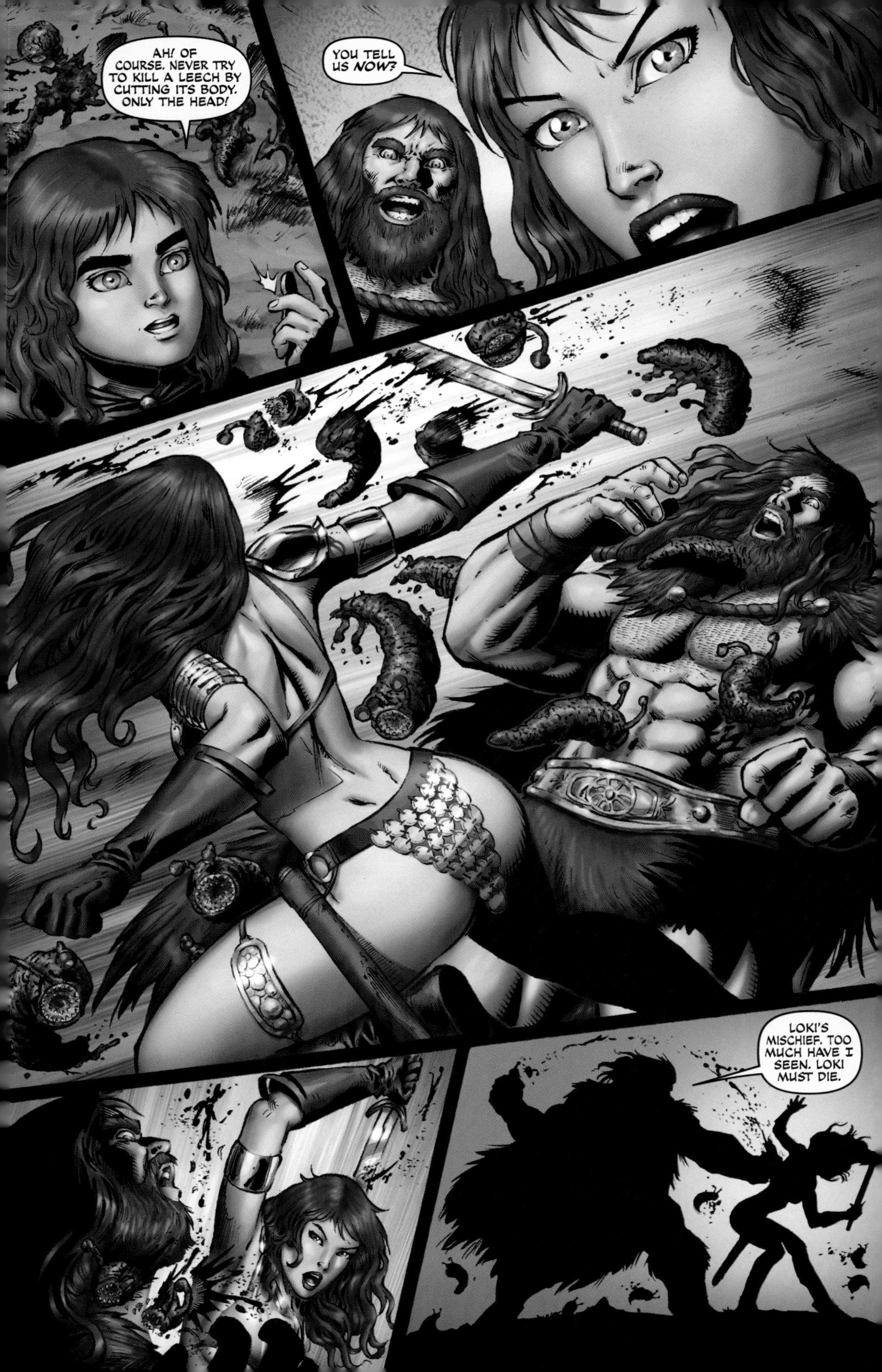
AH! OF COURSE. NEVER TRY TO KILL A LEECH BY CUTTING ITS BODY. ONLY THE HEAD!
YOU TELL US NOW?
LOKI'S MISCHIEF. TOO MUCH HAVE I SEEN. LOKI MUST DIE.

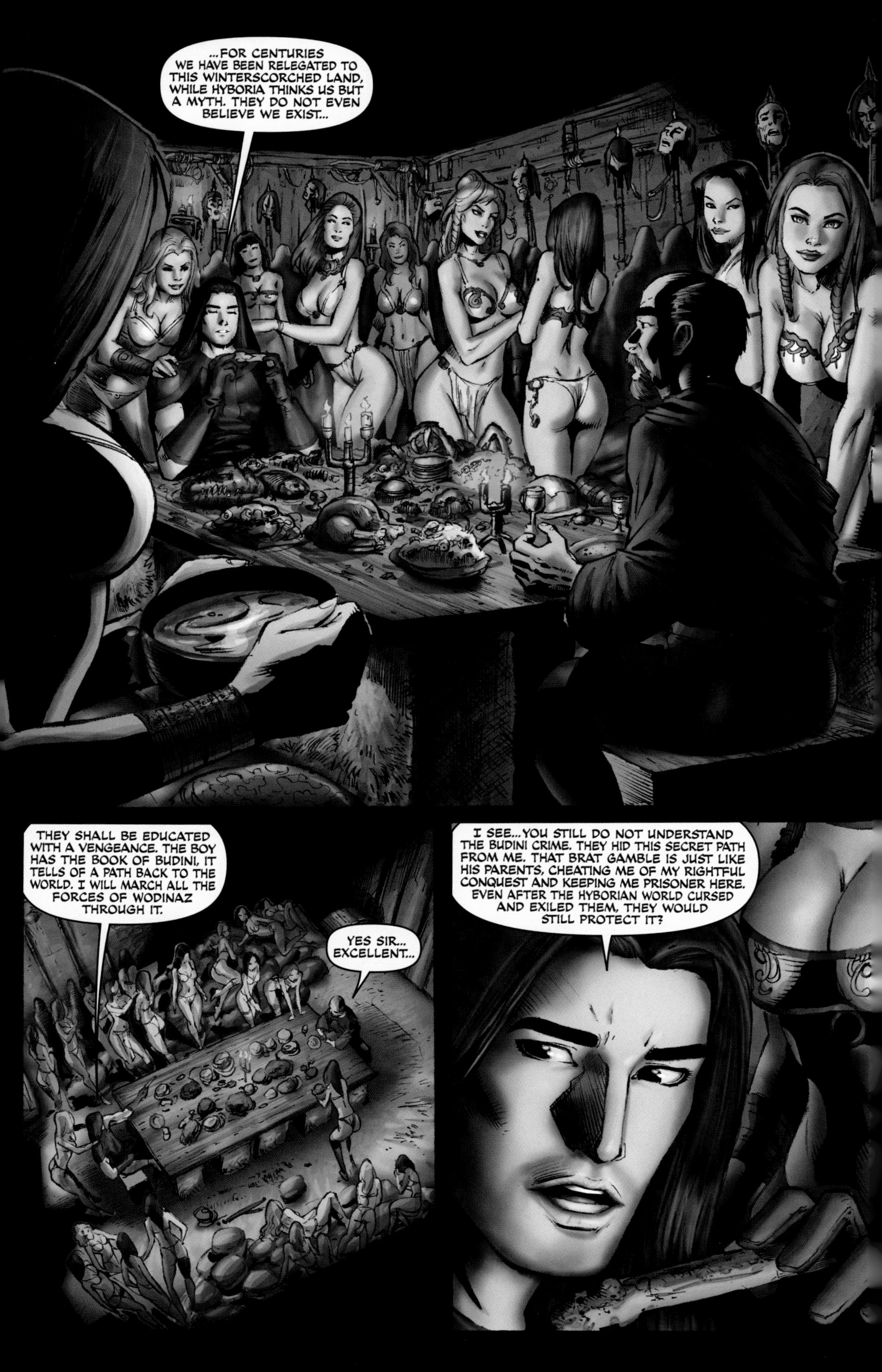
...FOR CENTURIES WE HAVE BEEN RELEGATED TO THIS WINTERSCORCHED LAND, WHILE HYBORIA THINKS US BUT A MYTH. THEY DO NOT EVEN BELIEVE WE EXIST...
THEY SHALL BE EDUCATED WITH A VENGEANCE. THE BOY HAS THE BOOK OF BUDINI, IT TELLS OF A PATH BACK TO THE WORLD. I WILL MARCH ALL THE FORCES OF WODINAZ THROUGH IT.
YES SIR... EXCELLENT...
I SEE... YOU STILL DO NOT UNDERSTAND THE BUDINI CRIME. THEY HID THIS SECRET PATH FROM ME. THAT BRAT GAMBLE IS JUST LIKE HIS PARENTS, CHEATING ME OF MY RIGHTFUL CONQUEST AND KEEPING ME PRISONER HERE. EVEN AFTER THE HYBORIAN WORLD CURSED AND EXILED THEM, THEY WOULD STILL PROTECT IT?

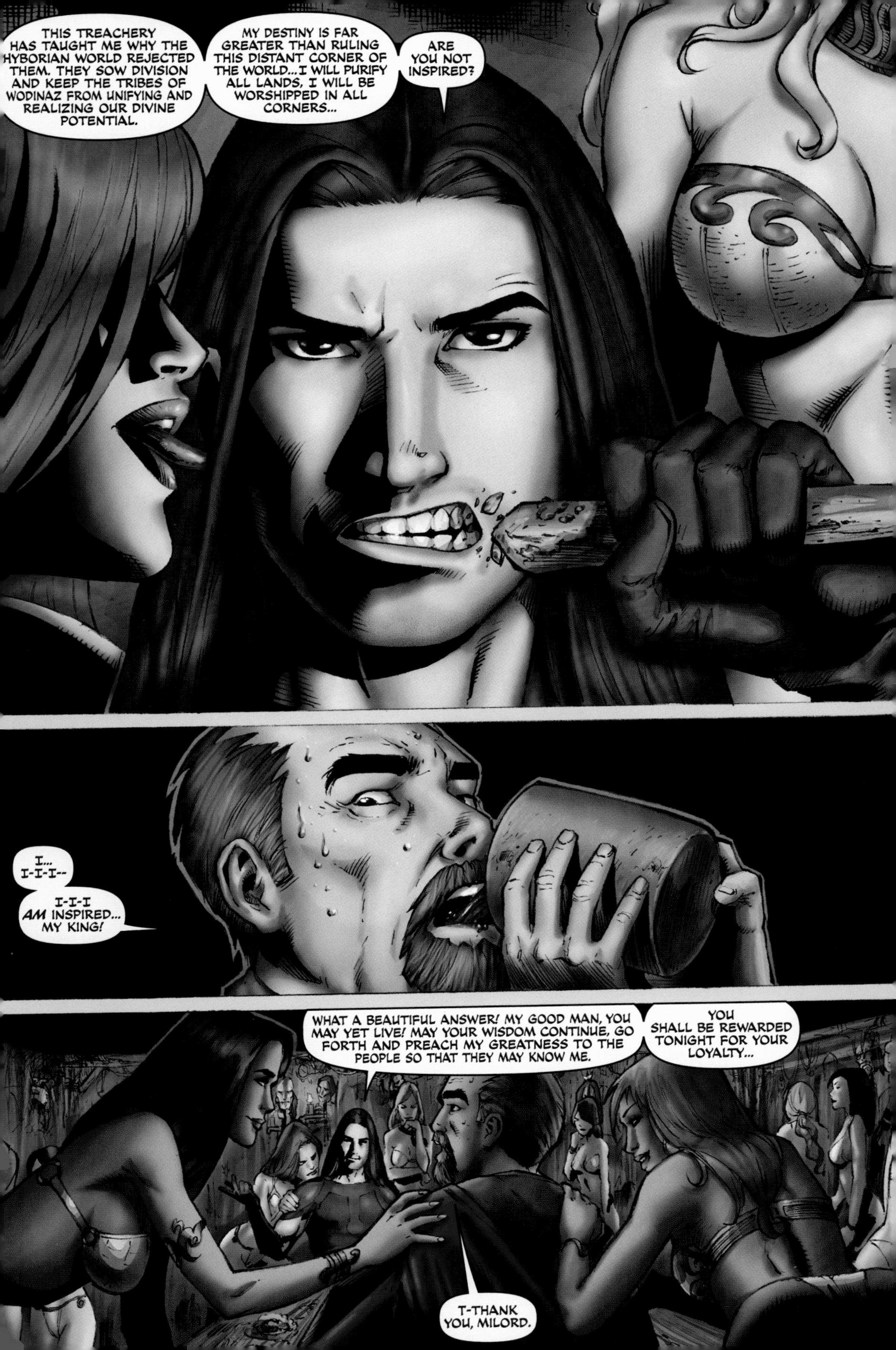
THIS TREACHERY HAS TAUGHT ME WHY THE HYBORIAN WORLD REJECTED THEM. THEY SOW DIVISION AND KEEP THE TRIBES OF WODINAZ FROM UNIFYING AND REALIZING OUR DIVINE POTENTIAL.
MY DESTINY IS FAR GREATER THAN RULING THIS DISTANT CORNER OF THE WORLD...I WILL PURIFY ALL LANDS, I WILL BE WORSHIPPED IN ALL CORNERS...
ARE YOU NOT INSPIRED?
I... I-I-I--
I-I-I AM INSPIRED... MY KING!
WHAT A BEAUTIFUL ANSWER! MY GOOD MAN, YOU MAY YET LIVE! MAY YOUR WISDOM CONTINUE, GO FORTH AND PREACH MY GREATNESS TO THE PEOPLE SO THAT THEY MAY KNOW ME.
YOU SHALL BE REWARDED TONIGHT FOR YOUR LOYALTY...
T-THANK YOU, MILORD.

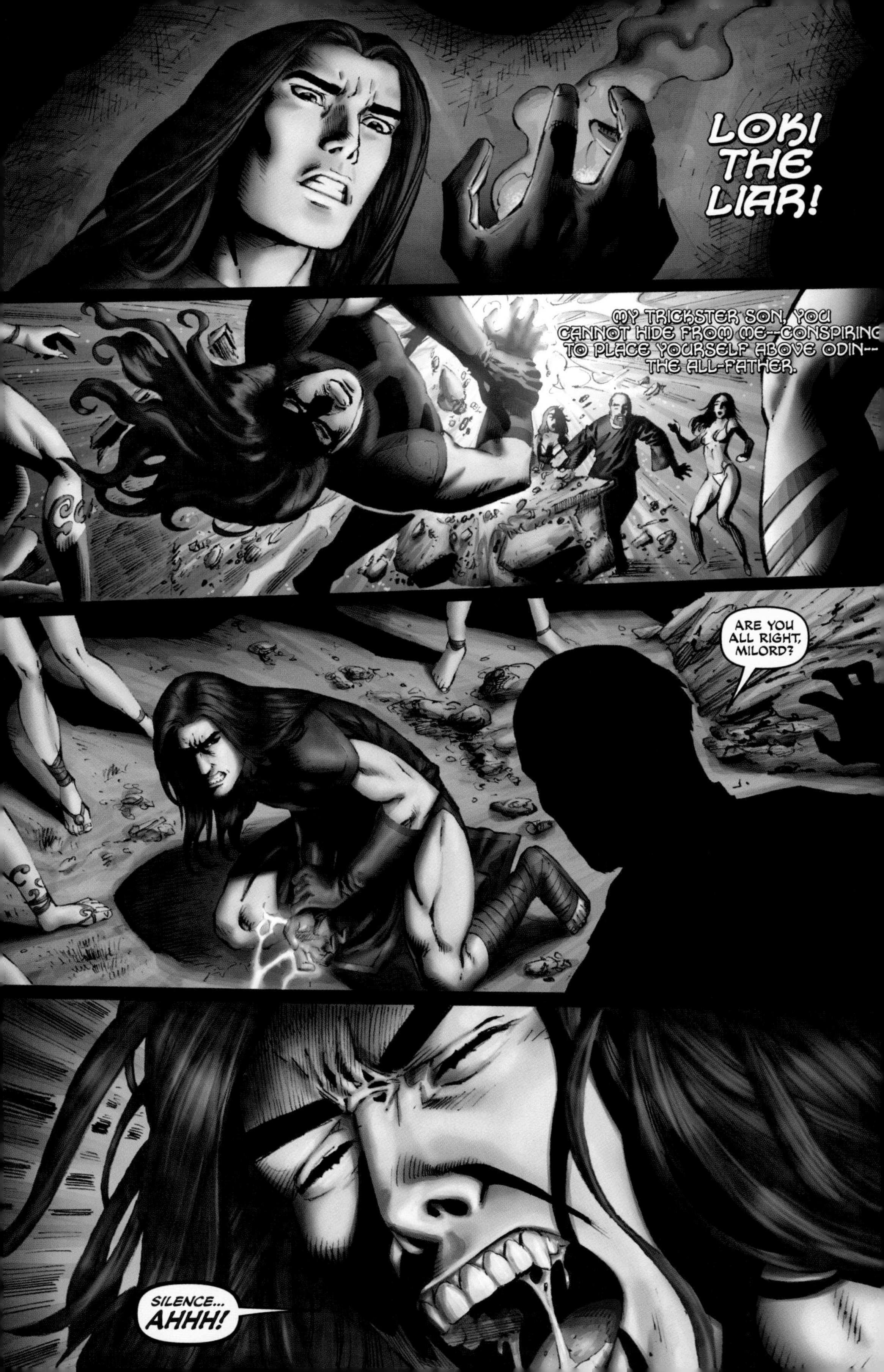
LOKI THE LIAR!
MY TRICKSTER SON, YOU CANNOT HIDE FROM ME--CONSPIRING TO PLACE YOURSELF ABOVE ODIN--THE ALL-FATHER.
ARE YOU ALL RIGHT, MILORD?
SILENCE... AHHH!

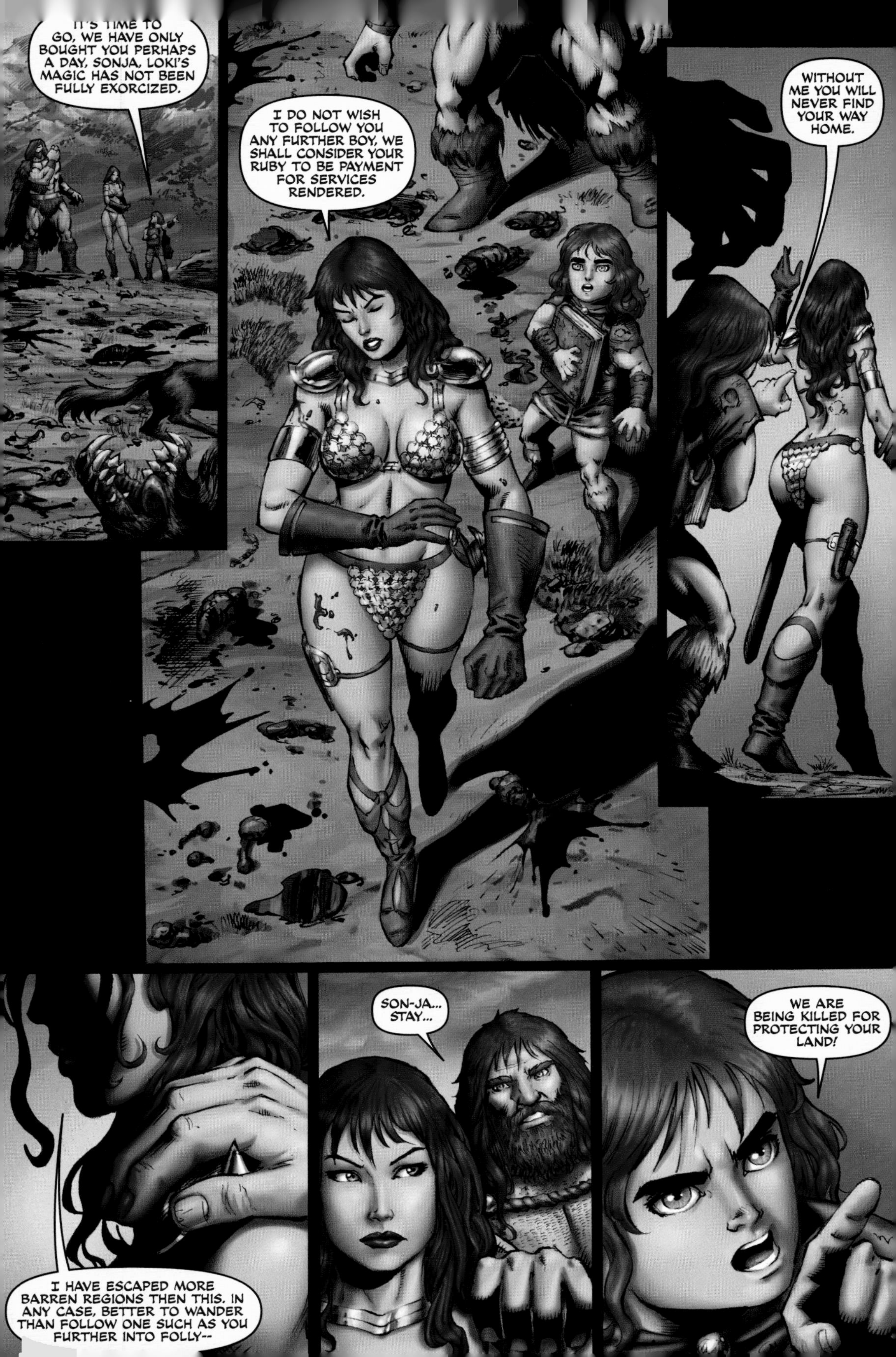
IT'S TIME TO GO, WE HAVE ONLY BOUGHT YOU PERHAPS A DAY, SONJA, LOKI'S MAGIC HAS NOT BEEN FULLY EXORCIZED.
I DO NOT WISH TO FOLLOW YOU ANY FURTHER BOY, WE SHALL CONSIDER YOUR RUBY TO BE PAYMENT FOR SERVICES RENDERED.
WITHOUT ME YOU WILL NEVER FIND YOUR WAY HOME.
I HAVE ESCAPED MORE BARREN REGIONS THEN THIS. IN ANY CASE, BETTER TO WANDER THAN FOLLOW ONE SUCH AS YOU FURTHER INTO FOLLY--
SON-JA... STAY...
WE ARE BEING KILLED FOR PROTECTING YOUR LAND!

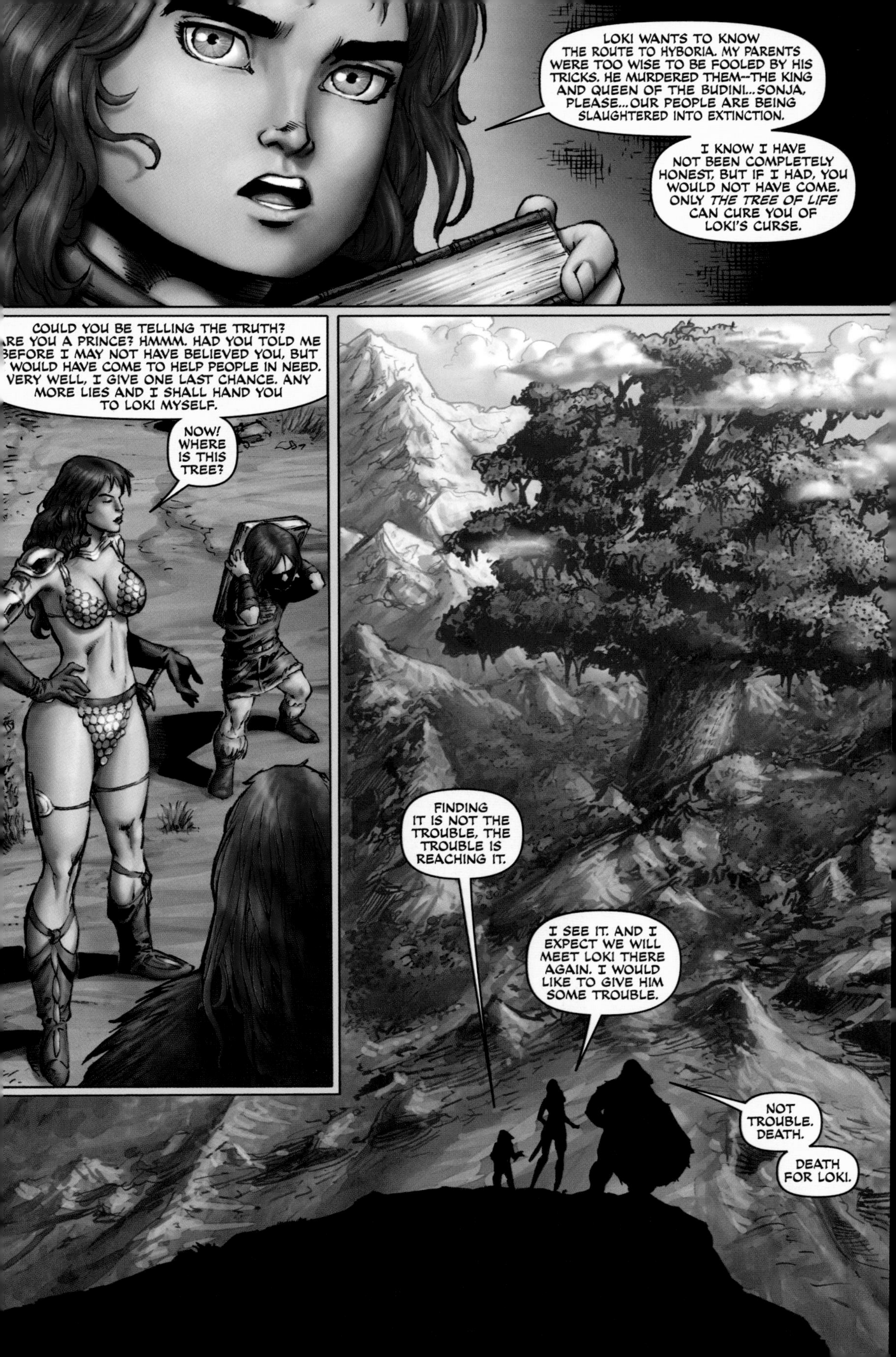
LOKI WANTS TO KNOW THE ROUTE TO HYBORIA. MY PARENTS WERE TOO WISE TO BE FOOLED BY HIS TRICKS. HE MURDERED THEM--THE KING AND QUEEN OF THE BUDINI...SONJA, PLEASE...OUR PEOPLE ARE BEING SLAUGHTERED INTO EXTINCTION.
I KNOW I HAVE NOT BEEN COMPLETELY HONEST, BUT IF I HAD, YOU WOULD NOT HAVE COME. ONLY *THE TREE OF LIFE* CAN CURE YOU OF LOKI'S CURSE.
COULD YOU BE TELLING THE TRUTH? ARE YOU A PRINCE? HMMM. HAD YOU TOLD ME BEFORE I MAY NOT HAVE BELIEVED YOU, BUT I WOULD HAVE COME TO HELP PEOPLE IN NEED. VERY WELL, I GIVE ONE LAST CHANCE. ANY MORE LIES AND I SHALL HAND YOU TO LOKI MYSELF.
NOW! WHERE IS THIS TREE?
FINDING IT IS NOT THE TROUBLE, THE TROUBLE IS REACHING IT.
I SEE IT. AND I EXPECT WE WILL MEET LOKI THERE AGAIN. I WOULD LIKE TO GIVE HIM SOME TROUBLE.
NOT TROUBLE. DEATH.
DEATH FOR LOKI.

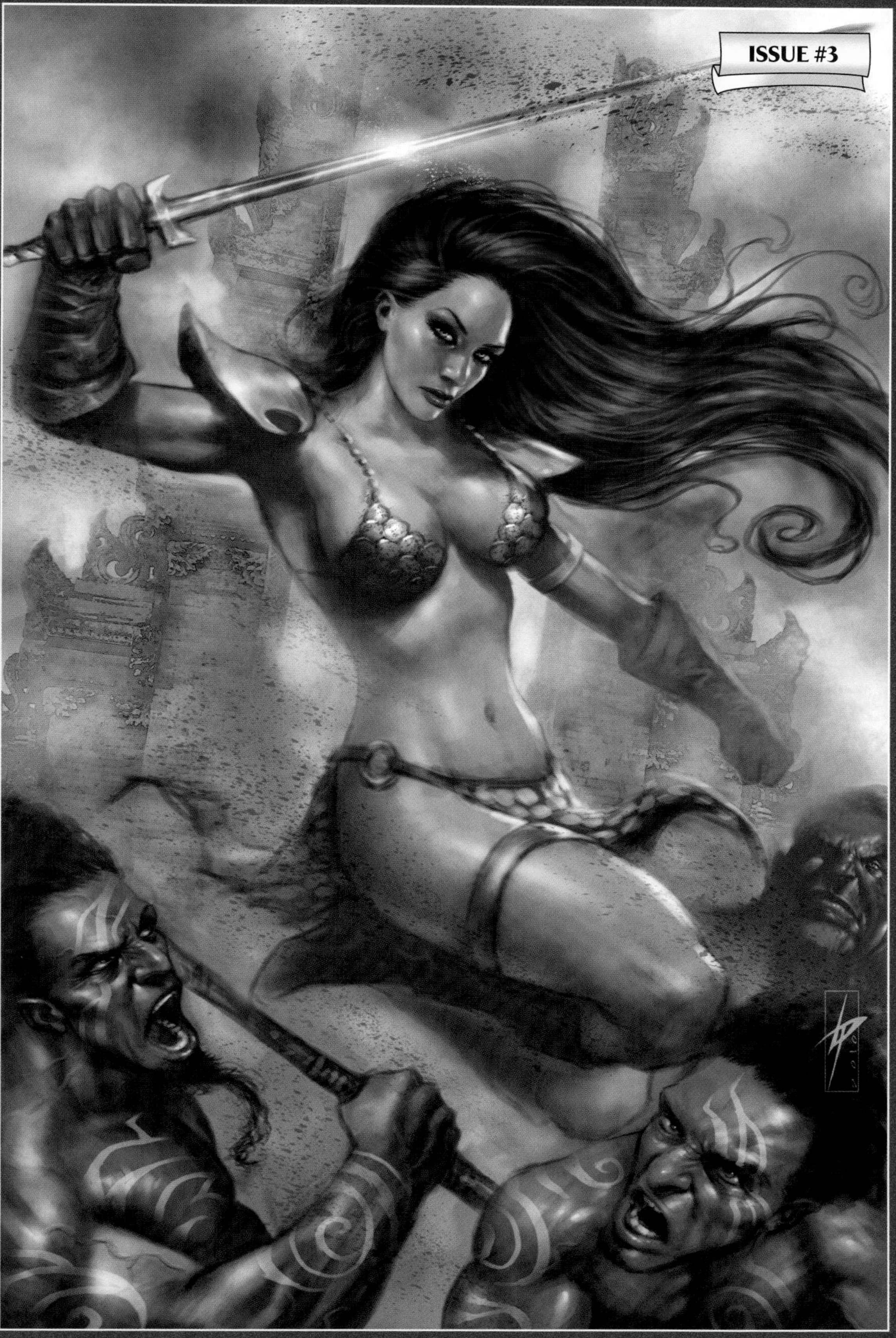
ISSUE #3

ISSUE #3 COVER BY LUCIO PARRILLO

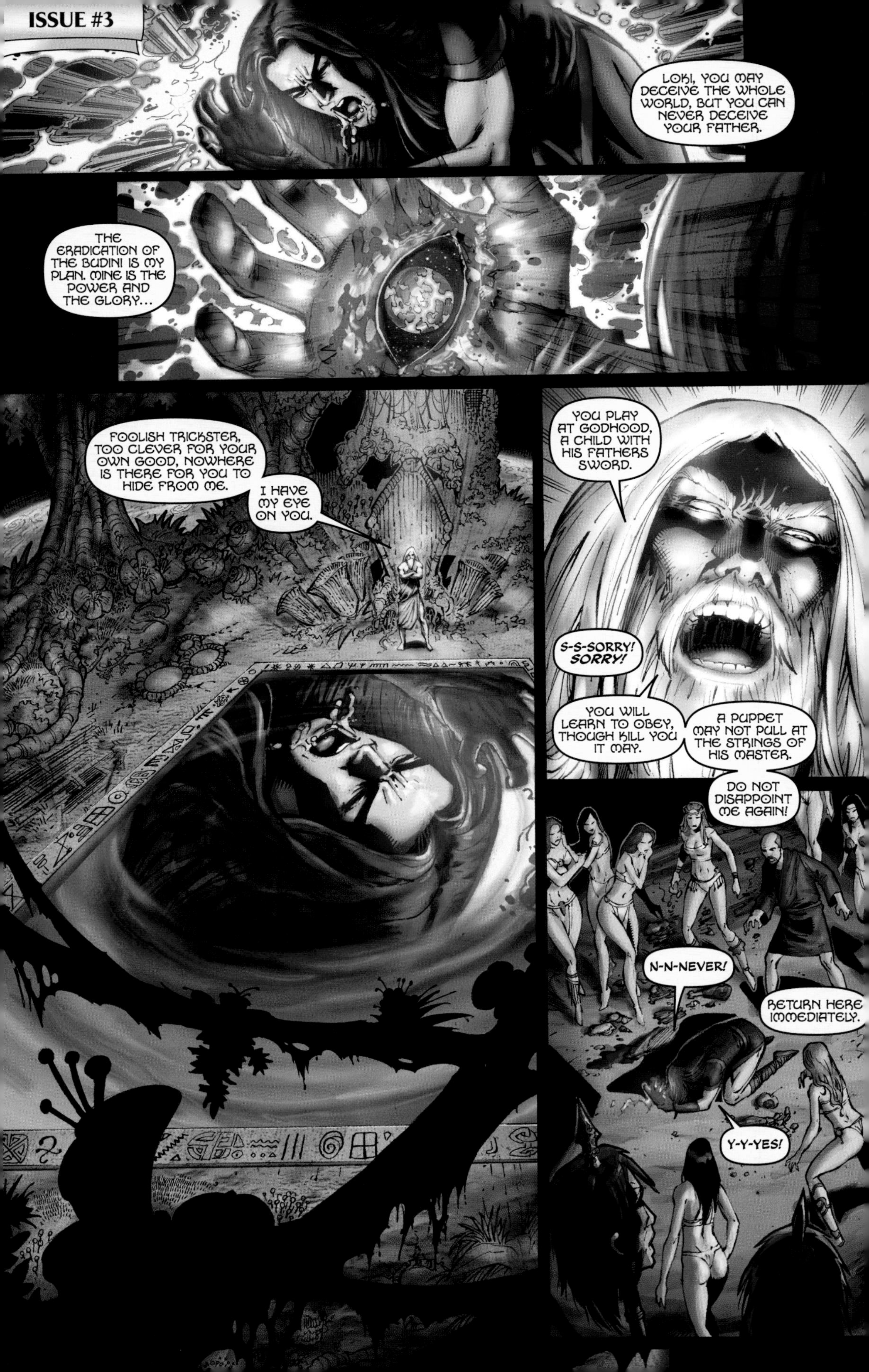
LOKI, YOU MAY DECEIVE THE WHOLE WORLD, BUT YOU CAN NEVER DECEIVE YOUR FATHER.
THE ERADICATION OF THE BUDINI IS MY PLAN. MINE IS THE POWER AND THE GLORY...
FOOLISH TRICKSTER, TOO CLEVER FOR YOUR OWN GOOD, NOWHERE IS THERE FOR YOU TO HIDE FROM ME.
I HAVE MY EYE ON YOU.
YOU PLAY AT GODHOOD, A CHILD WITH HIS FATHERS SWORD.
S-S-SORRY! SORRY!
YOU WILL LEARN TO OBEY, THOUGH KILL YOU IT MAY.
A PUPPET MAY NOT PULL AT THE STRINGS OF HIS MASTER.
DO NOT DISAPPOINT ME AGAIN!
N-N-NEVER!
RETURN HERE IMMEDIATELY.
Y-Y-YES!

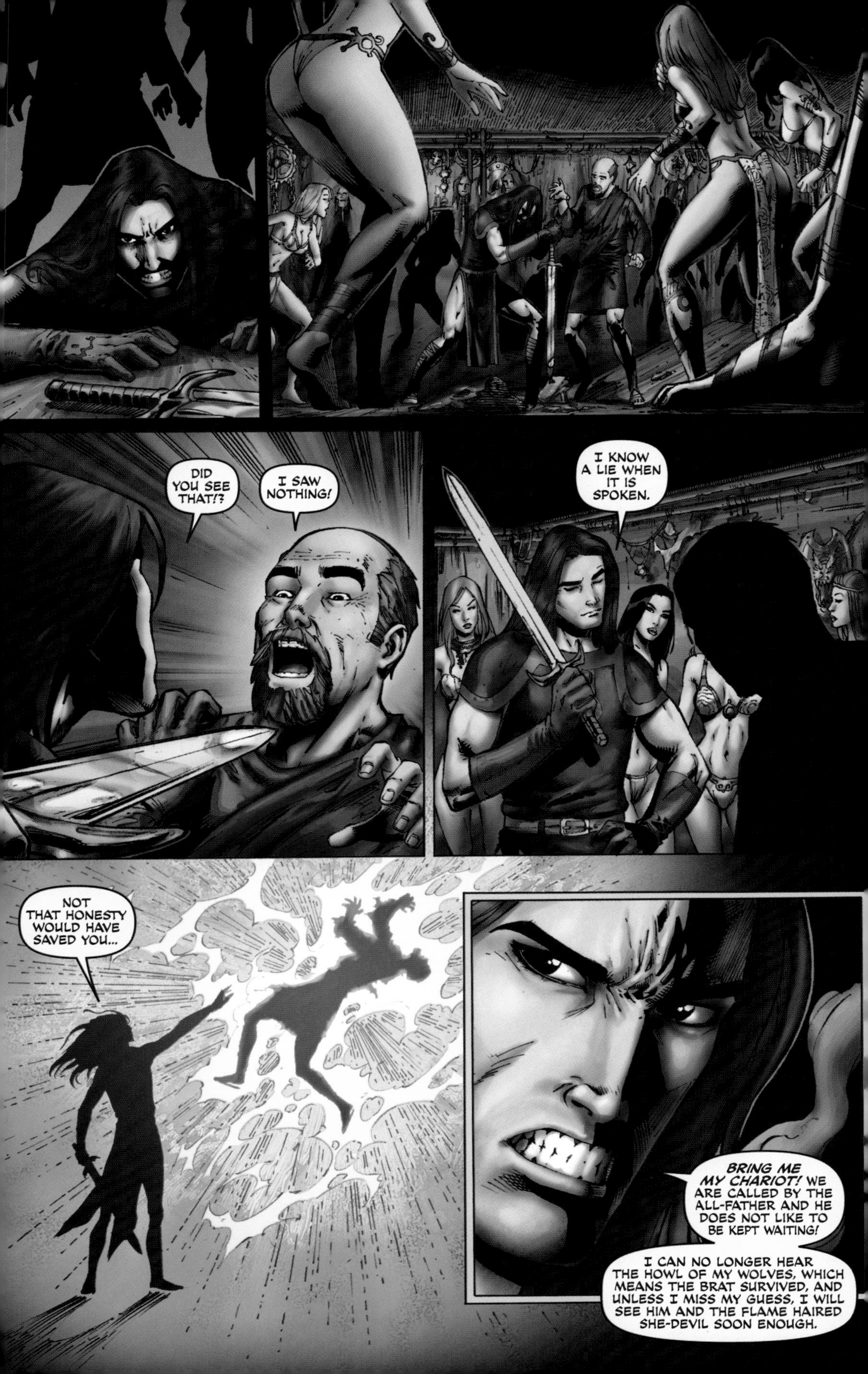
DID YOU SEE THAT!?
I SAW NOTHING!
I KNOW A LIE WHEN IT IS SPOKEN.
NOT THAT HONESTY WOULD HAVE SAVED YOU...
BRING ME MY CHARIOT! WE ARE CALLED BY THE ALL-FATHER AND HE DOES NOT LIKE TO BE KEPT WAITING!
I CAN NO LONGER HEAR THE HOWL OF MY WOLVES, WHICH MEANS THE BRAT SURVIVED, AND UNLESS I MISS MY GUESS, I WILL SEE HIM AND THE FLAME HAIRED SHE-DEVIL SOON ENOUGH.

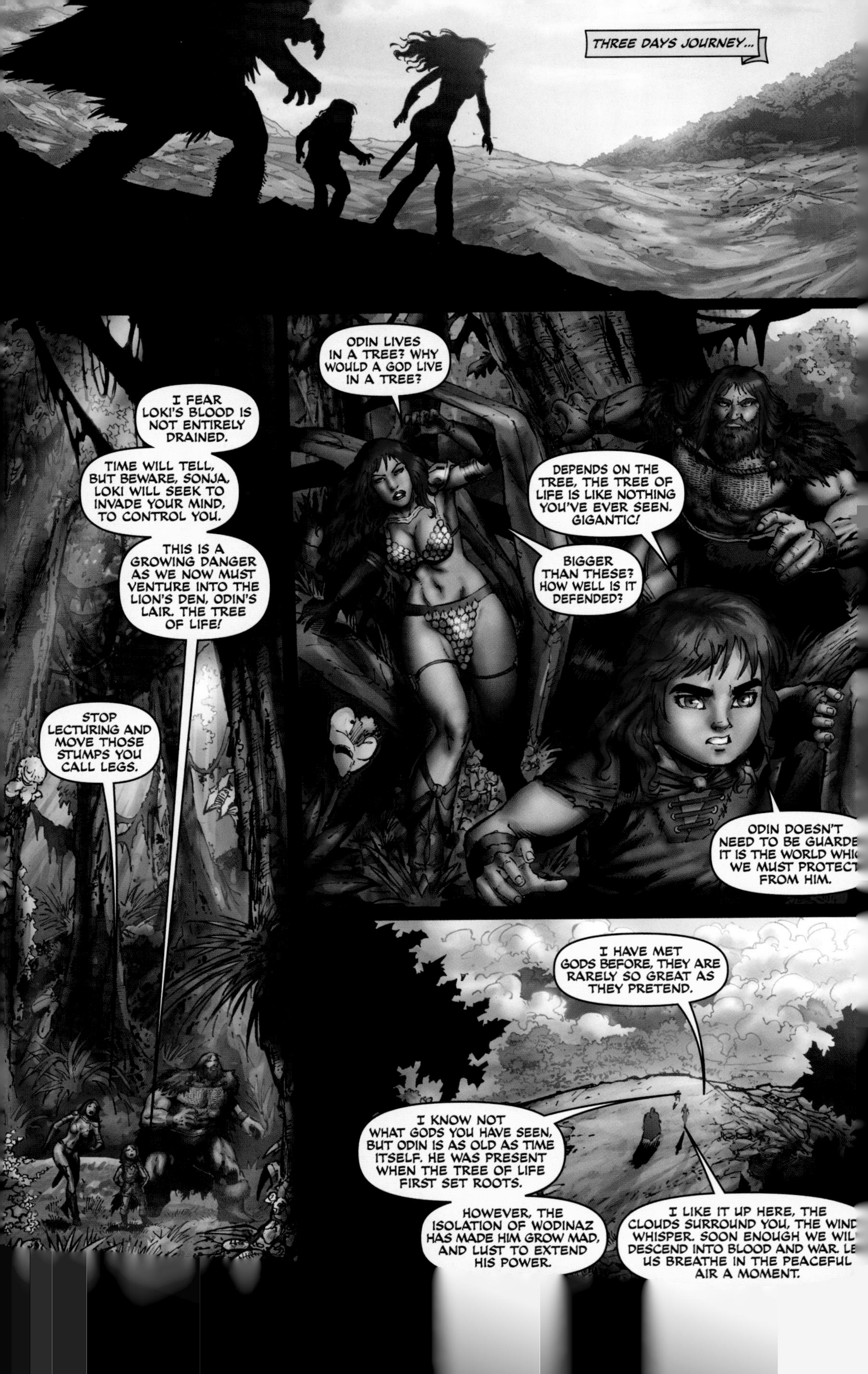
THREE DAYS JOURNEY...
I FEAR LOKI'S BLOOD IS NOT ENTIRELY DRAINED.
TIME WILL TELL, BUT BEWARE, SONJA, LOKI WILL SEEK TO INVADE YOUR MIND, TO CONTROL YOU.
THIS IS A GROWING DANGER AS WE NOW MUST VENTURE INTO THE LION'S DEN, ODIN'S LAIR. THE TREE OF LIFE!
STOP LECTURING AND MOVE THOSE STUMPS YOU CALL LEGS.
ODIN LIVES IN A TREE? WHY WOULD A GOD LIVE IN A TREE?
DEPENDS ON THE TREE. THE TREE OF LIFE IS LIKE NOTHING YOU'VE EVER SEEN. GIGANTIC!
BIGGER THAN THESE? HOW WELL IS IT DEFENDED?
ODIN DOESN'T NEED TO BE GUARDE IT IS THE WORLD WHIC WE MUST PROTECT FROM HIM.
I HAVE MET GODS BEFORE, THEY ARE RARELY SO GREAT AS THEY PRETEND.
I KNOW NOT WHAT GODS YOU HAVE SEEN, BUT ODIN IS AS OLD AS TIME ITSELF. HE WAS PRESENT WHEN THE TREE OF LIFE FIRST SET ROOTS.
HOWEVER, THE ISOLATION OF WODINAZ HAS MADE HIM GROW MAD, AND LUST TO EXTEND HIS POWER.
I LIKE IT UP HERE, THE CLOUDS SURROUND YOU, THE WIND WHISPER. SOON ENOUGH WE WIL DESCEND INTO BLOOD AND WAR. LE US BREATHE IN THE PEACEFUL AIR A MOMENT.

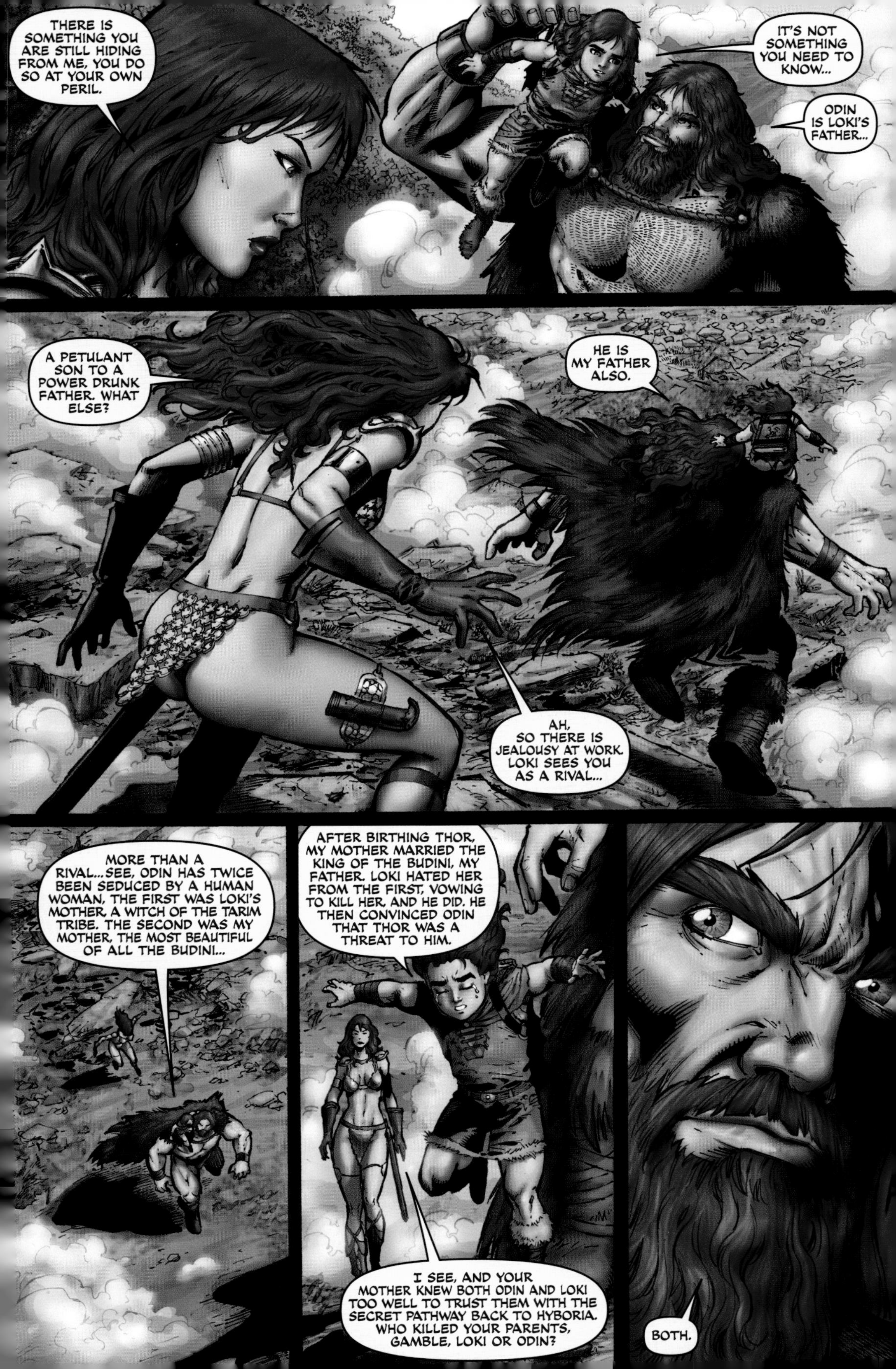
THERE IS SOMETHING YOU ARE STILL HIDING FROM ME, YOU DO SO AT YOUR OWN PERIL.
IT'S NOT SOMETHING YOU NEED TO KNOW...
ODIN IS LOKI'S FATHER...
A PETULANT SON TO A POWER DRUNK FATHER. WHAT ELSE?
HE IS MY FATHER ALSO.
AH, SO THERE IS JEALOUSY AT WORK. LOKI SEES YOU AS A RIVAL...
MORE THAN A RIVAL...SEE, ODIN HAS TWICE BEEN SEDUCED BY A HUMAN WOMAN, THE FIRST WAS LOKI'S MOTHER, A WITCH OF THE TARIM TRIBE. THE SECOND WAS MY MOTHER, THE MOST BEAUTIFUL OF ALL THE BUDINI...
AFTER BIRTHING THOR, MY MOTHER MARRIED THE KING OF THE BUDINI, MY FATHER. LOKI HATED HER FROM THE FIRST, VOWING TO KILL HER, AND HE DID. HE THEN CONVINCED ODIN THAT THOR WAS A THREAT TO HIM.
I SEE, AND YOUR MOTHER KNEW BOTH ODIN AND LOKI TOO WELL TO TRUST THEM WITH THE SECRET PATHWAY BACK TO HYBORIA. WHO KILLED YOUR PARENTS, GAMBLE, LOKI OR ODIN?
BOTH.

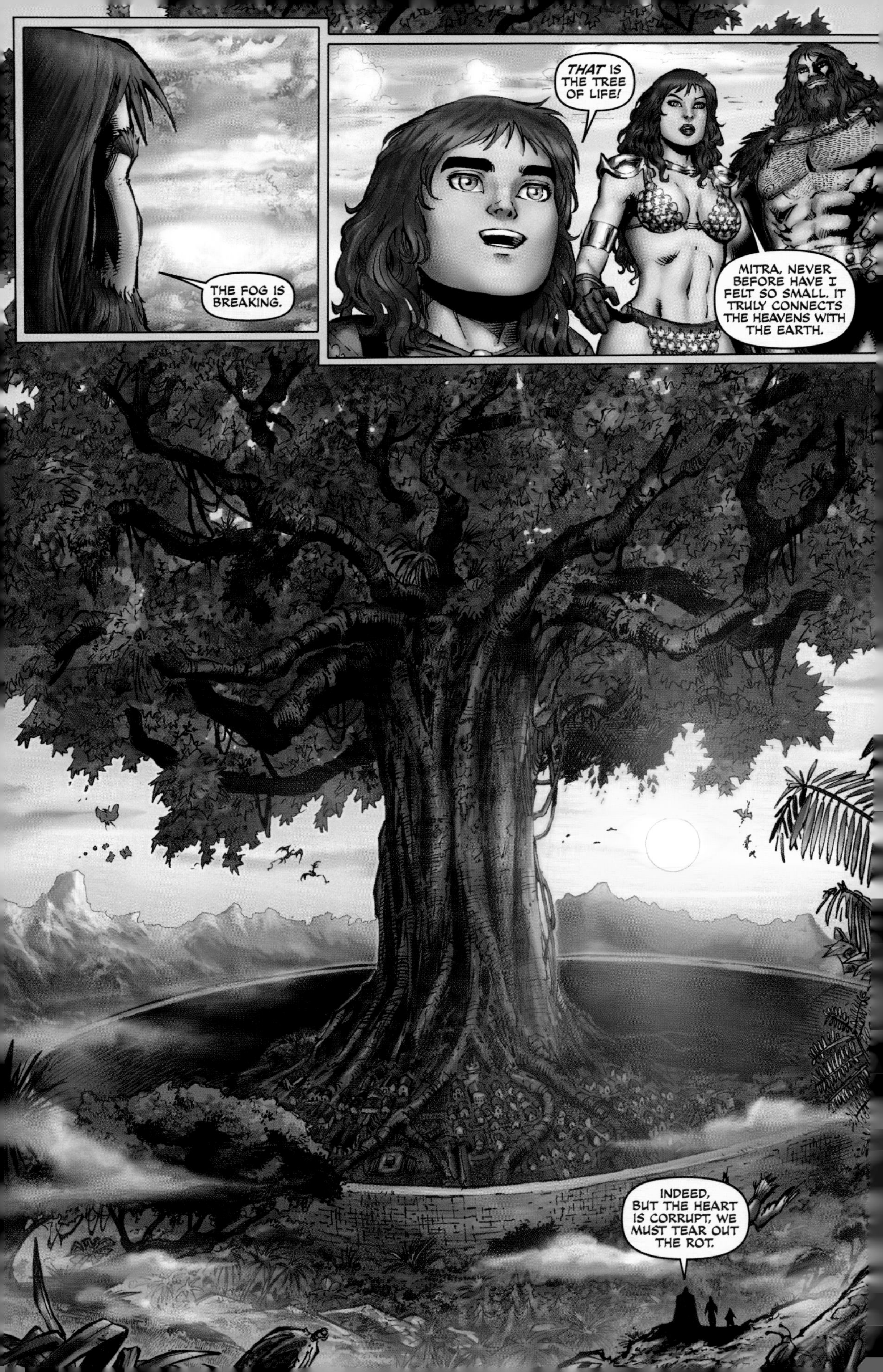
THE FOG IS BREAKING.
THAT IS THE TREE OF LIFE!
MITRA, NEVER BEFORE HAVE I FELT SO SMALL. IT TRULY CONNECTS THE HEAVENS WITH THE EARTH.
INDEED, BUT THE HEART IS CORRUPT, WE MUST TEAR OUT THE ROT.

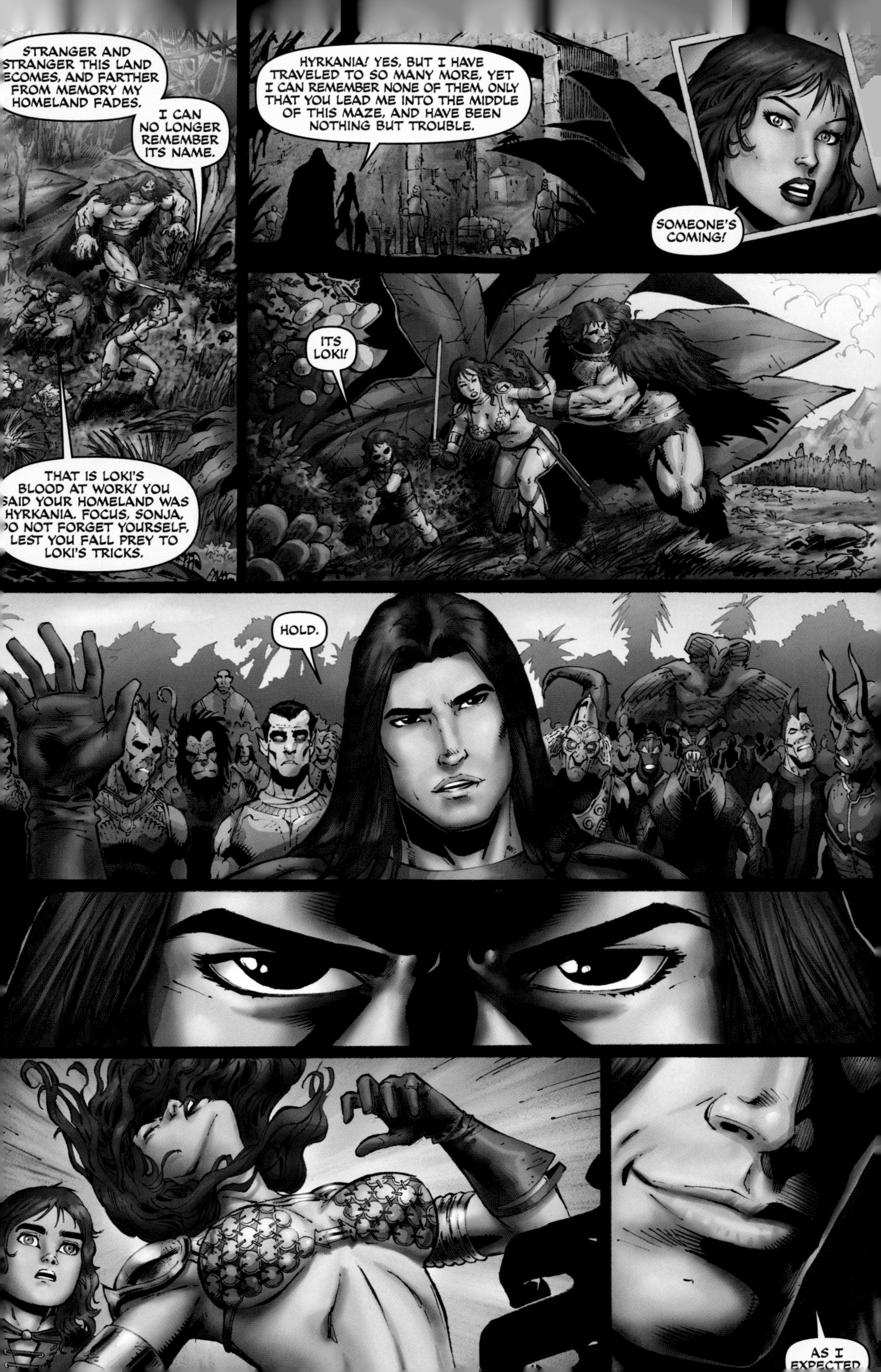
STRANGER AND STRANGER THIS LAND BECOMES, AND FARTHER FROM MEMORY MY HOMELAND FADES.
I CAN NO LONGER REMEMBER ITS NAME.
THAT IS LOKI'S BLOOD AT WORK! YOU SAID YOUR HOMELAND WAS HYRKANIA. FOCUS, SONJA, DO NOT FORGET YOURSELF, LEST YOU FALL PREY TO LOKI'S TRICKS.
HYRKANIA! YES, BUT I HAVE TRAVELED TO SO MANY MORE, YET I CAN REMEMBER NONE OF THEM, ONLY THAT YOU LEAD ME INTO THE MIDDLE OF THIS MAZE, AND HAVE BEEN NOTHING BUT TROUBLE.
SOMEONE'S COMING!
ITS LOKI!
HOLD.
AS I EXPECTED.

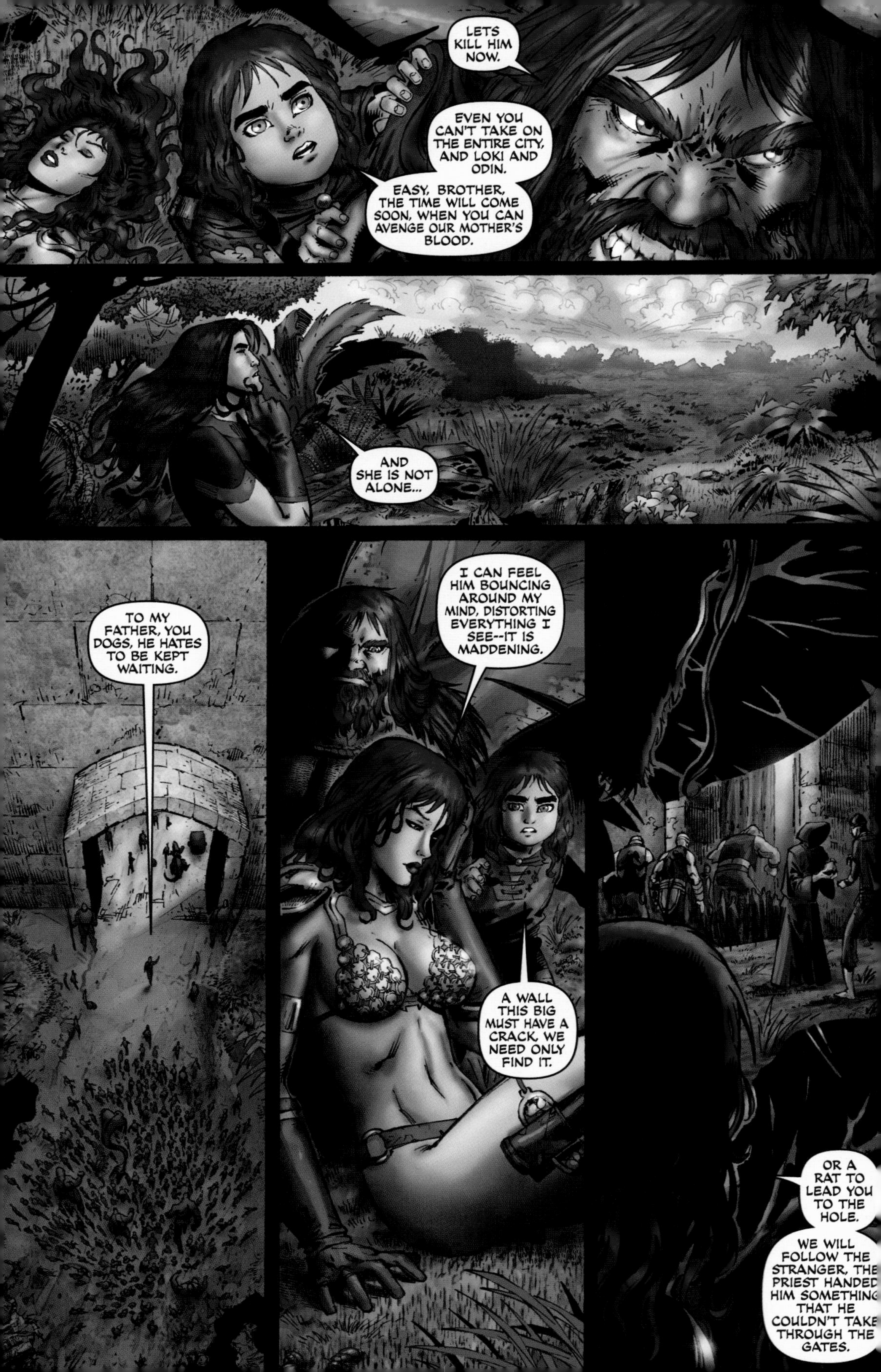
LETS KILL HIM NOW.
EVEN YOU CAN'T TAKE ON THE ENTIRE CITY, AND LOKI AND ODIN.
EASY, BROTHER, THE TIME WILL COME SOON, WHEN YOU CAN AVENGE OUR MOTHER'S BLOOD.
AND SHE IS NOT ALONE...
TO MY FATHER, YOU DOGS, HE HATES TO BE KEPT WAITING.
I CAN FEEL HIM BOUNCING AROUND MY MIND, DISTORTING EVERYTHING I SEE--IT IS MADDENING.
A WALL THIS BIG MUST HAVE A CRACK, WE NEED ONLY FIND IT.
OR A RAT TO LEAD YOU TO THE HOLE.
WE WILL FOLLOW THE STRANGER, THE PRIEST HANDED HIM SOMETHING THAT HE COULDN'T TAKE THROUGH THE GATES.

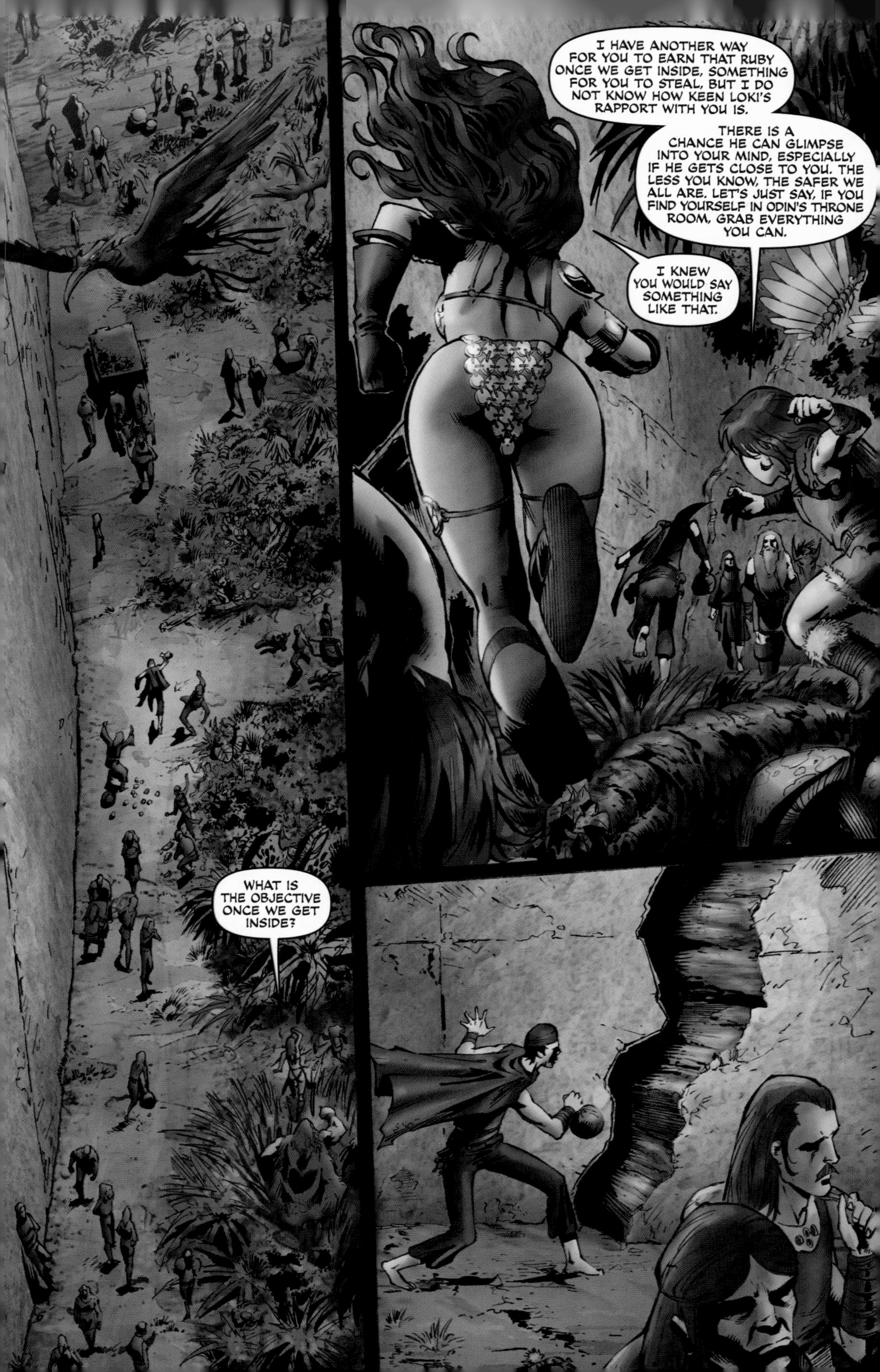
I HAVE ANOTHER WAY FOR YOU TO EARN THAT RUBY ONCE WE GET INSIDE, SOMETHING FOR YOU TO STEAL, BUT I DO NOT KNOW HOW KEEN LOKI'S RAPPORT WITH YOU IS.
THERE IS A CHANCE HE CAN GLIMPSE INTO YOUR MIND, ESPECIALLY IF HE GETS CLOSE TO YOU. THE LESS YOU KNOW, THE SAFER WE ALL ARE. LET'S JUST SAY, IF YOU FIND YOURSELF IN ODIN'S THRONE ROOM, GRAB EVERYTHING YOU CAN.
I KNEW YOU WOULD SAY SOMETHING LIKE THAT.
WHAT IS THE OBJECTIVE ONCE WE GET INSIDE?

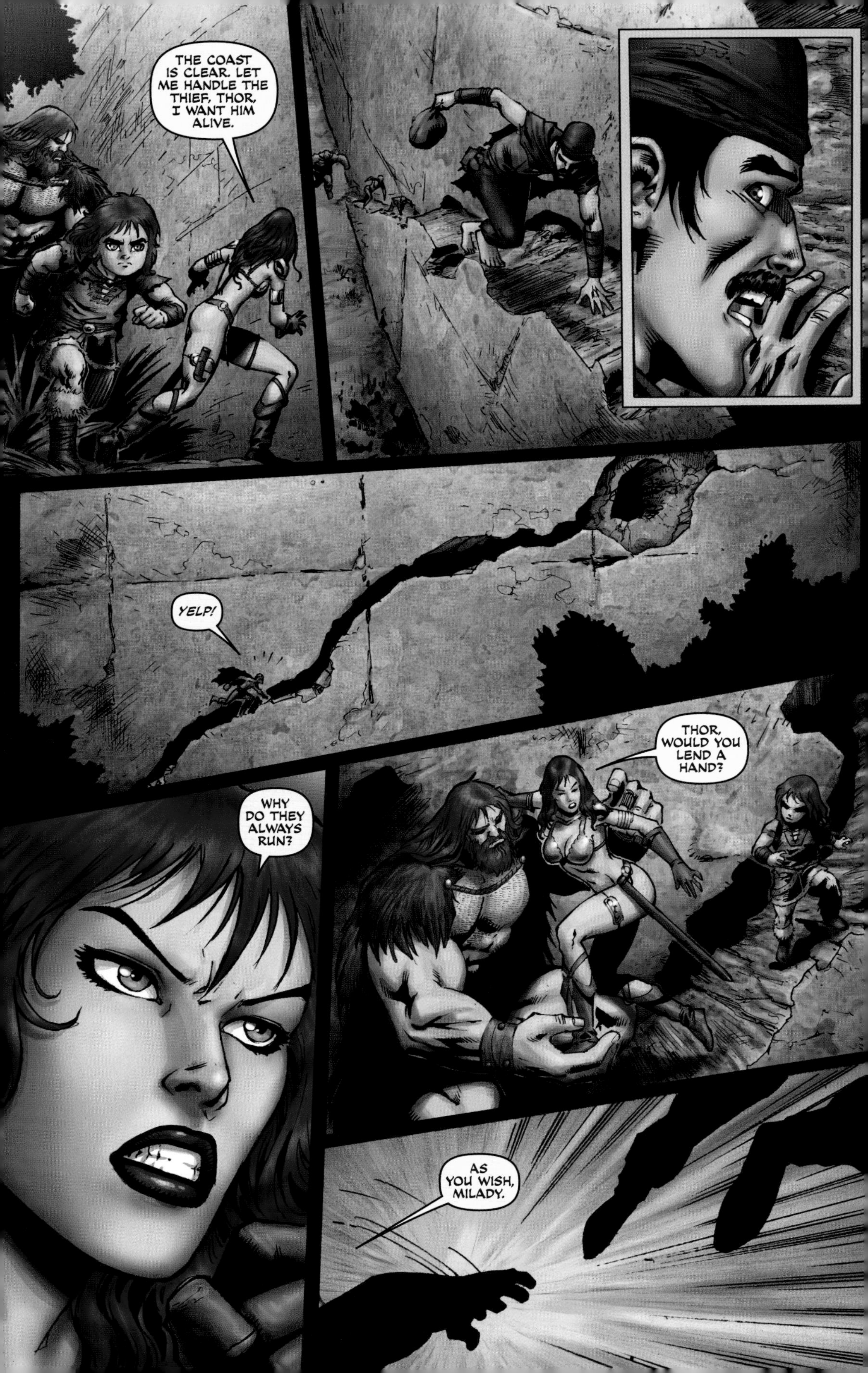
THE COAST IS CLEAR. LET ME HANDLE THE THIEF, THOR, I WANT HIM ALIVE.
YELP!
WHY DO THEY ALWAYS RUN?
THOR, WOULD YOU LEND A HAND?
AS YOU WISH, MILADY.

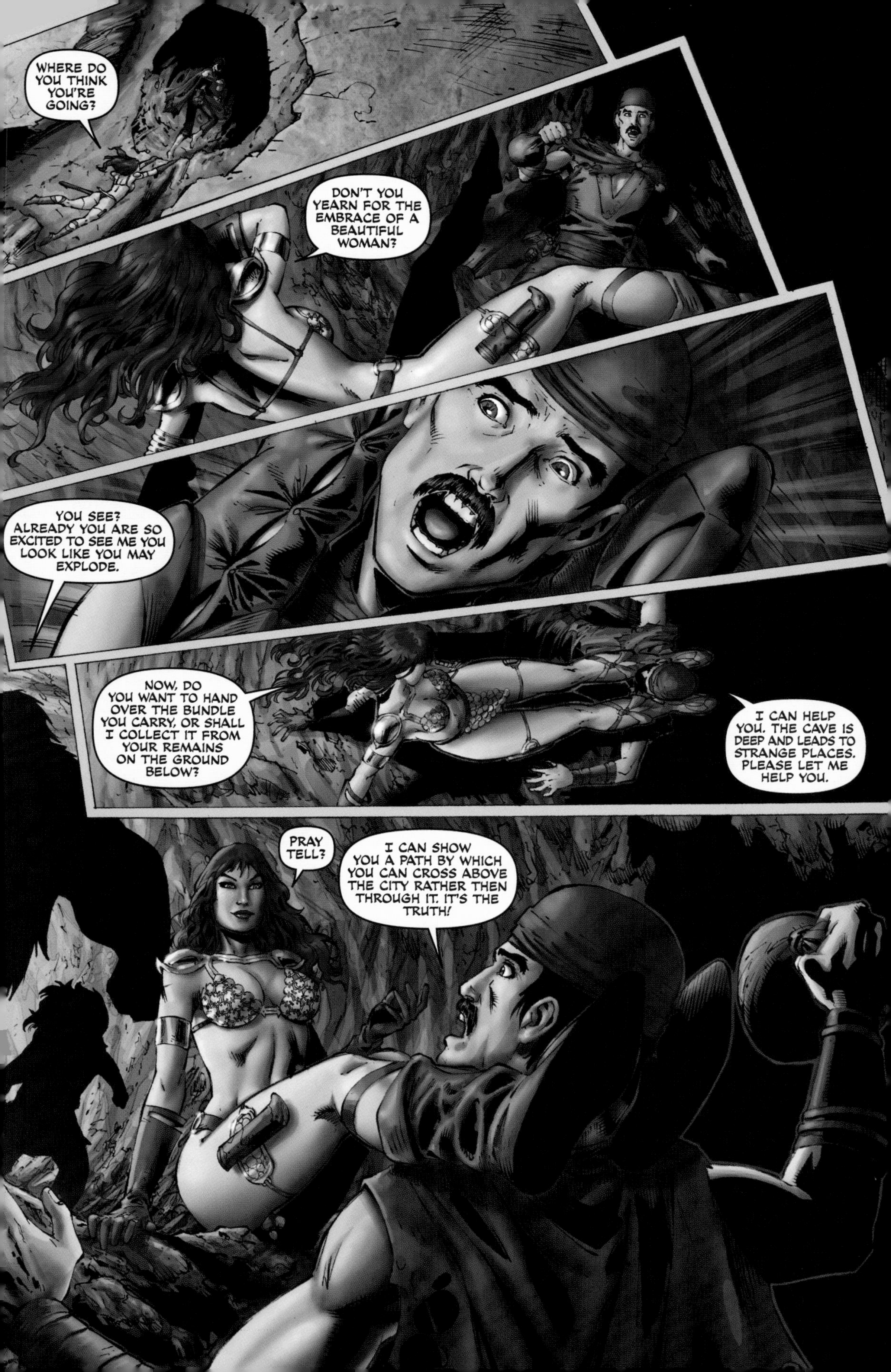
WHERE DO YOU THINK YOU'RE GOING?
DON'T YOU YEARN FOR THE EMBRACE OF A BEAUTIFUL WOMAN?
YOU SEE? ALREADY YOU ARE SO EXCITED TO SEE ME YOU LOOK LIKE YOU MAY EXPLODE.
NOW, DO YOU WANT TO HAND OVER THE BUNDLE YOU CARRY, OR SHALL I COLLECT IT FROM YOUR REMAINS ON THE GROUND BELOW?
I CAN HELP YOU. THE CAVE IS DEEP AND LEADS TO STRANGE PLACES. PLEASE LET ME HELP YOU.
PRAY TELL?
I CAN SHOW YOU A PATH BY WHICH YOU CAN CROSS ABOVE THE CITY RATHER THEN THROUGH IT. IT'S THE TRUTH!

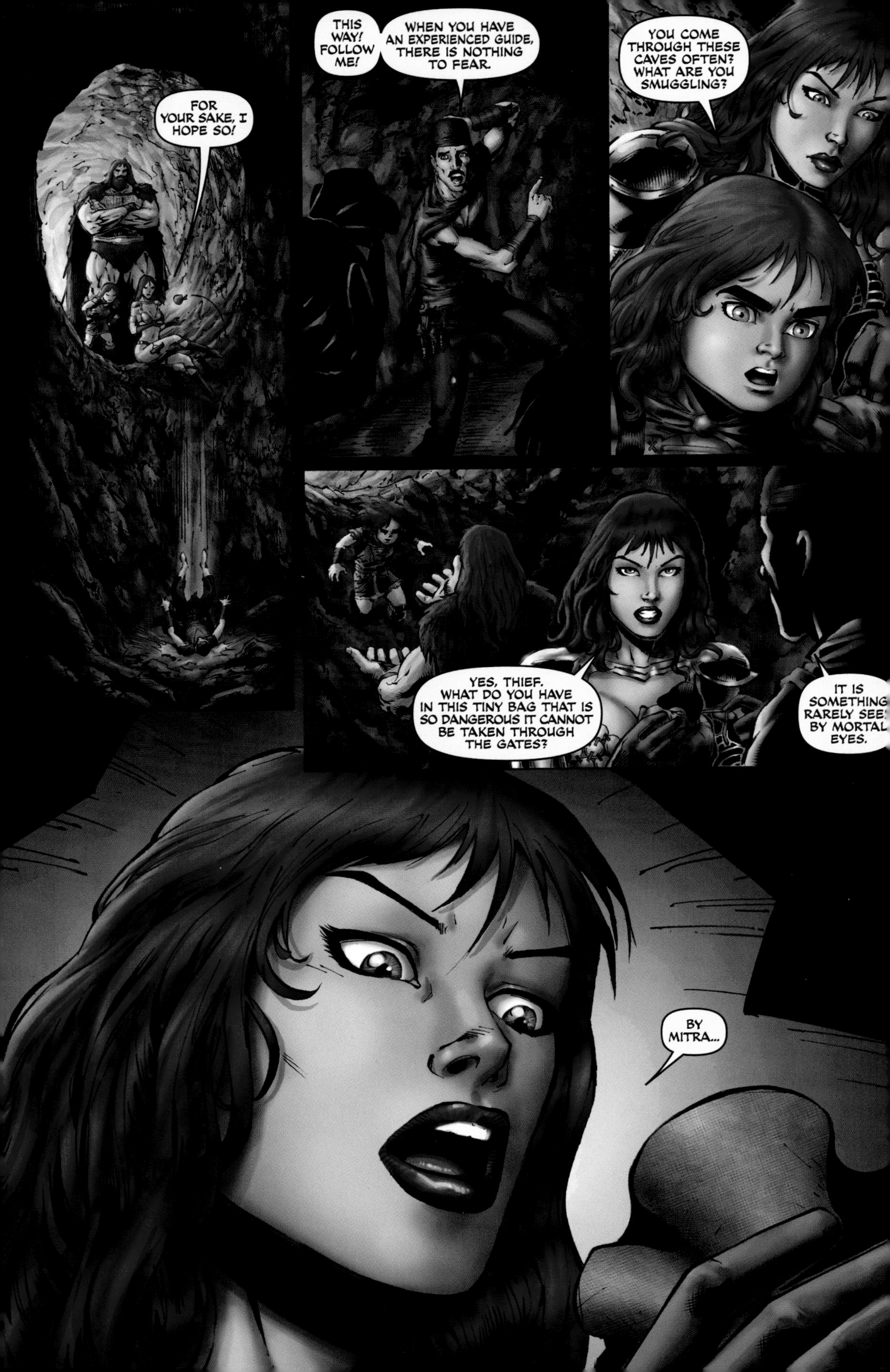
FOR YOUR SAKE, I HOPE SO!
THIS WAY! FOLLOW ME!
WHEN YOU HAVE AN EXPERIENCED GUIDE, THERE IS NOTHING TO FEAR.
YOU COME THROUGH THESE CAVES OFTEN? WHAT ARE YOU SMUGGLING?
YES, THIEF. WHAT DO YOU HAVE IN THIS TINY BAG THAT IS SO DANGEROUS IT CANNOT BE TAKEN THROUGH THE GATES?
IT IS SOMETHING RARELY SEE BY MORTAL EYES.
BY MITRA...

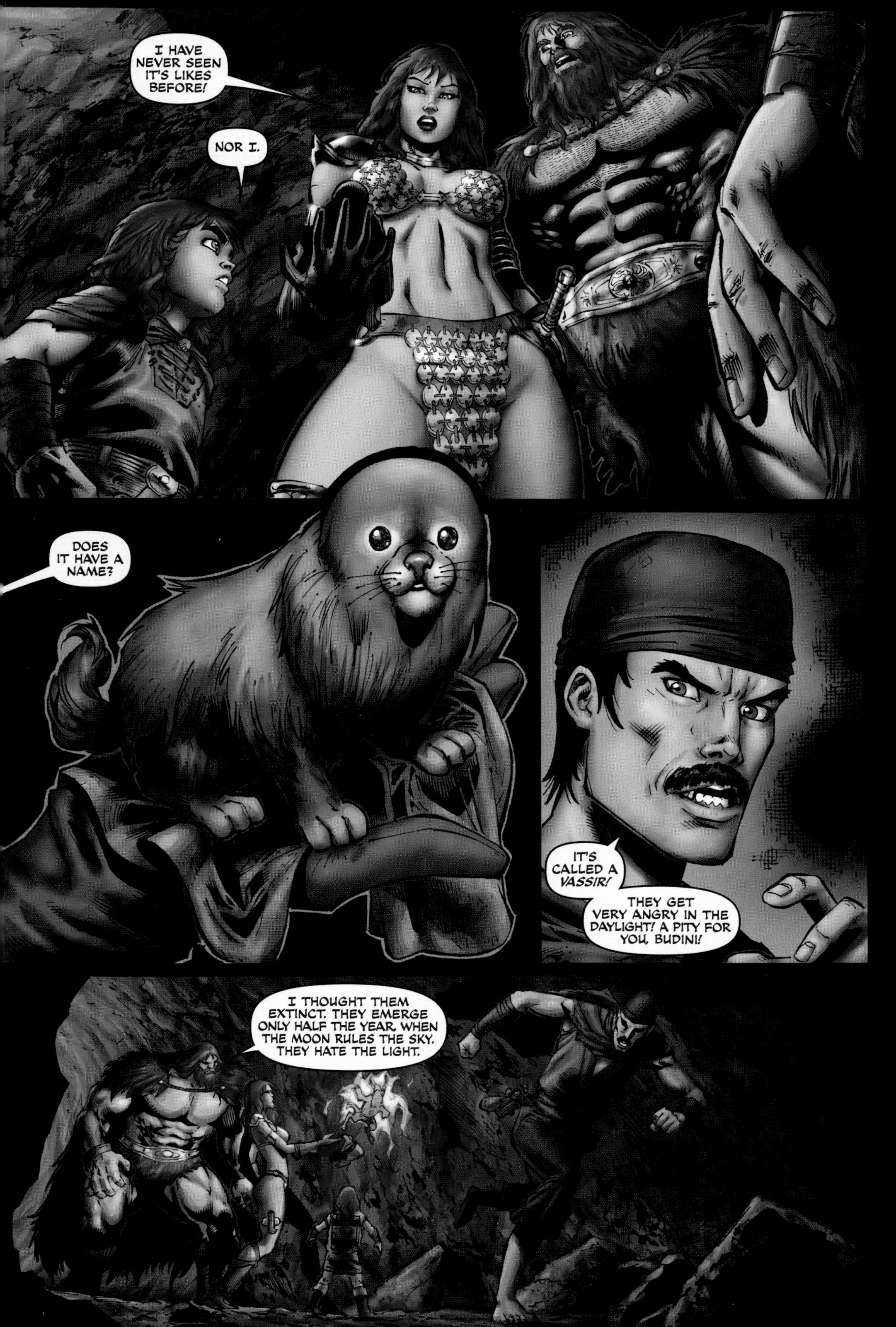
I HAVE NEVER SEEN IT'S LIKES BEFORE!
NOR I.
DOES IT HAVE A NAME?
IT'S CALLED A *VASSIR!*
THEY GET VERY ANGRY IN THE DAYLIGHT! A PITY FOR YOU, BUDINI!
I THOUGHT THEM EXTINCT. THEY EMERGE ONLY HALF THE YEAR WHEN THE MOON RULES THE SKY. THEY HATE THE LIGHT.

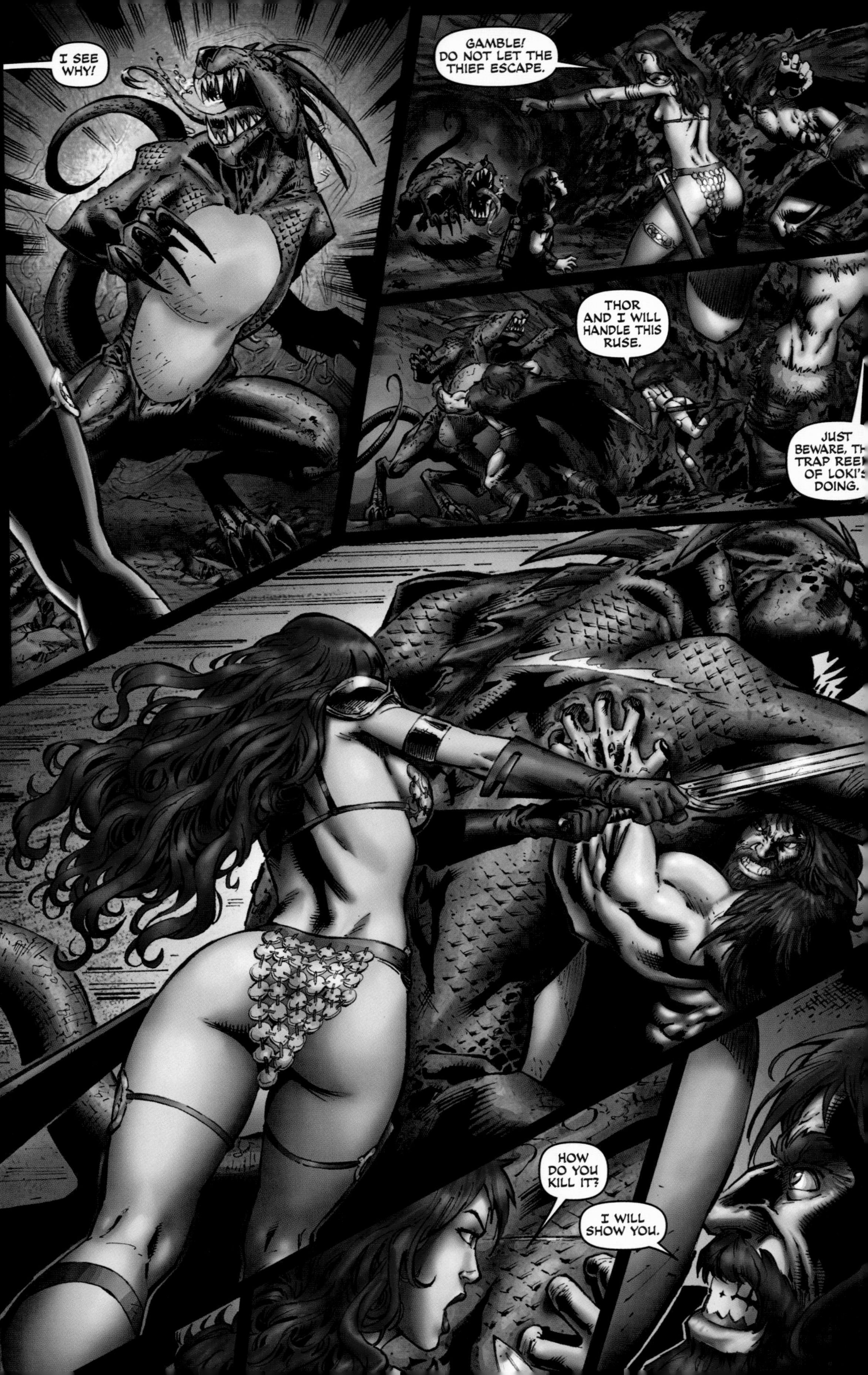
I SEE WHY!
GAMBLE! DO NOT LET THE THIEF ESCAPE.
THOR AND I WILL HANDLE THIS RUSE.
JUST BEWARE, TH TRAP REE OF LOKI'S DOING.
HOW DO YOU KILL IT?
I WILL SHOW YOU.

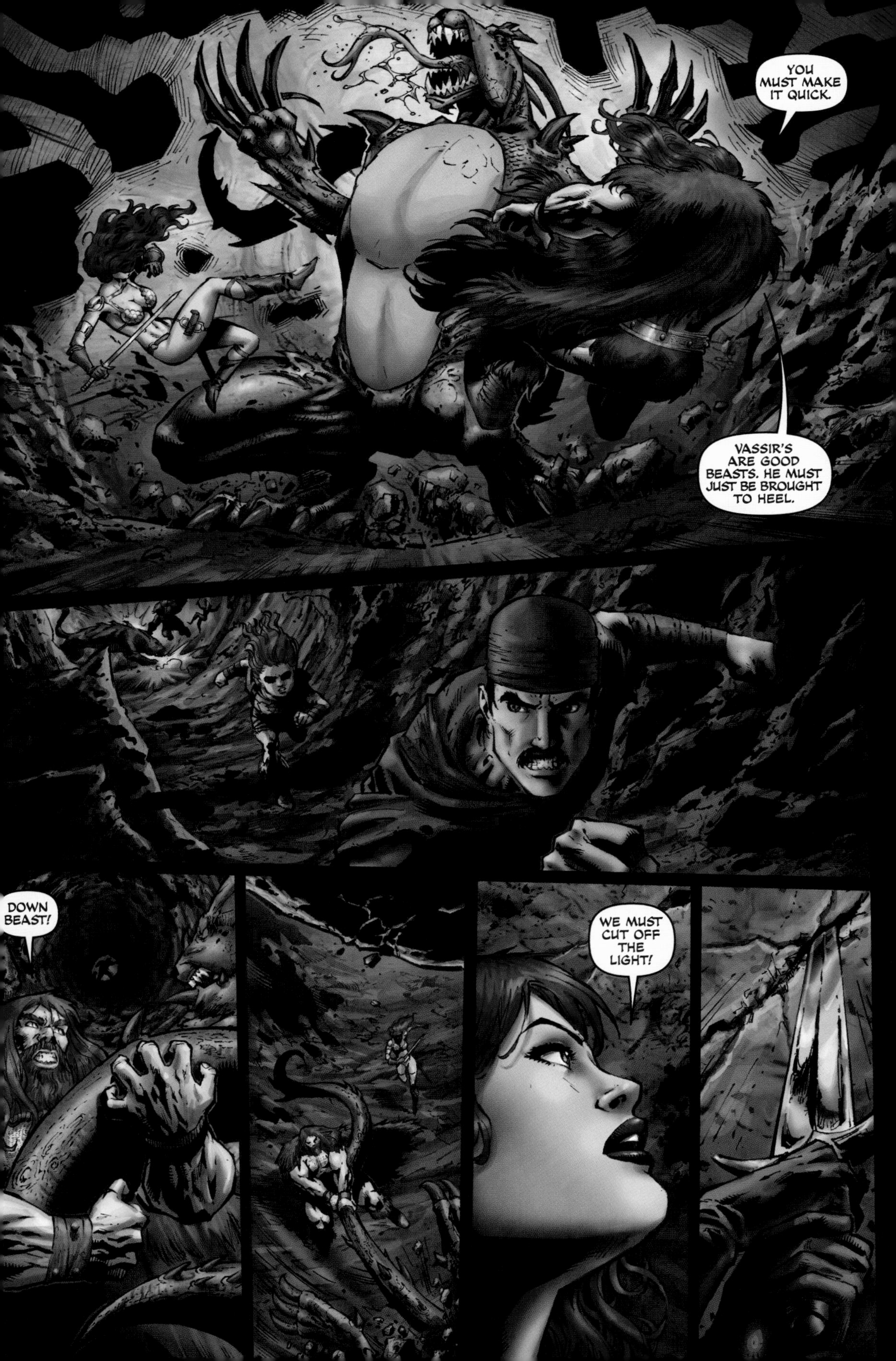
YOU MUST MAKE IT QUICK.
VASSIR'S ARE GOOD BEASTS. HE MUST JUST BE BROUGHT TO HEEL.
DOWN BEAST!
WE MUST CUT OFF THE LIGHT!

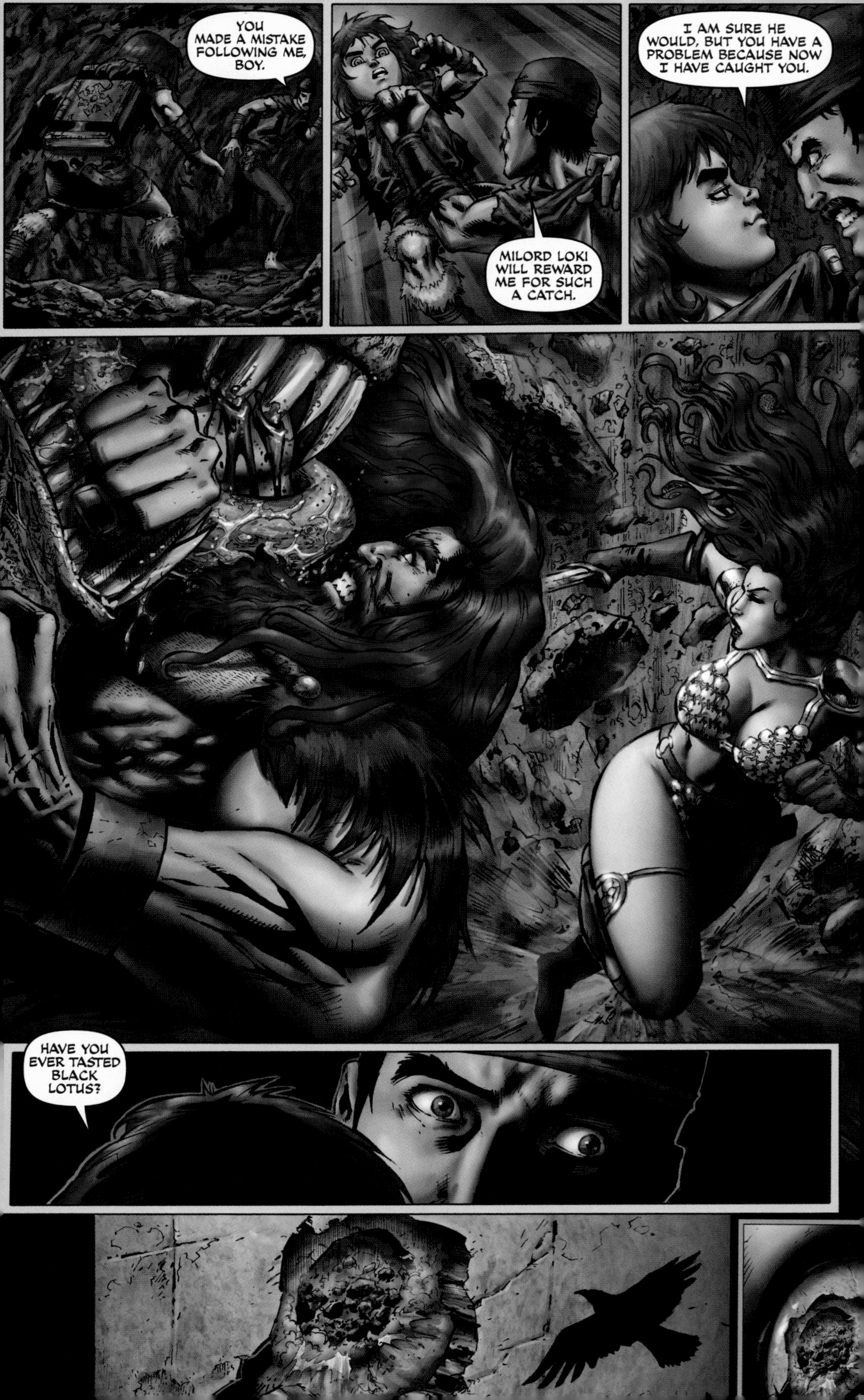

YOU MADE A MISTAKE FOLLOWING ME, BOY.
MILORD LOKI WILL REWARD ME FOR SUCH A CATCH.
I AM SURE HE WOULD, BUT YOU HAVE A PROBLEM BECAUSE NOW I HAVE CAUGHT YOU.
HAVE YOU EVER TASTED BLACK LOTUS?

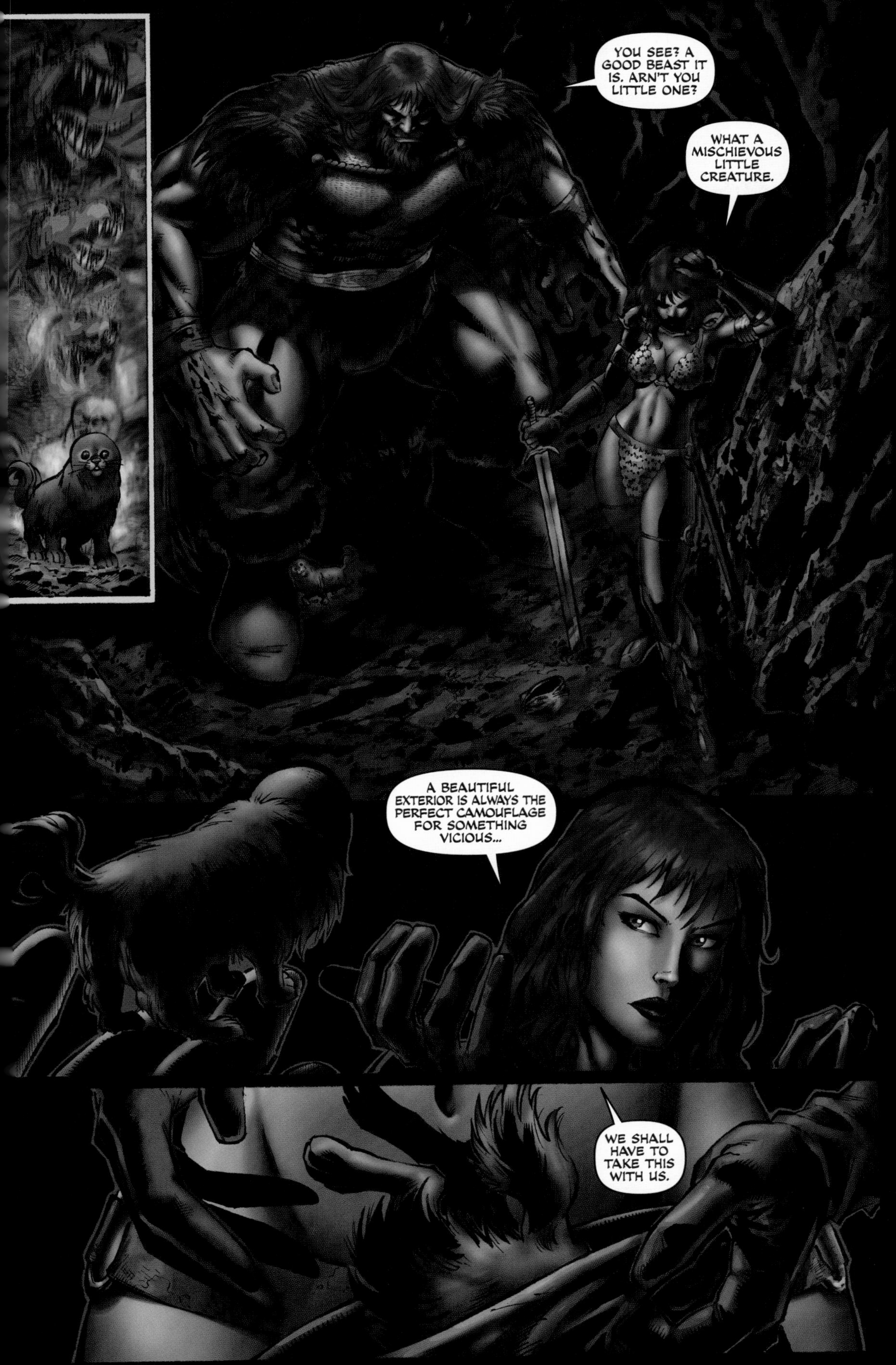
YOU SEE? A GOOD BEAST IT IS. ARN'T YOU LITTLE ONE?
WHAT A MISCHIEVOUS LITTLE CREATURE.
A BEAUTIFUL EXTERIOR IS ALWAYS THE PERFECT CAMOUFLAGE FOR SOMETHING VICIOUS...
WE SHALL HAVE TO TAKE THIS WITH US.

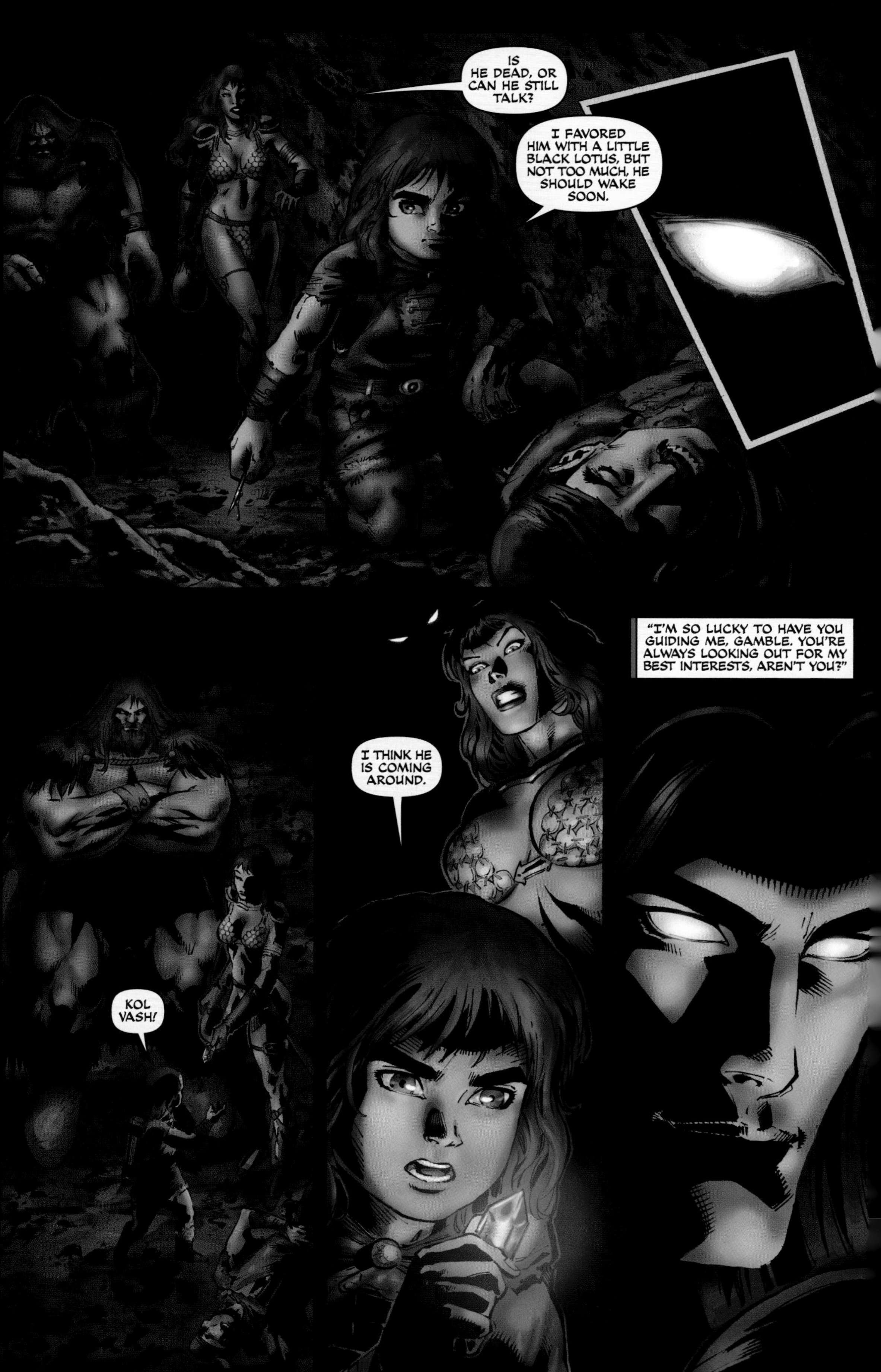
IS HE DEAD, OR CAN HE STILL TALK?
I FAVORED HIM WITH A LITTLE BLACK LOTUS, BUT NOT TOO MUCH, HE SHOULD WAKE SOON.
KOL VASH!
I THINK HE IS COMING AROUND.
"I'M SO LUCKY TO HAVE YOU GUIDING ME, GAMBLE. YOU'RE ALWAYS LOOKING OUT FOR MY BEST INTERESTS, AREN'T YOU?"

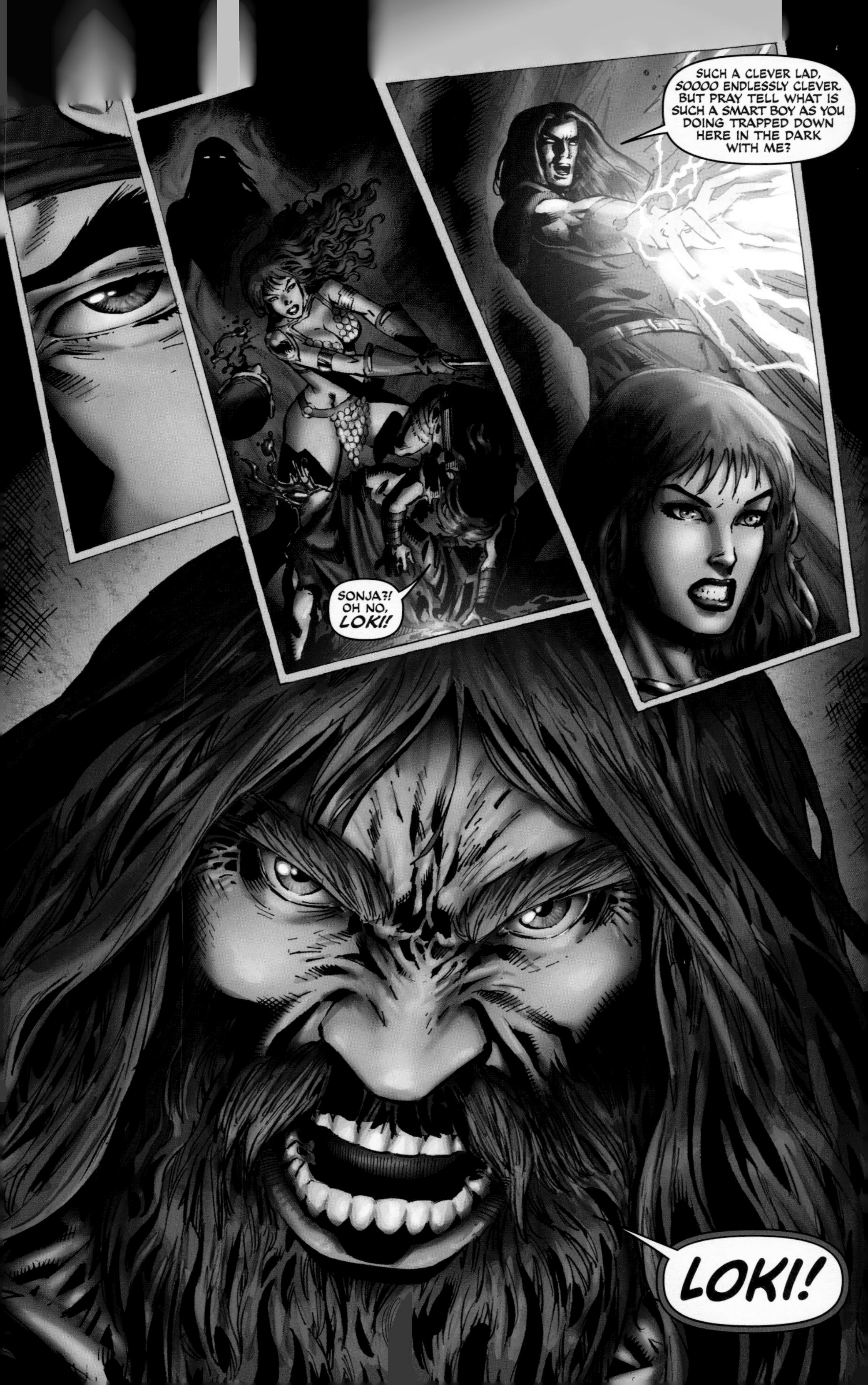
SUCH A CLEVER LAD, SOOOO ENDLESSLY CLEVER. BUT PRAY TELL WHAT IS SUCH A SMART BOY AS YOU DOING TRAPPED DOWN HERE IN THE DARK WITH ME?
SONJA?! OH NO, LOKI!
LOKI!

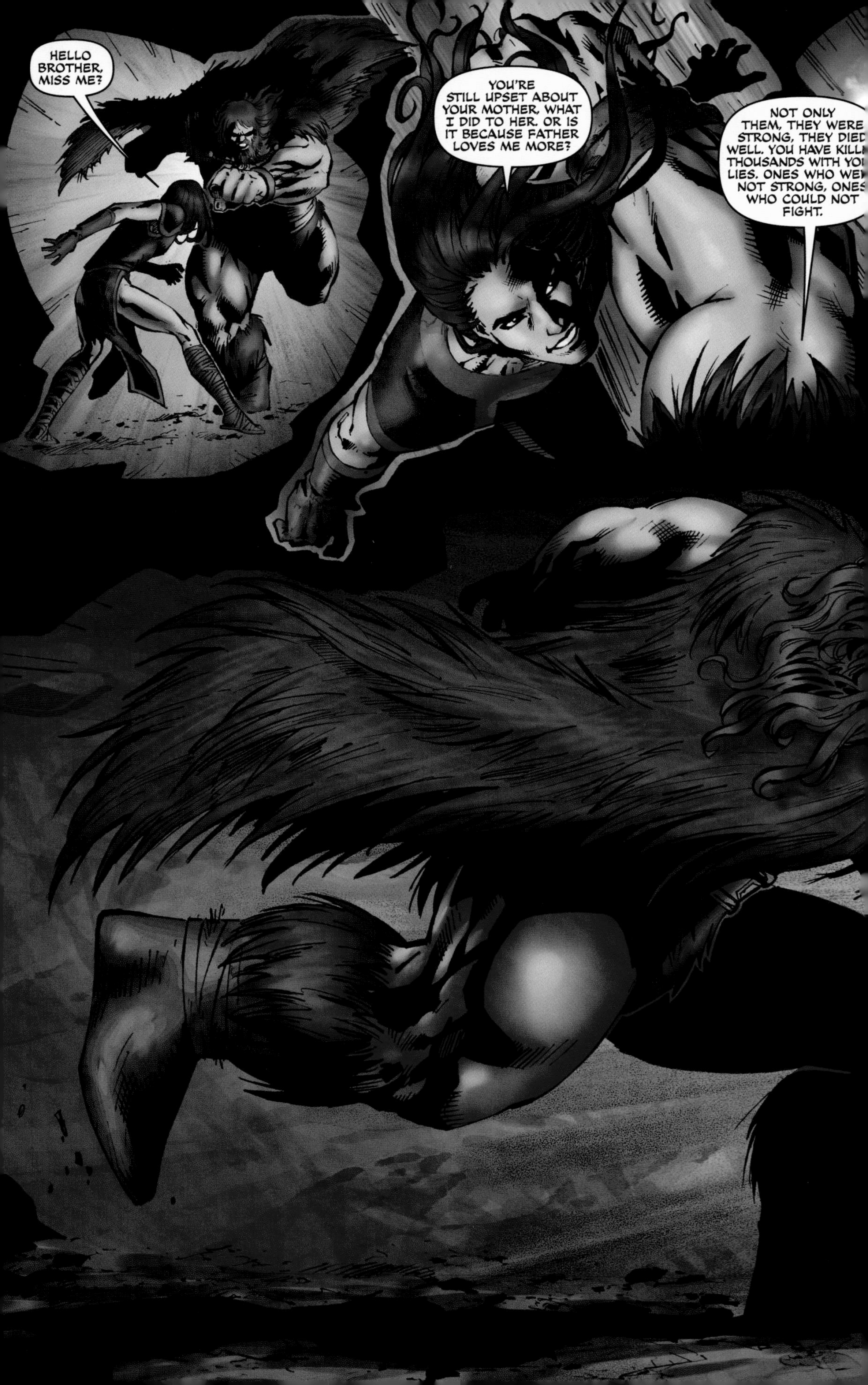
HELLO BROTHER, MISS ME?
YOU'RE STILL UPSET ABOUT YOUR MOTHER, WHAT I DID TO HER. OR IS IT BECAUSE FATHER LOVES ME MORE?
NOT ONLY THEM, THEY WERE STRONG, THEY DIED WELL. YOU HAVE KILL THOUSANDS WITH YO LIES. ONES WHO WE NOT STRONG, ONES WHO COULD NOT FIGHT.

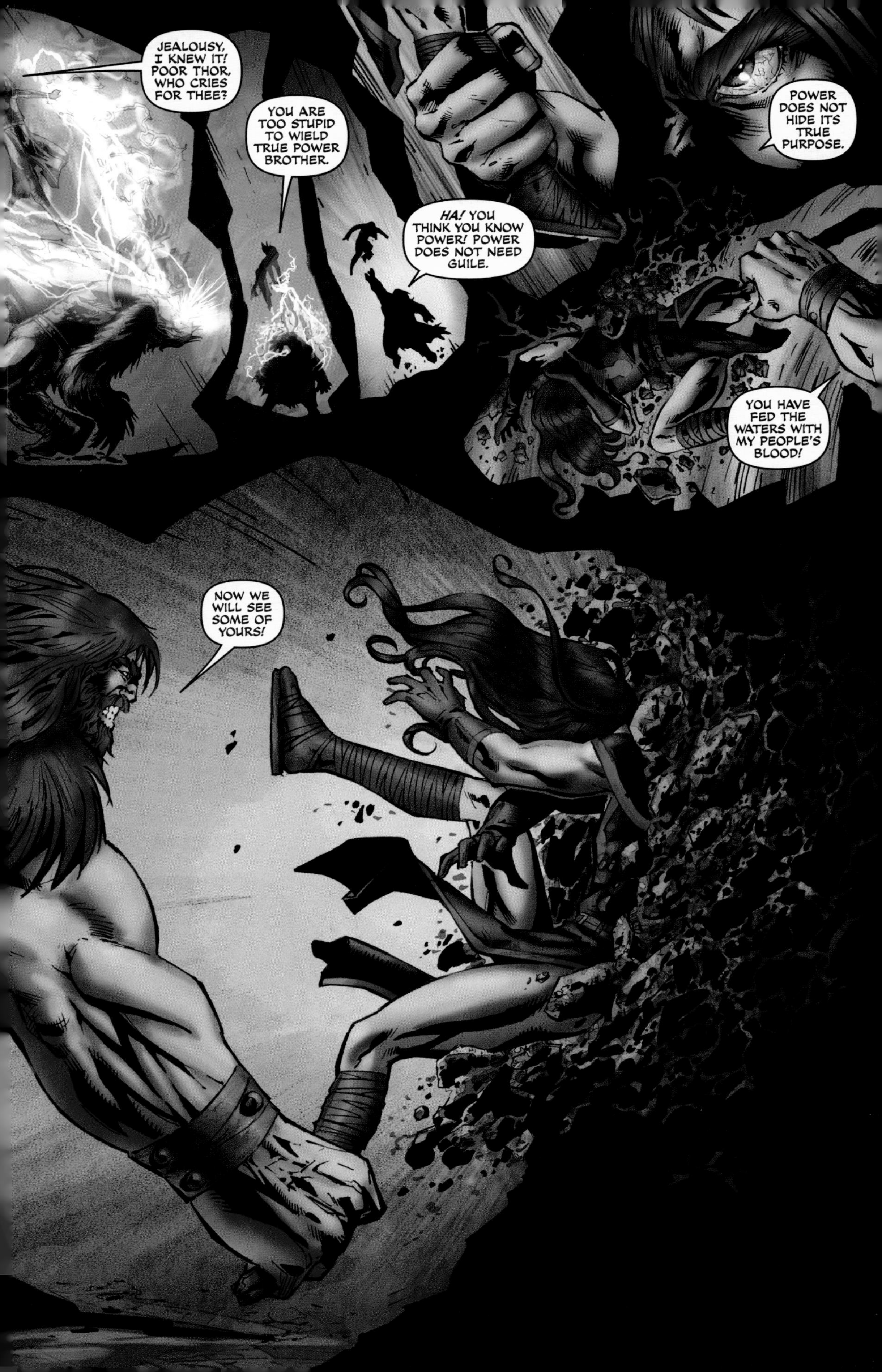
JEALOUSY, I KNEW IT! POOR THOR, WHO CRIES FOR THEE?
YOU ARE TOO STUPID TO WIELD TRUE POWER BROTHER.
HA! YOU THINK YOU KNOW POWER! POWER DOES NOT NEED GUILE.
POWER DOES NOT HIDE ITS TRUE PURPOSE.
YOU HAVE FED THE WATERS WITH MY PEOPLE'S BLOOD!
NOW WE WILL SEE SOME OF YOURS!

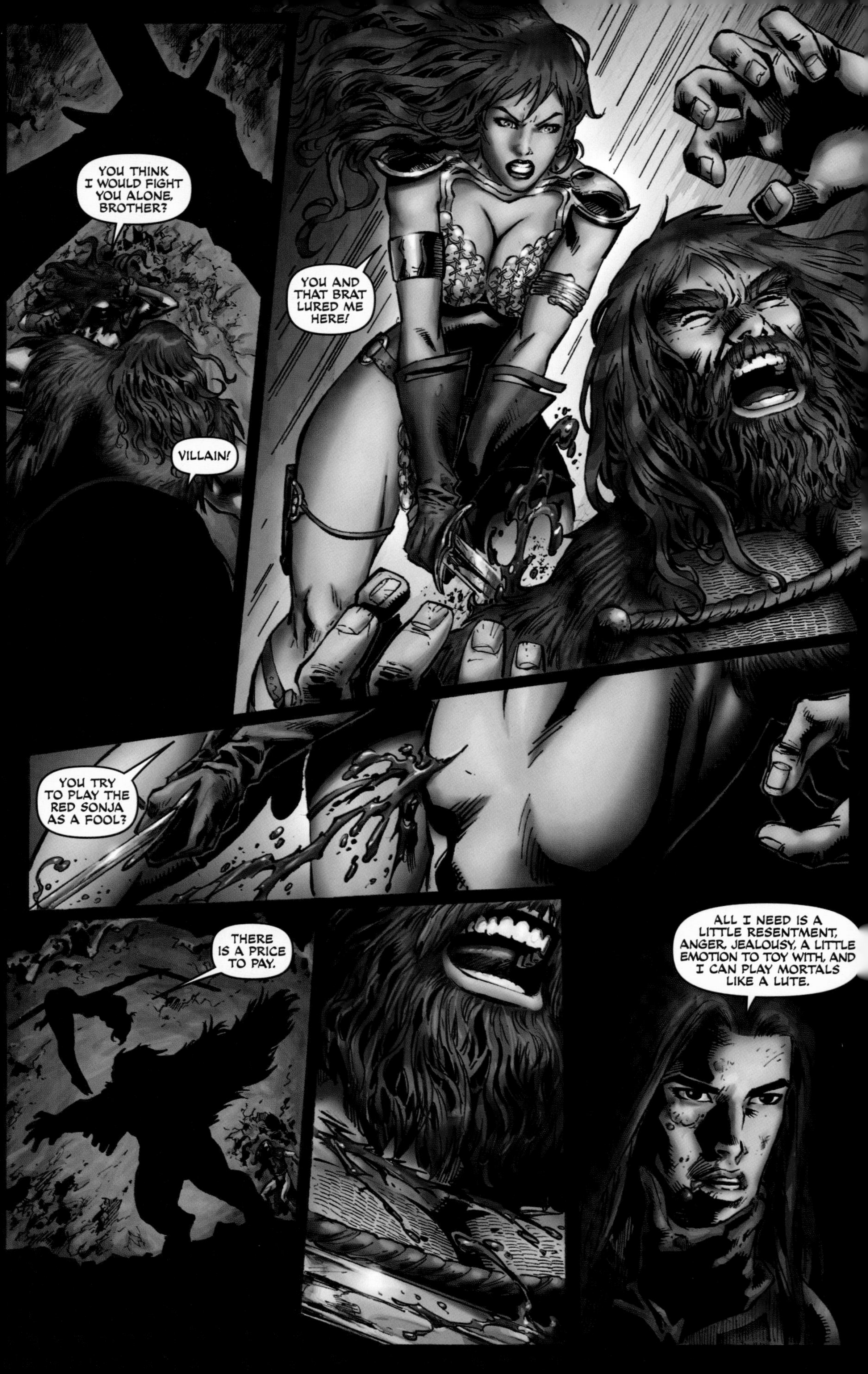
YOU THINK I WOULD FIGHT YOU ALONE, BROTHER?
VILLAIN!
YOU AND THAT BRAT LURED ME HERE!
YOU TRY TO PLAY THE RED SONJA AS A FOOL?
THERE IS A PRICE TO PAY.
ALL I NEED IS A LITTLE RESENTMENT, ANGER, JEALOUSY, A LITTLE EMOTION TO TOY WITH, AND I CAN PLAY MORTALS LIKE A LUTE.

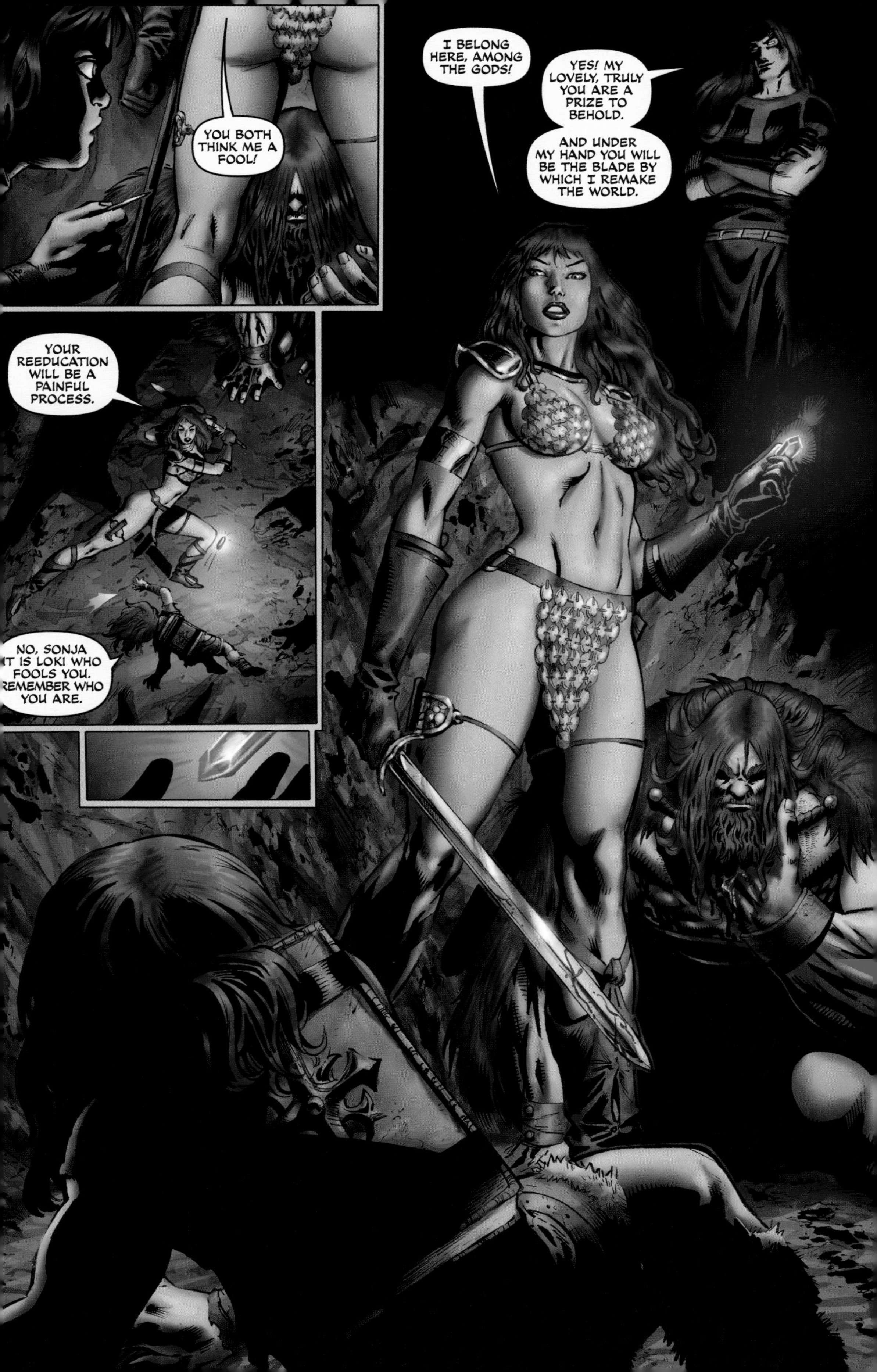
YOU BOTH THINK ME A FOOL!
YOUR REEDUCATION WILL BE A PAINFUL PROCESS.
NO, SONJA IT IS LOKI WHO FOOLS YOU. REMEMBER WHO YOU ARE.
I BELONG HERE, AMONG THE GODS!
YES! MY LOVELY, TRULY YOU ARE A PRIZE TO BEHOLD.
AND UNDER MY HAND YOU WILL BE THE BLADE BY WHICH I REMAKE THE WORLD.

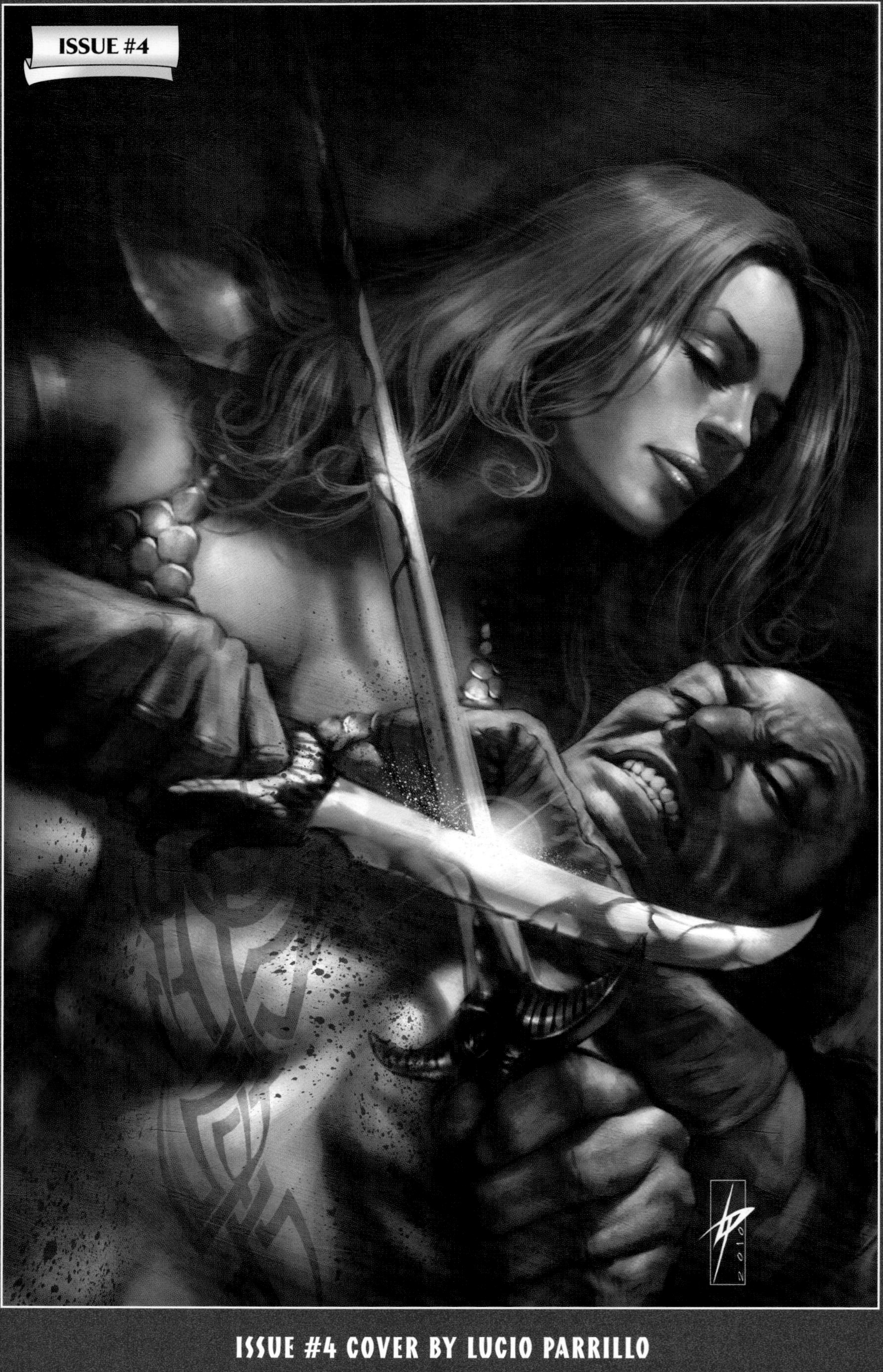
ISSUE #4

ISSUE #4 COVER BY LUCIO PARRILLO

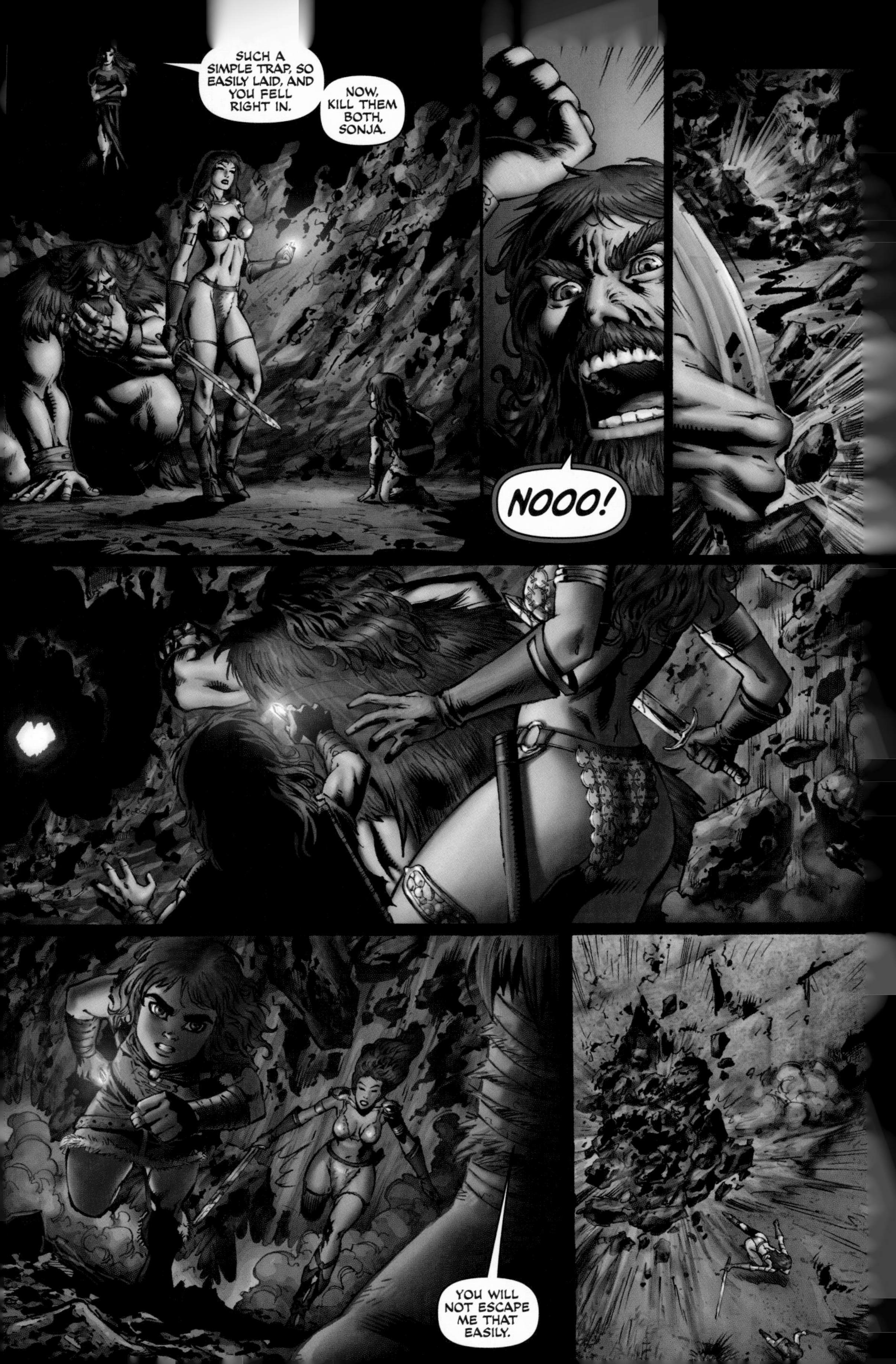

SUCH A SIMPLE TRAP, SO EASILY LAID, AND YOU FELL RIGHT IN.
NOW, KILL THEM BOTH, SONJA.
NOOO!
YOU WILL NOT ESCAPE ME THAT EASILY.

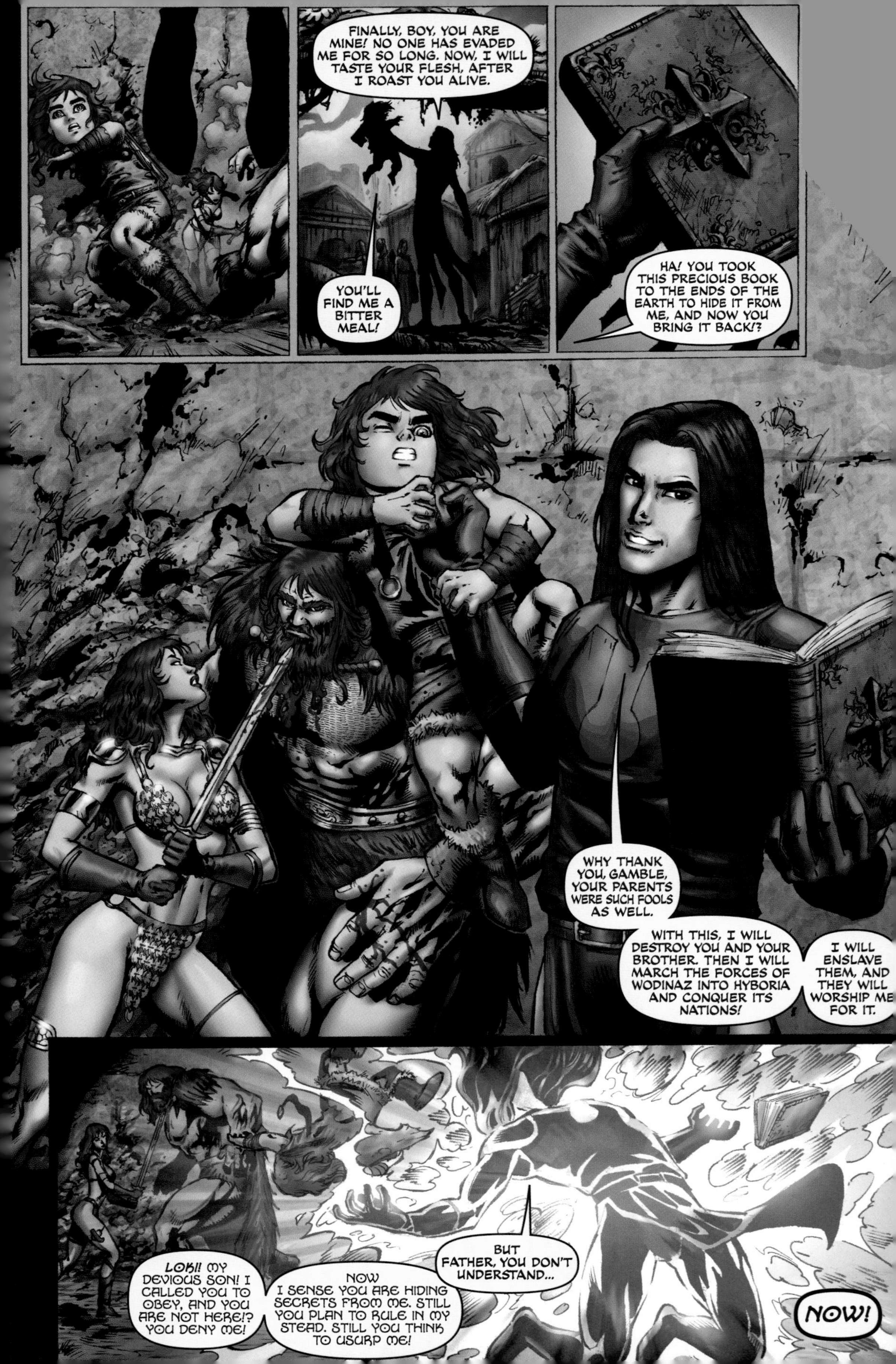
FINALLY, BOY, YOU ARE MINE! NO ONE HAS EVADED ME FOR SO LONG. NOW, I WILL TASTE YOUR FLESH, AFTER I ROAST YOU ALIVE.
YOU'LL FIND ME A BITTER MEAL!
HA! YOU TOOK THIS PRECIOUS BOOK TO THE ENDS OF THE EARTH TO HIDE IT FROM ME, AND NOW YOU BRING IT BACK!?
WHY THANK YOU, GAMBLE, YOUR PARENTS WERE SUCH FOOLS AS WELL.
WITH THIS, I WILL DESTROY YOU AND YOUR BROTHER. THEN I WILL MARCH THE FORCES OF WODINAZ INTO HYBORIA AND CONQUER ITS NATIONS!
I WILL ENSLAVE THEM, AND THEY WILL WORSHIP ME FOR IT.
LOKI! MY DEVIOUS SON! I CALLED YOU TO OBEY, AND YOU ARE NOT HERE!? YOU DENY ME!
NOW I SENSE YOU ARE HIDING SECRETS FROM ME. STILL YOU PLAN TO RULE IN MY STEAD. STILL YOU THINK TO USURP ME!
BUT FATHER, YOU DON'T UNDERSTAND...
NOW!

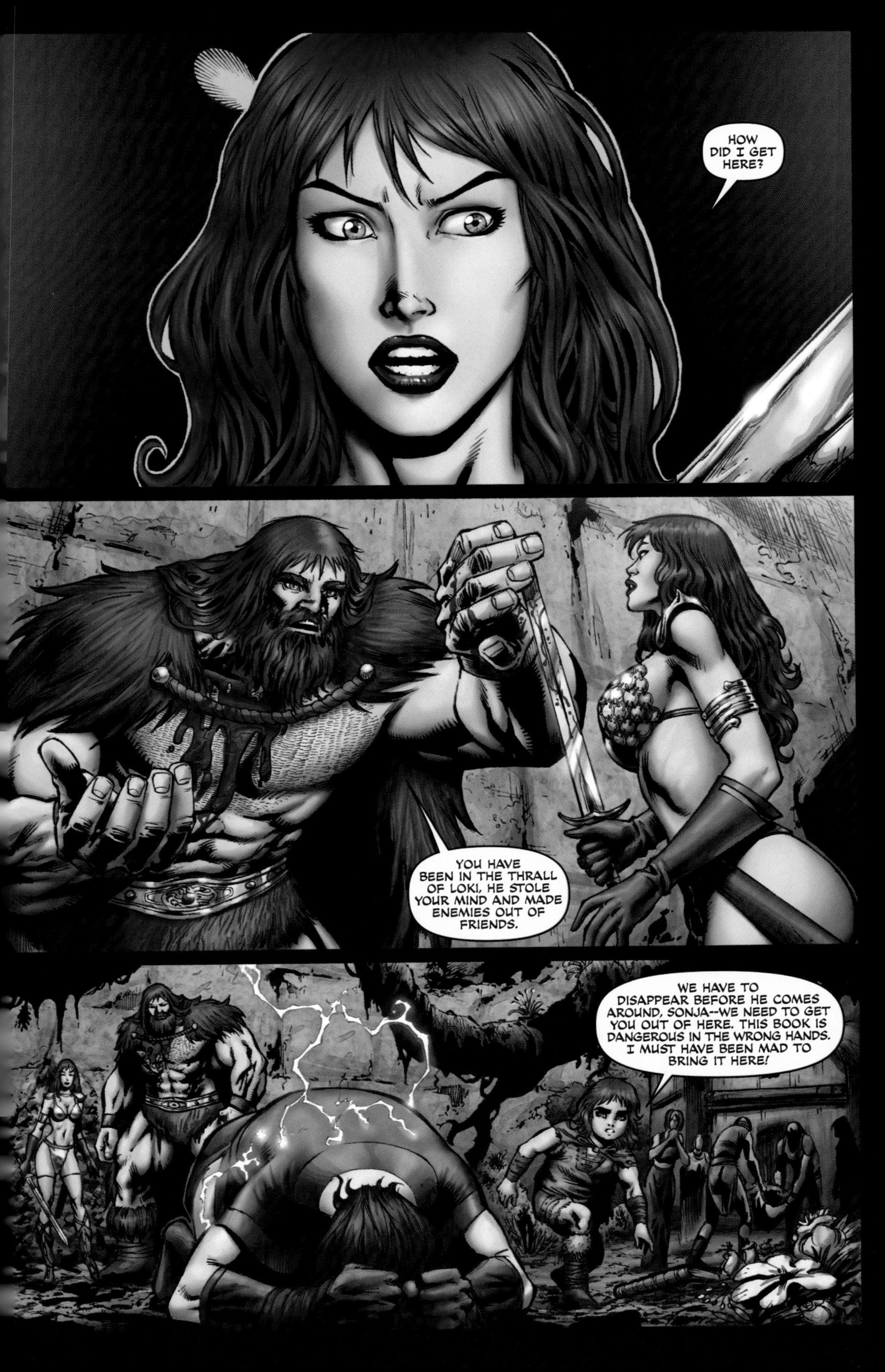
HOW DID I GET HERE?
YOU HAVE BEEN IN THE THRALL OF LOKI, HE STOLE YOUR MIND AND MADE ENEMIES OUT OF FRIENDS.
WE HAVE TO DISAPPEAR BEFORE HE COMES AROUND, SONJA--WE NEED TO GET YOU OUT OF HERE. THIS BOOK IS DANGEROUS IN THE WRONG HANDS. I MUST HAVE BEEN MAD TO BRING IT HERE!

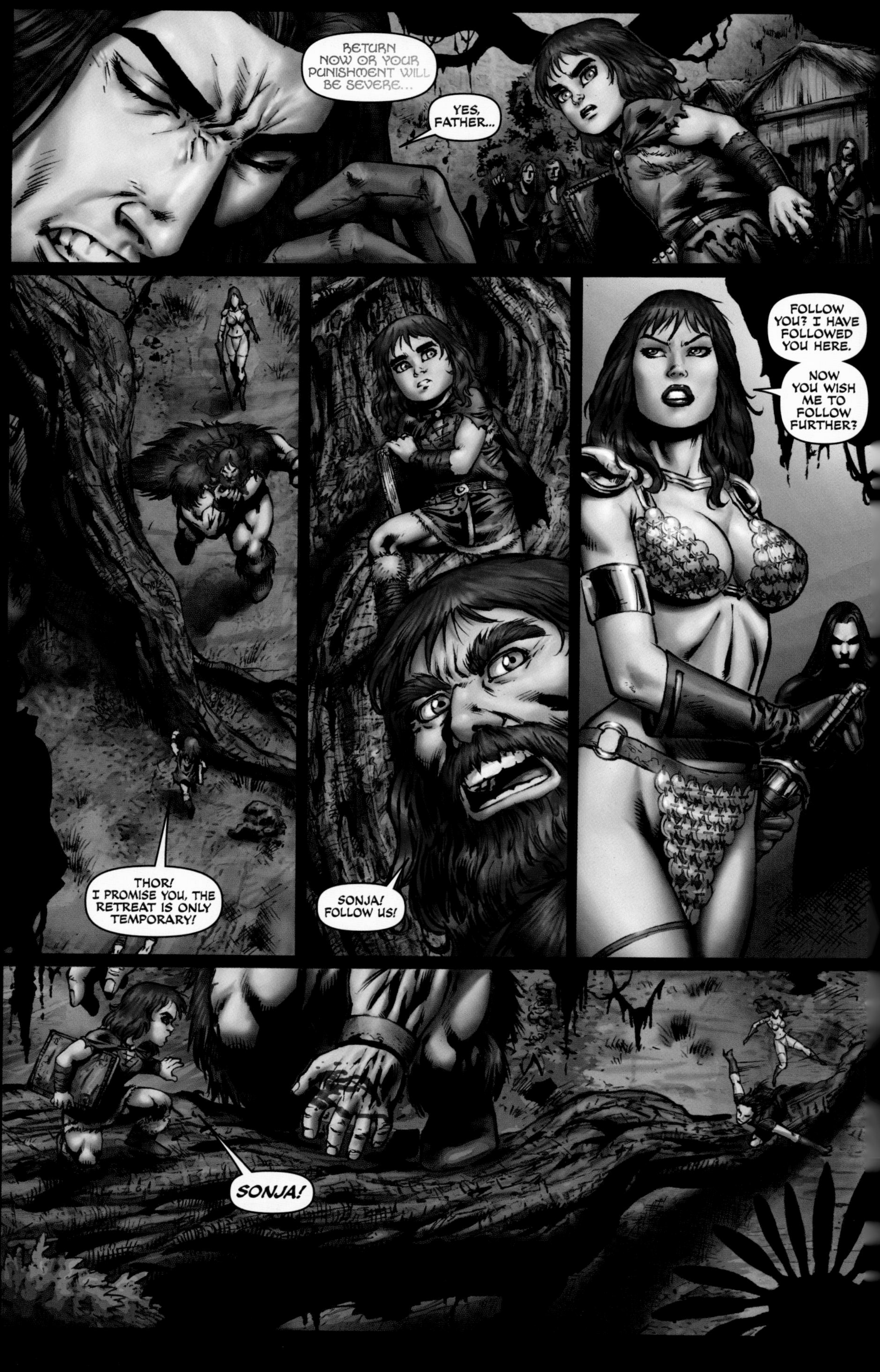
RETURN NOW OR YOUR PUNISHMENT WILL BE SEVERE...
YES, FATHER...
THOR! I PROMISE YOU, THE RETREAT IS ONLY TEMPORARY!
SONJA! FOLLOW US!
FOLLOW YOU? I HAVE FOLLOWED YOU HERE.
NOW YOU WISH ME TO FOLLOW FURTHER?
SONJA!

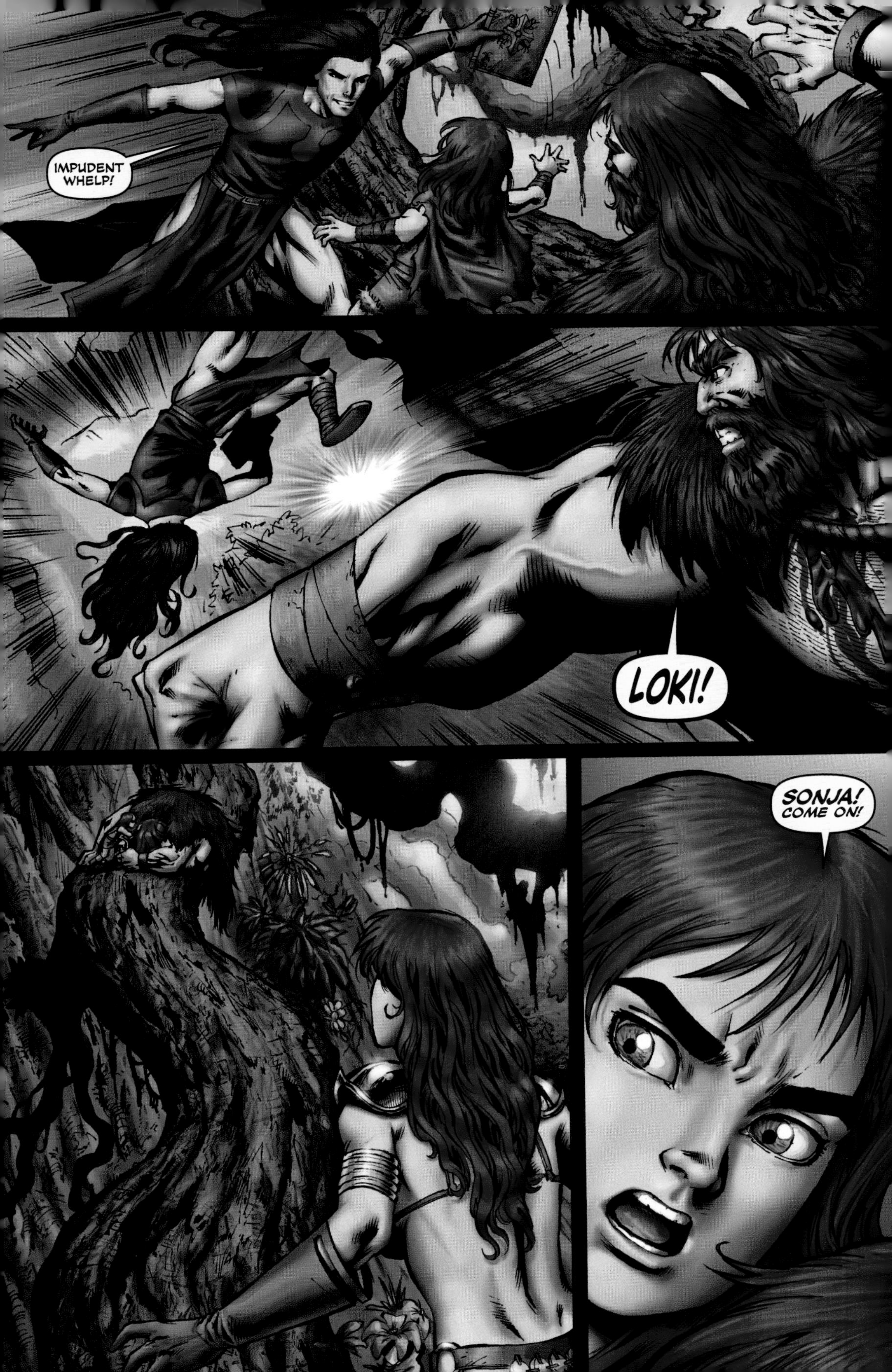
IMPUDENT WHELP!
LOKI!
SONJA! COME ON!

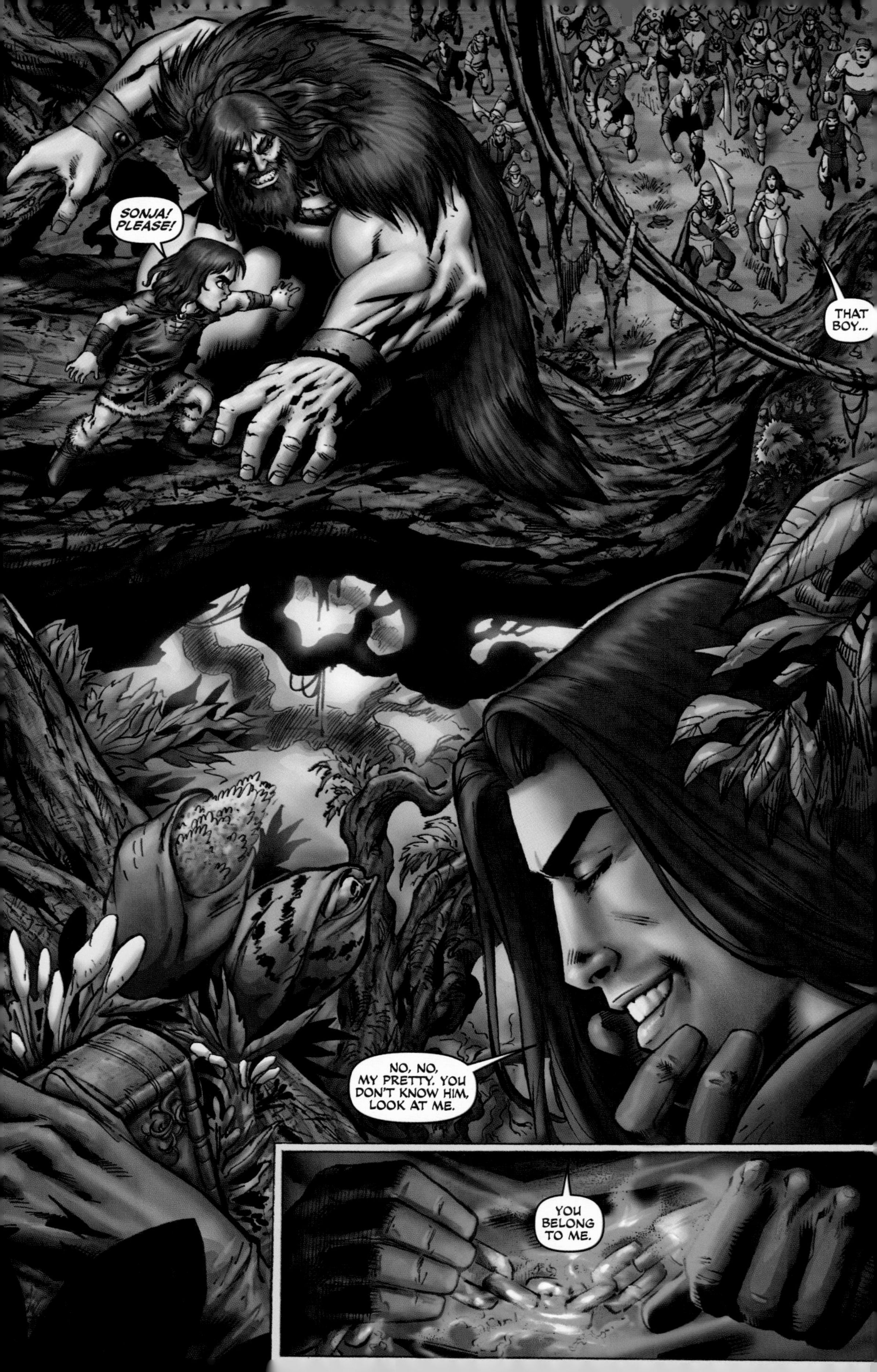
SONJA! PLEASE!
THAT BOY...
NO, NO, MY PRETTY. YOU DON'T KNOW HIM. LOOK AT ME.
YOU BELONG TO ME.

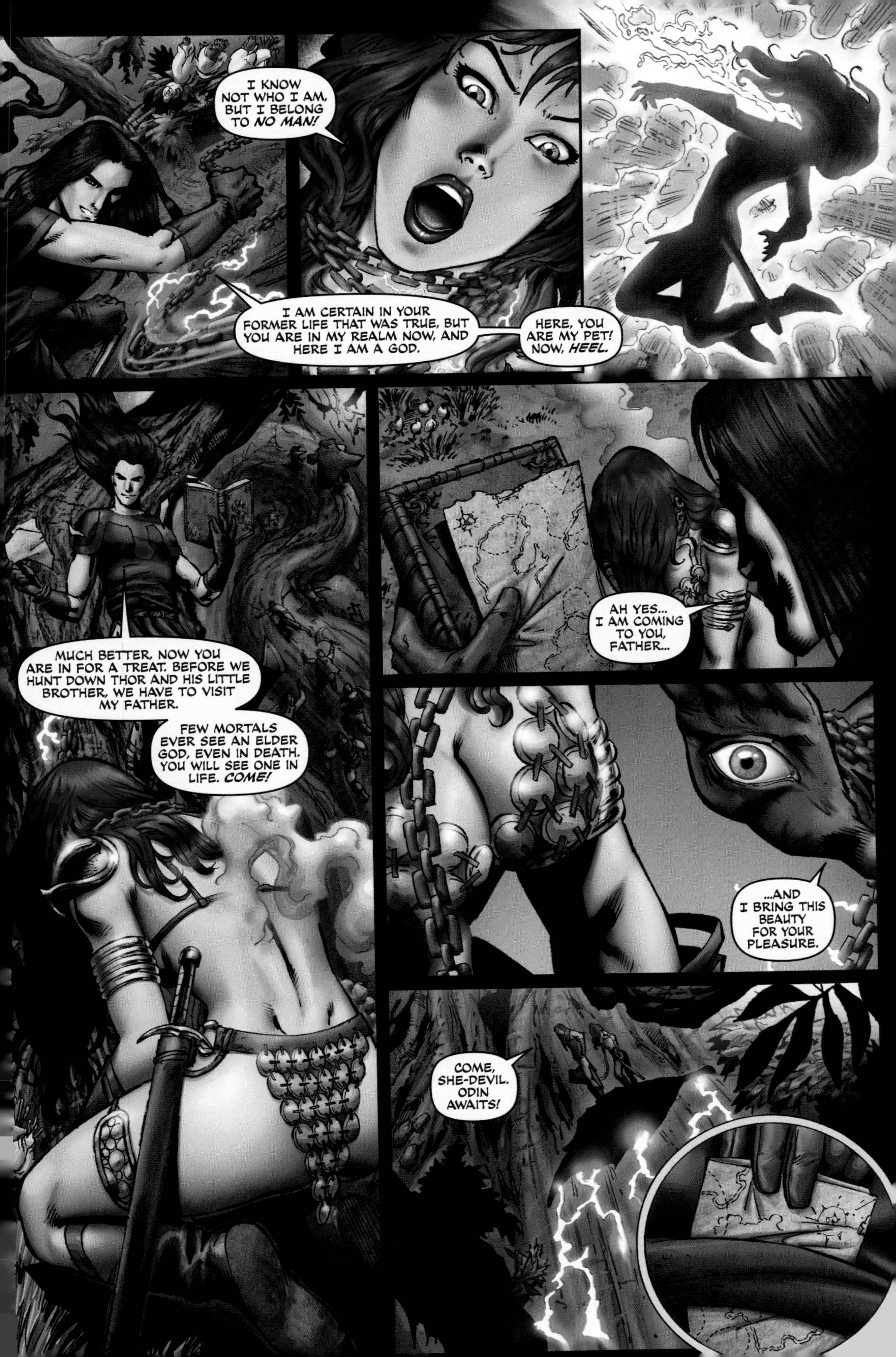
I KNOW NOT WHO I AM, BUT I BELONG TO *NO MAN!*
I AM CERTAIN IN YOUR FORMER LIFE THAT WAS TRUE, BUT YOU ARE IN MY REALM NOW, AND HERE I AM A GOD.
HERE, YOU ARE MY PET! NOW, *HEEL.*
MUCH BETTER, NOW YOU ARE IN FOR A TREAT. BEFORE WE HUNT DOWN THOR AND HIS LITTLE BROTHER, WE HAVE TO VISIT MY FATHER.
FEW MORTALS EVER SEE AN ELDER GOD, EVEN IN DEATH. YOU WILL SEE ONE IN LIFE. *COME!*
AH YES... I AM COMING TO YOU, FATHER...
...AND I BRING THIS BEAUTY FOR YOUR PLEASURE.
COME, SHE-DEVIL. ODIN AWAITS!

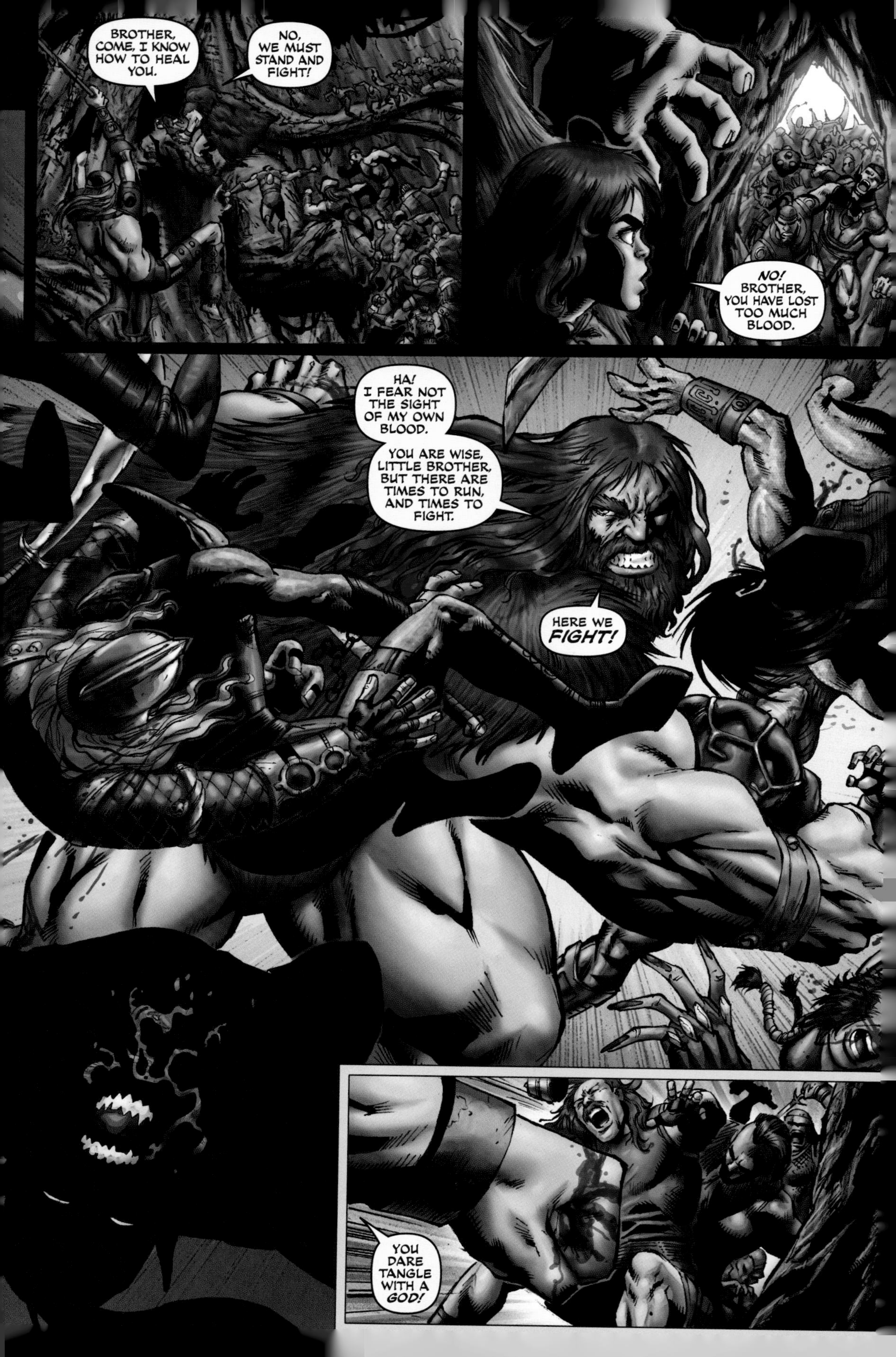
BROTHER, COME, I KNOW HOW TO HEAL YOU.
NO, WE MUST STAND AND FIGHT!
NO! BROTHER, YOU HAVE LOST TOO MUCH BLOOD.
HA! I FEAR NOT THE SIGHT OF MY OWN BLOOD.
YOU ARE WISE, LITTLE BROTHER, BUT THERE ARE TIMES TO RUN, AND TIMES TO FIGHT.
HERE WE FIGHT!
YOU DARE TANGLE WITH A GOD!

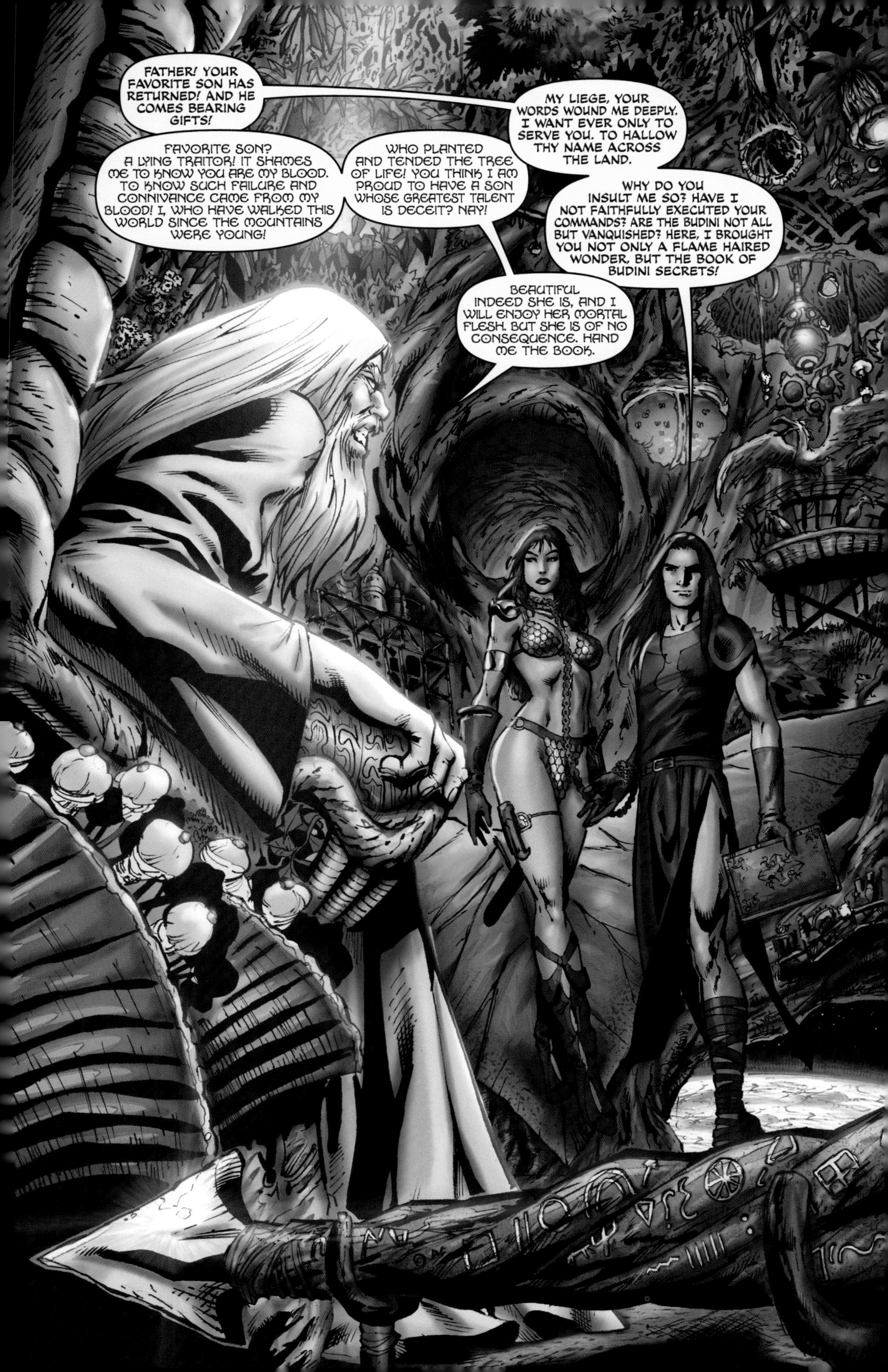
FATHER! YOUR FAVORITE SON HAS RETURNED! AND HE COMES BEARING GIFTS!
FAVORITE SON? A LYING TRAITOR! IT SHAMES ME TO KNOW YOU ARE MY BLOOD. TO KNOW SUCH FAILURE AND CONNIVANCE CAME FROM MY BLOOD! I, WHO HAVE WALKED THIS WORLD SINCE THE MOUNTAINS WERE YOUNG!
WHO PLANTED AND TENDED THE TREE OF LIFE! YOU THINK I AM PROUD TO HAVE A SON WHOSE GREATEST TALENT IS DECEIT? NAY!
MY LIEGE, YOUR WORDS WOUND ME DEEPLY. I WANT EVER ONLY TO SERVE YOU. TO HALLOW THY NAME ACROSS THE LAND.
WHY DO YOU INSULT ME SO? HAVE I NOT FAITHFULLY EXECUTED YOUR COMMANDS? ARE THE BUDINI NOT ALL BUT VANQUISHED? HERE, I BROUGHT YOU NOT ONLY A FLAME HAIRED WONDER, BUT THE BOOK OF BUDINI SECRETS!
BEAUTIFUL INDEED SHE IS, AND I WILL ENJOY HER MORTAL FLESH. BUT SHE IS OF NO CONSEQUENCE. HAND ME THE BOOK.

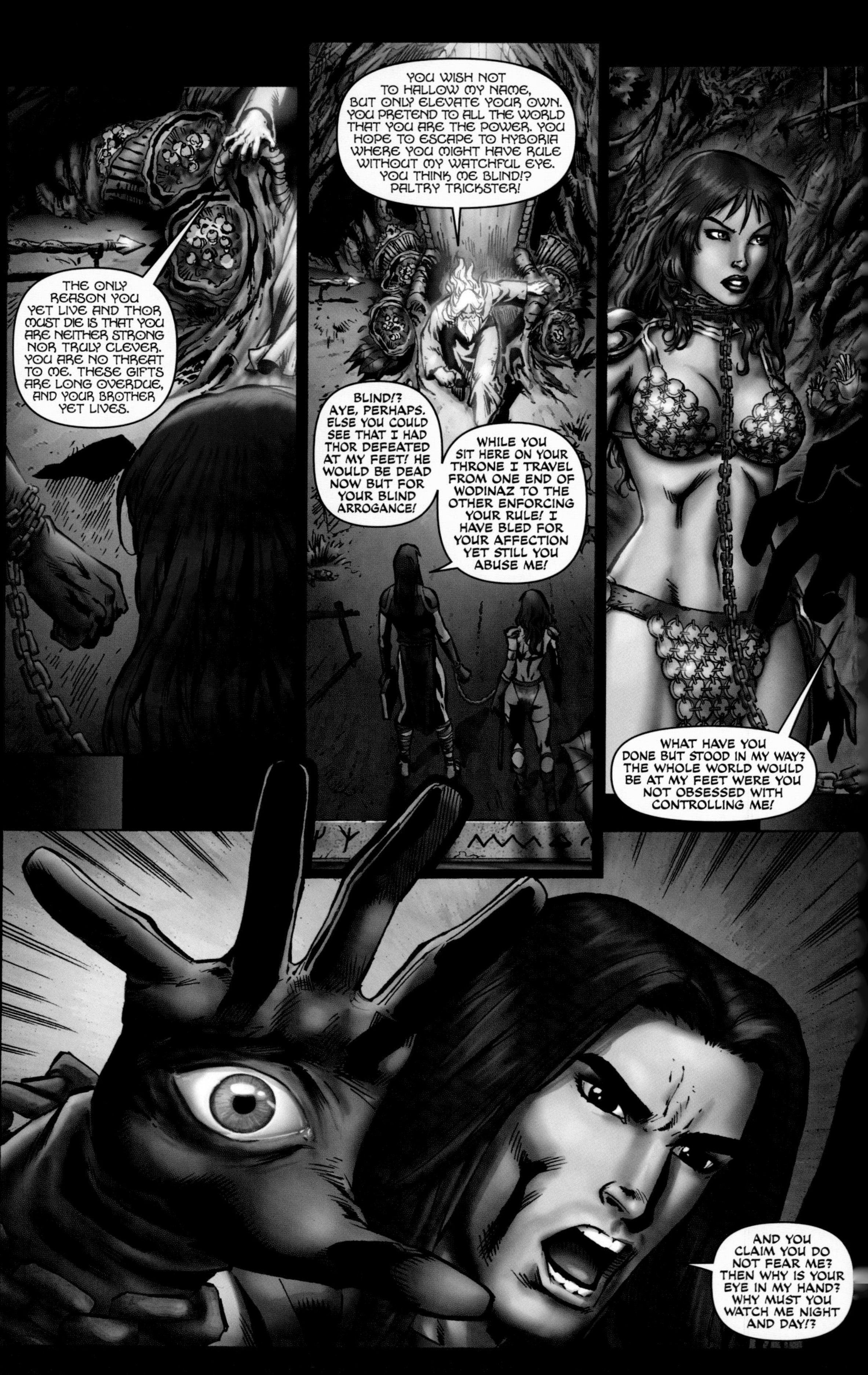
THE ONLY REASON YOU YET LIVE AND THOR MUST DIE IS THAT YOU ARE NEITHER STRONG NOR TRULY CLEVER. YOU ARE NO THREAT TO ME. THESE GIFTS ARE LONG OVERDUE, AND YOUR BROTHER YET LIVES.
YOU WISH NOT TO HALLOW MY NAME, BUT ONLY ELEVATE YOUR OWN. YOU PRETEND TO ALL THE WORLD THAT YOU ARE THE POWER. YOU HOPE TO ESCAPE TO HYBORIA WHERE YOU MIGHT HAVE RULE WITHOUT MY WATCHFUL EYE. YOU THINK ME BLIND!? PALTRY TRICKSTER!
BLIND!? AYE, PERHAPS. ELSE YOU COULD SEE THAT I HAD THOR DEFEATED AT MY FEET! HE WOULD BE DEAD NOW BUT FOR YOUR BLIND ARROGANCE!
WHILE YOU SIT HERE ON YOUR THRONE I TRAVEL FROM ONE END OF WODINAZ TO THE OTHER ENFORCING YOUR RULE! I HAVE BLED FOR YOUR AFFECTION YET STILL YOU ABUSE ME!
WHAT HAVE YOU DONE BUT STOOD IN MY WAY? THE WHOLE WORLD WOULD BE AT MY FEET WERE YOU NOT OBSESSED WITH CONTROLLING ME!
AND YOU CLAIM YOU DO NOT FEAR ME? THEN WHY IS YOUR EYE IN MY HAND? WHY MUST YOU WATCH ME NIGHT AND DAY!?

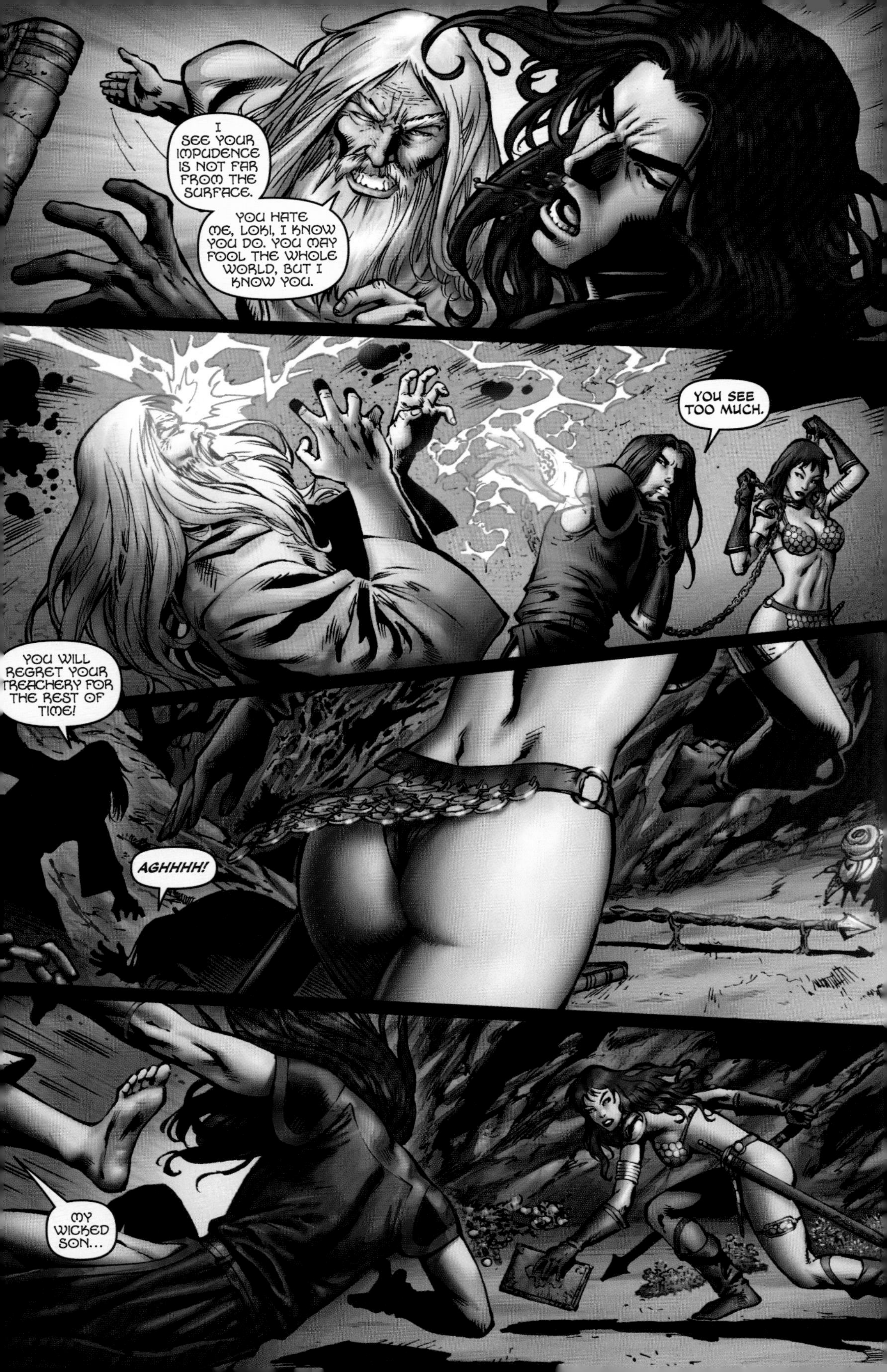
I SEE YOUR IMPUDENCE IS NOT FAR FROM THE SURFACE.
YOU HATE ME, LOKI, I KNOW YOU DO. YOU MAY FOOL THE WHOLE WORLD, BUT I KNOW YOU.
YOU SEE TOO MUCH.
YOU WILL REGRET YOUR TREACHERY FOR THE REST OF TIME!
AGHHHH!
MY WICKED SON...

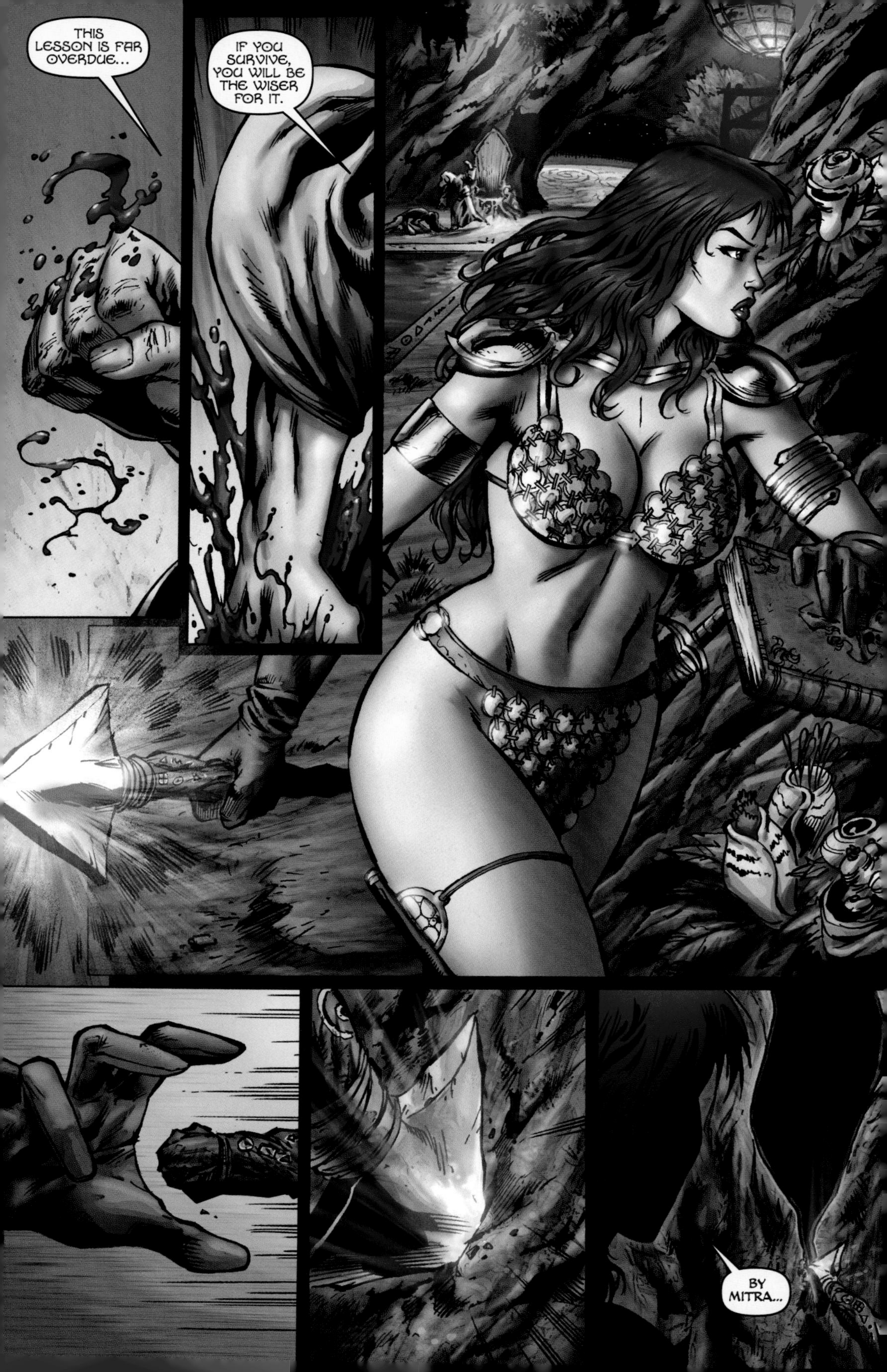
THIS LESSON IS FAR OVERDUE...
IF YOU SURVIVE, YOU WILL BE THE WISER FOR IT.
BY MITRA...

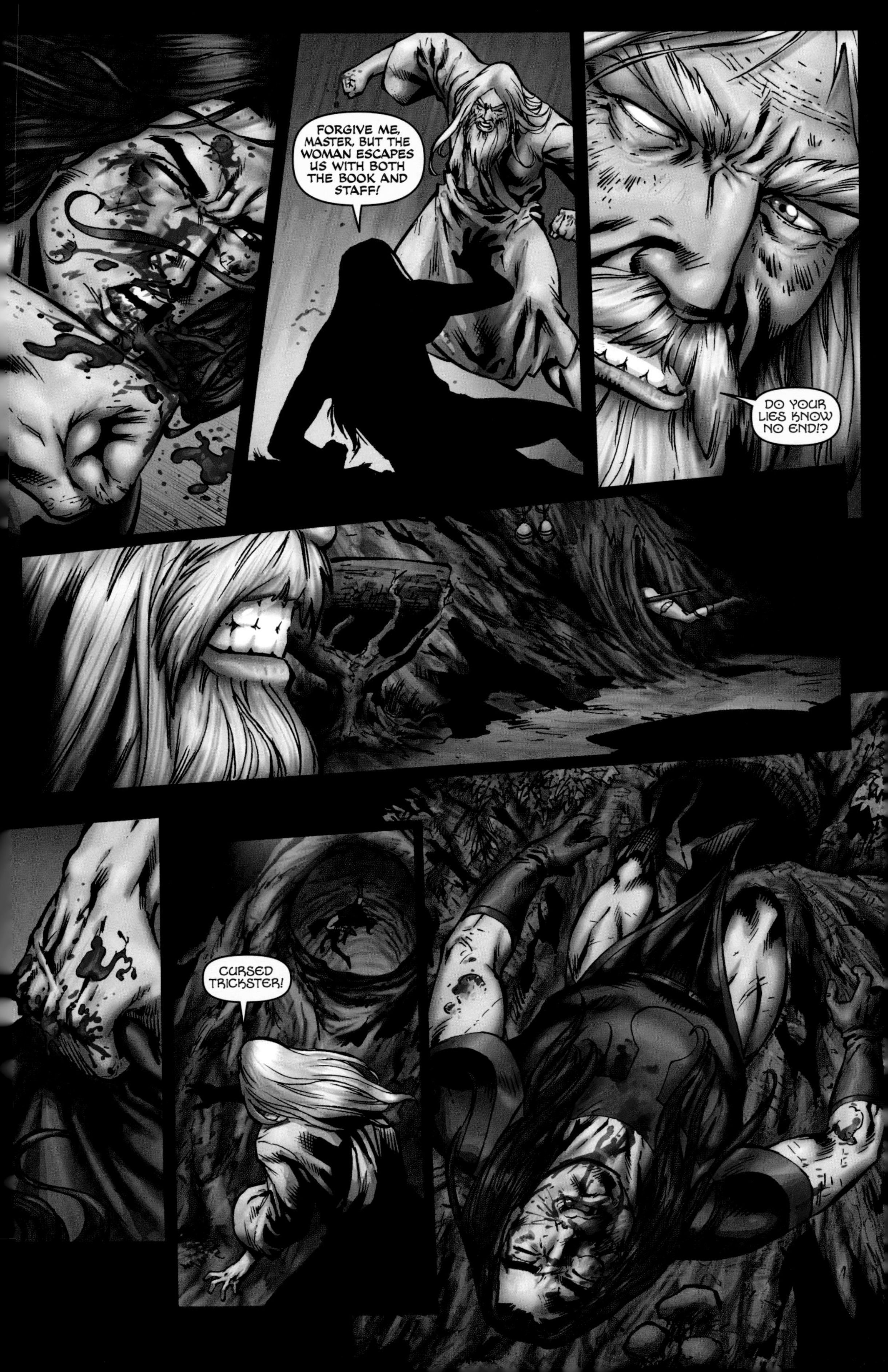
FORGIVE ME, MASTER, BUT THE WOMAN ESCAPES US WITH BOTH THE BOOK AND STAFF!
DO YOUR LIES KNOW NO END!?
CURSED TRICKSTER!

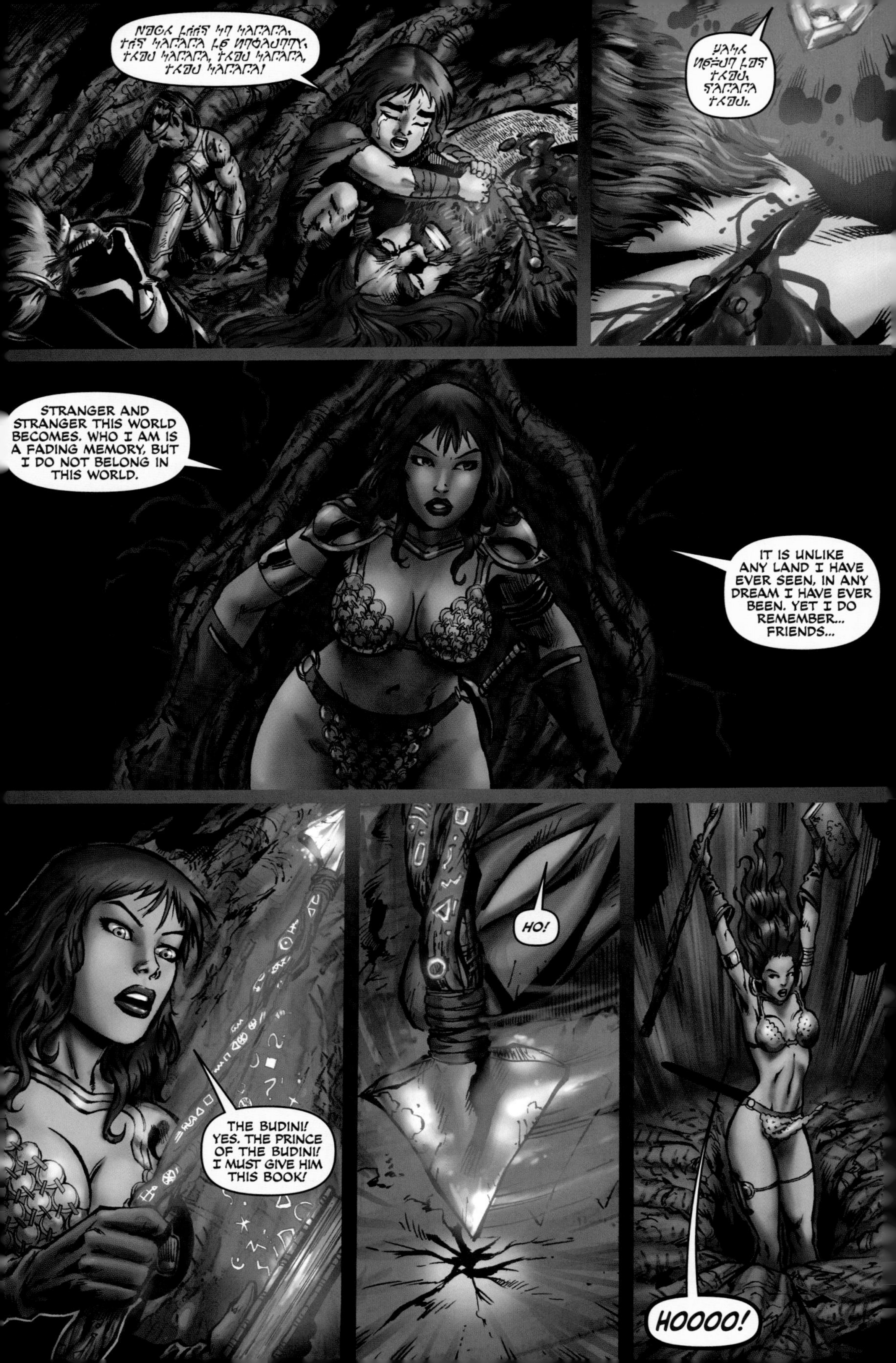
STRANGER AND STRANGER THIS WORLD BECOMES. WHO I AM IS A FADING MEMORY, BUT I DO NOT BELONG IN THIS WORLD.
IT IS UNLIKE ANY LAND I HAVE EVER SEEN, IN ANY DREAM I HAVE EVER BEEN. YET I DO REMEMBER... FRIENDS...
THE BUDINI! YES. THE PRINCE OF THE BUDINI! I MUST GIVE HIM THIS BOOK!
HO!
HOOOO!

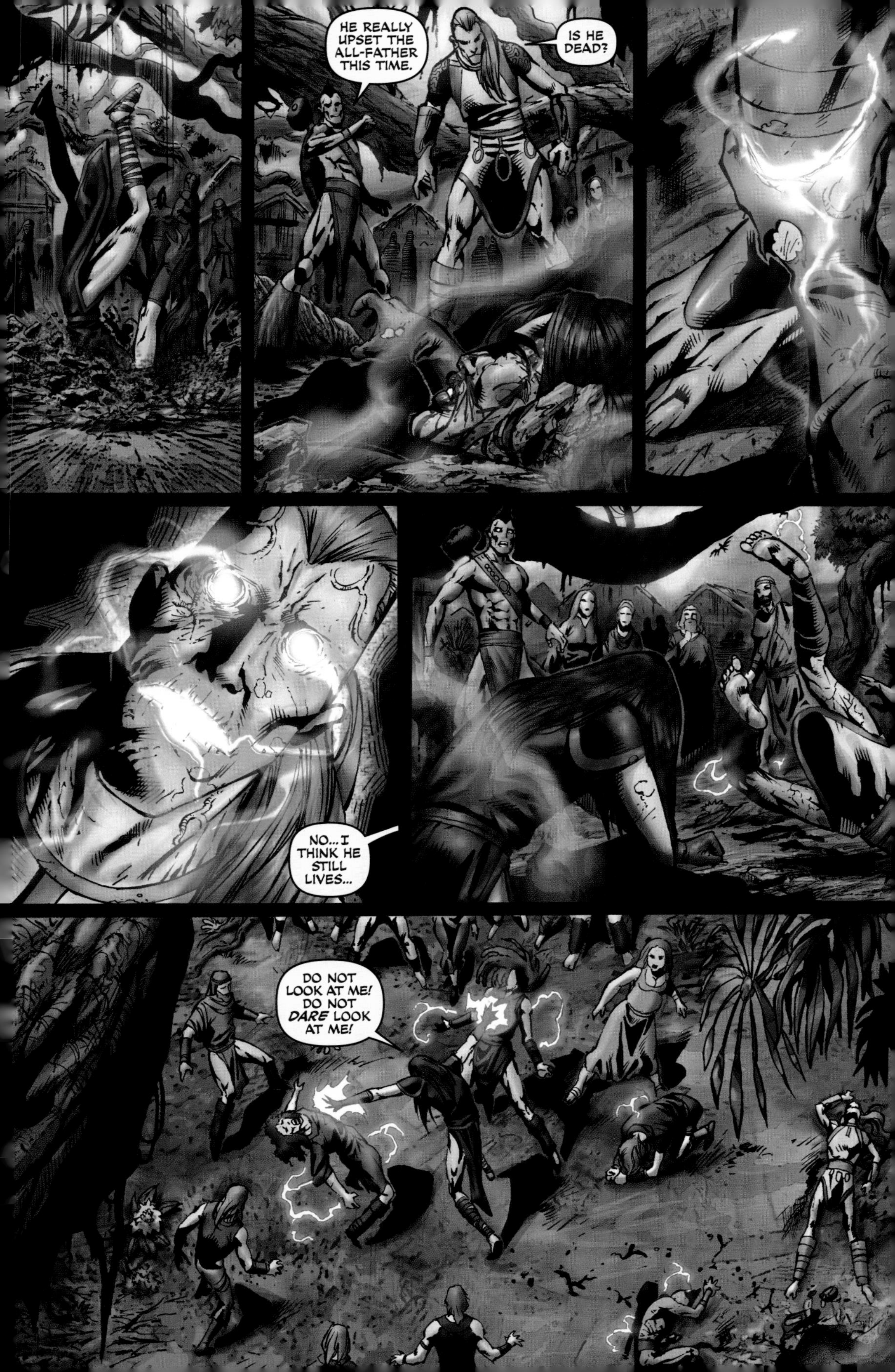
HE REALLY UPSET THE ALL-FATHER THIS TIME.
IS HE DEAD?
NO... I THINK HE STILL LIVES...
DO NOT LOOK AT ME! DO NOT *DARE* LOOK AT ME!

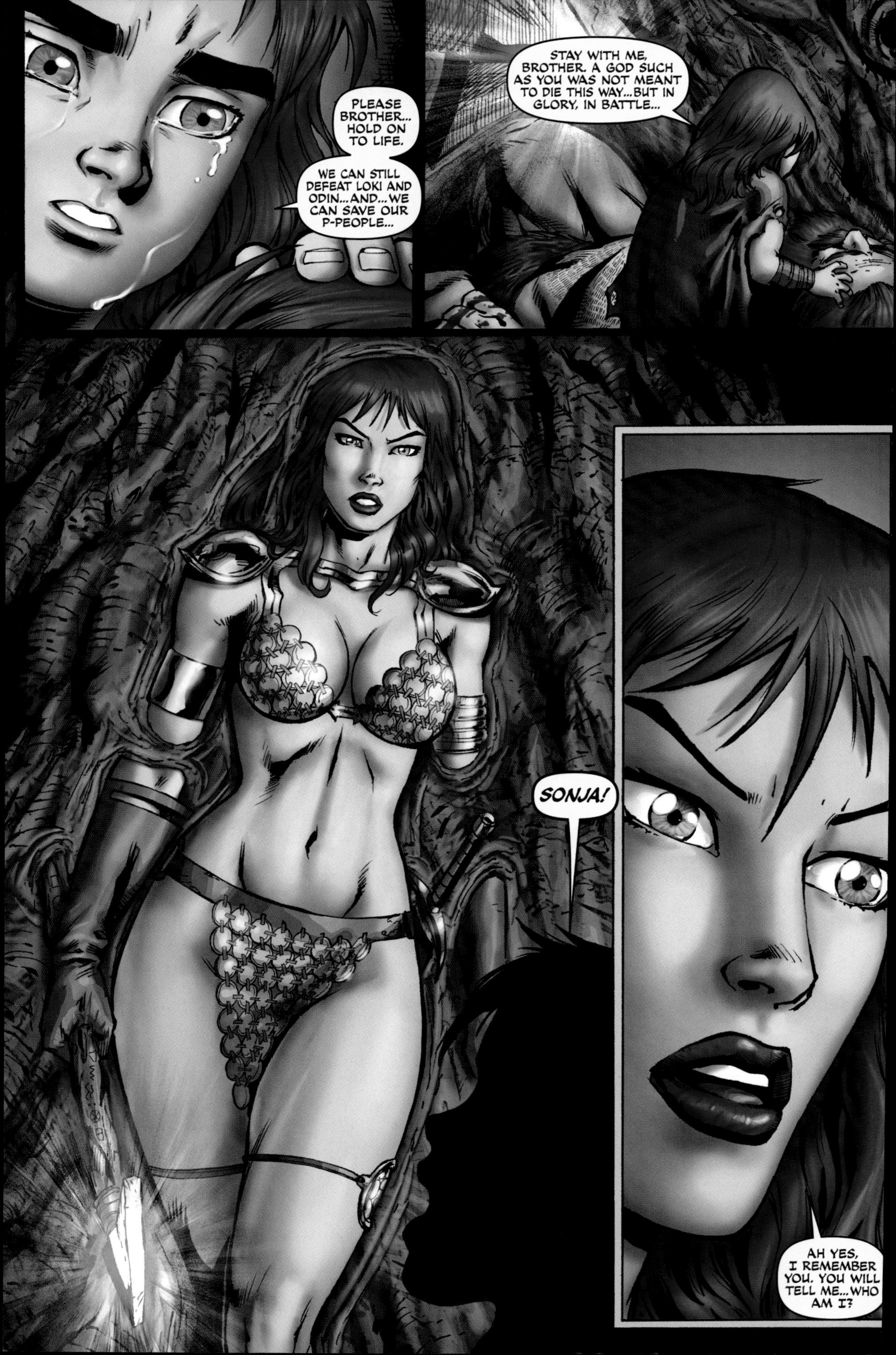
PLEASE BROTHER... HOLD ON TO LIFE.
WE CAN STILL DEFEAT LOKI AND ODIN...AND...WE CAN SAVE OUR P-PEOPLE...
STAY WITH ME, BROTHER. A GOD SUCH AS YOU WAS NOT MEANT TO DIE THIS WAY...BUT IN GLORY, IN BATTLE...
SONJA!
AH YES, I REMEMBER YOU. YOU WILL TELL ME...WHO AM I?

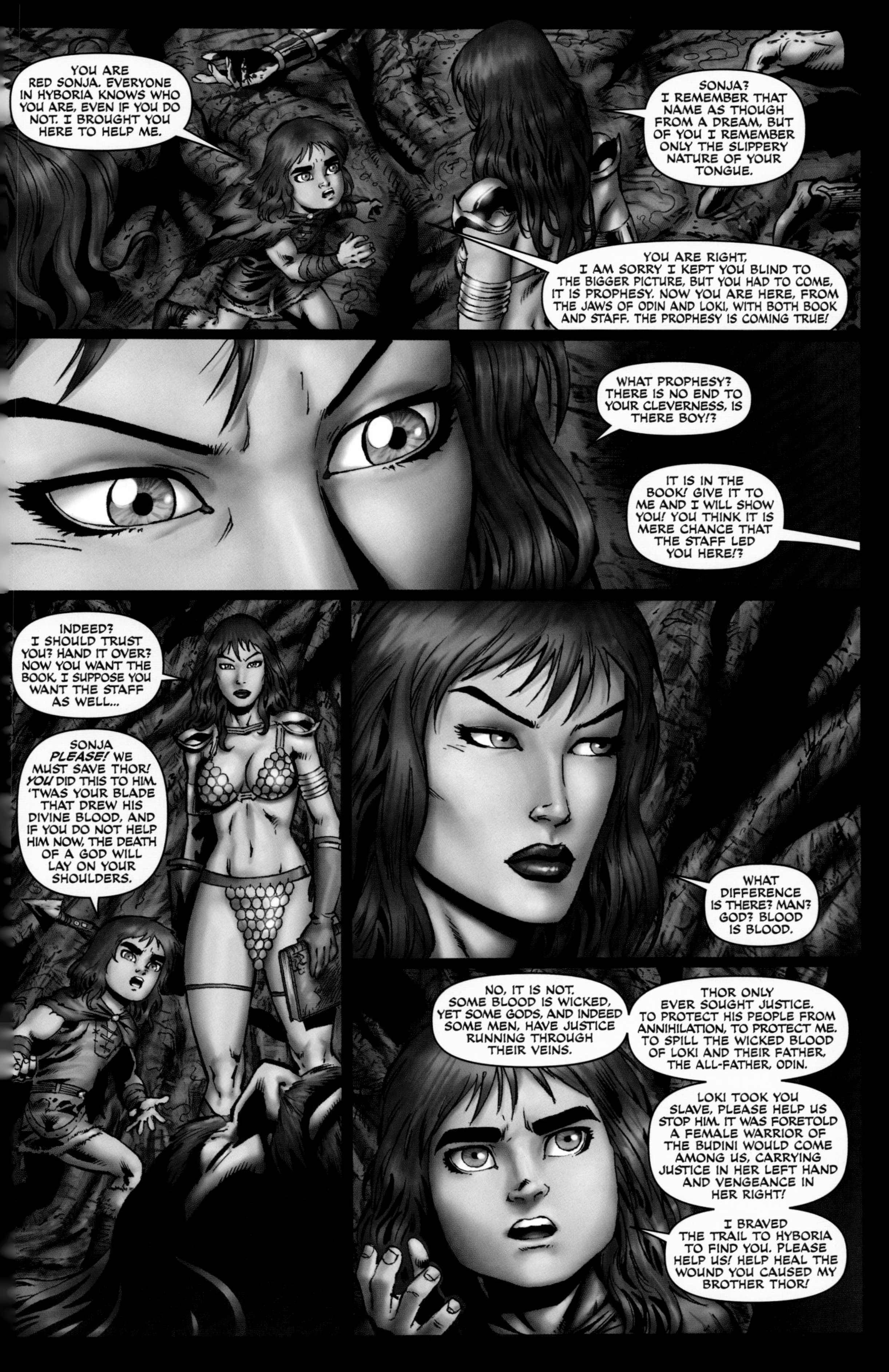
YOU ARE RED SONJA. EVERYONE IN HYBORIA KNOWS WHO YOU ARE, EVEN IF YOU DO NOT. I BROUGHT YOU HERE TO HELP ME.
SONJA? I REMEMBER THAT NAME AS THOUGH FROM A DREAM, BUT OF YOU I REMEMBER ONLY THE SLIPPERY NATURE OF YOUR TONGUE.
YOU ARE RIGHT, I AM SORRY I KEPT YOU BLIND TO THE BIGGER PICTURE, BUT YOU HAD TO COME, IT IS PROPHESY. NOW YOU ARE HERE, FROM THE JAWS OF ODIN AND LOKI, WITH BOTH BOOK AND STAFF. THE PROPHESY IS COMING TRUE!
WHAT PROPHESY? THERE IS NO END TO YOUR CLEVERNESS, IS THERE BOY!?
IT IS IN THE BOOK! GIVE IT TO ME AND I WILL SHOW YOU! YOU THINK IT IS MERE CHANCE THAT THE STAFF LED YOU HERE!?
INDEED? I SHOULD TRUST YOU? HAND IT OVER? NOW YOU WANT THE BOOK, I SUPPOSE YOU WANT THE STAFF AS WELL...
SONJA *PLEASE!* WE MUST SAVE THOR! *YOU* DID THIS TO HIM. 'TWAS YOUR BLADE THAT DREW HIS DIVINE BLOOD, AND IF YOU DO NOT HELP HIM NOW, THE DEATH OF A GOD WILL LAY ON YOUR SHOULDERS.
WHAT DIFFERENCE IS THERE? MAN? GOD? BLOOD IS BLOOD.
NO, IT IS NOT. SOME BLOOD IS WICKED, YET SOME GODS, AND INDEED SOME MEN, HAVE JUSTICE RUNNING THROUGH THEIR VEINS.
THOR ONLY EVER SOUGHT JUSTICE. TO PROTECT HIS PEOPLE FROM ANNIHILATION, TO PROTECT ME. TO SPILL THE WICKED BLOOD OF LOKI AND THEIR FATHER, THE ALL-FATHER, ODIN.
LOKI TOOK YOU SLAVE, PLEASE HELP US STOP HIM. IT WAS FORETOLD A FEMALE WARRIOR OF THE BUDINI WOULD COME AMONG US, CARRYING JUSTICE IN HER LEFT HAND AND VENGEANCE IN HER RIGHT!
I BRAVED THE TRAIL TO HYBORIA TO FIND YOU. PLEASE HELP US! HELP HEAL THE WOUND YOU CAUSED MY BROTHER THOR!

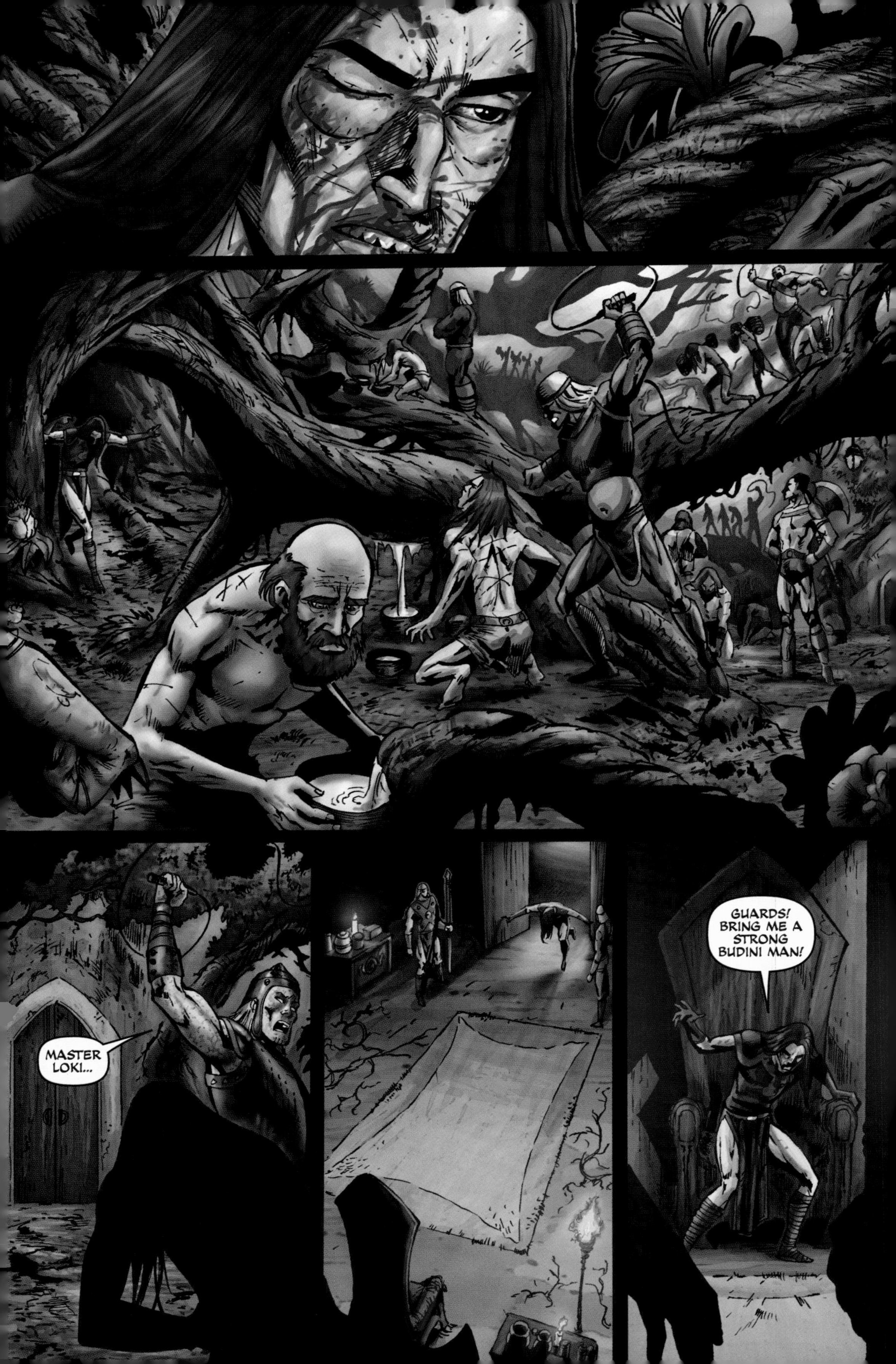
MASTER LOKI...
GUARDS! BRING ME A STRONG BUDINI MAN!

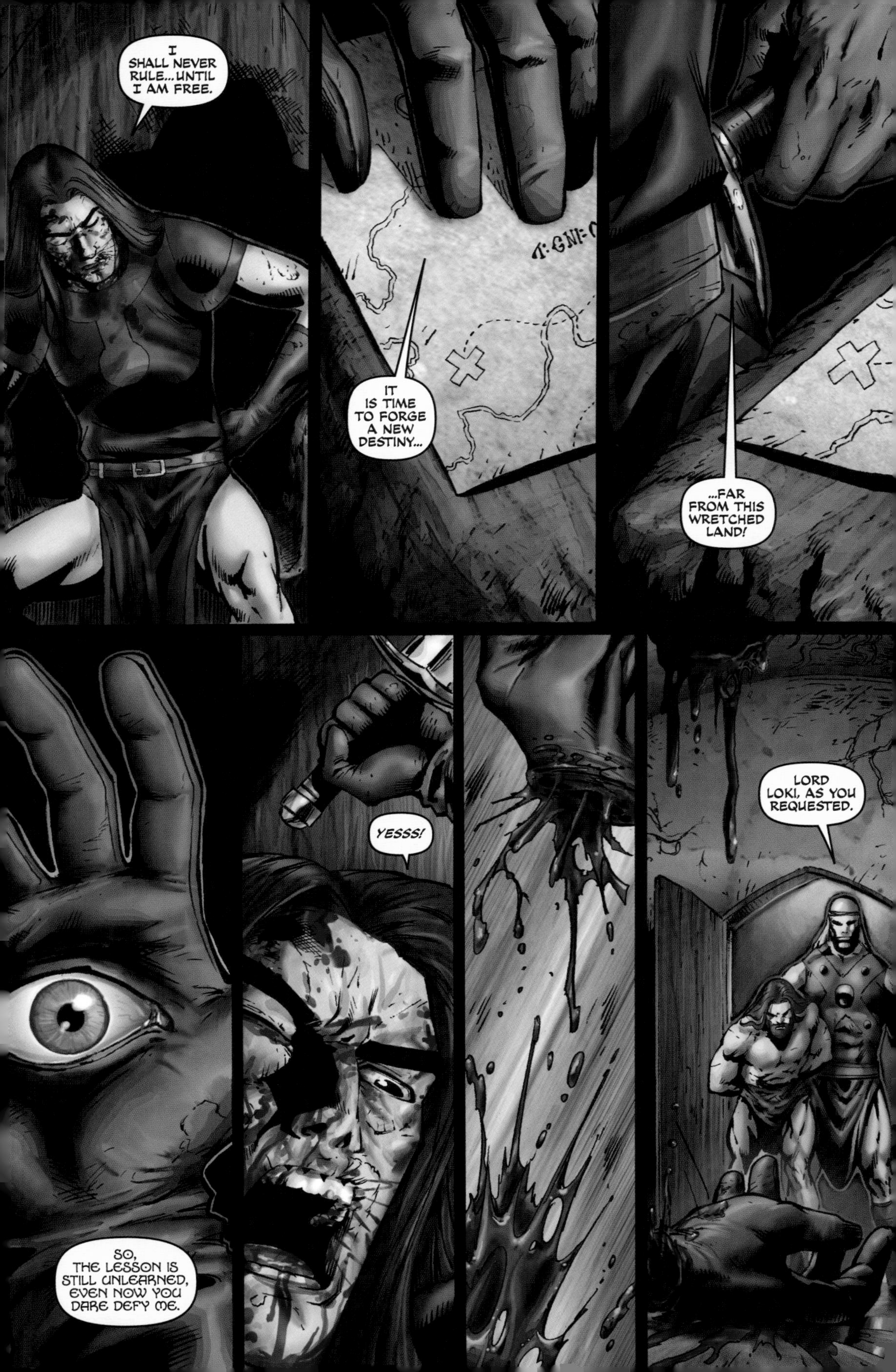
I SHALL NEVER RULE...UNTIL I AM FREE.
IT IS TIME TO FORGE A NEW DESTINY...
...FAR FROM THIS WRETCHED LAND!
SO, THE LESSON IS STILL UNLEARNED, EVEN NOW YOU DARE DEFY ME.
YESSS!
LORD LOKI, AS YOU REQUESTED.

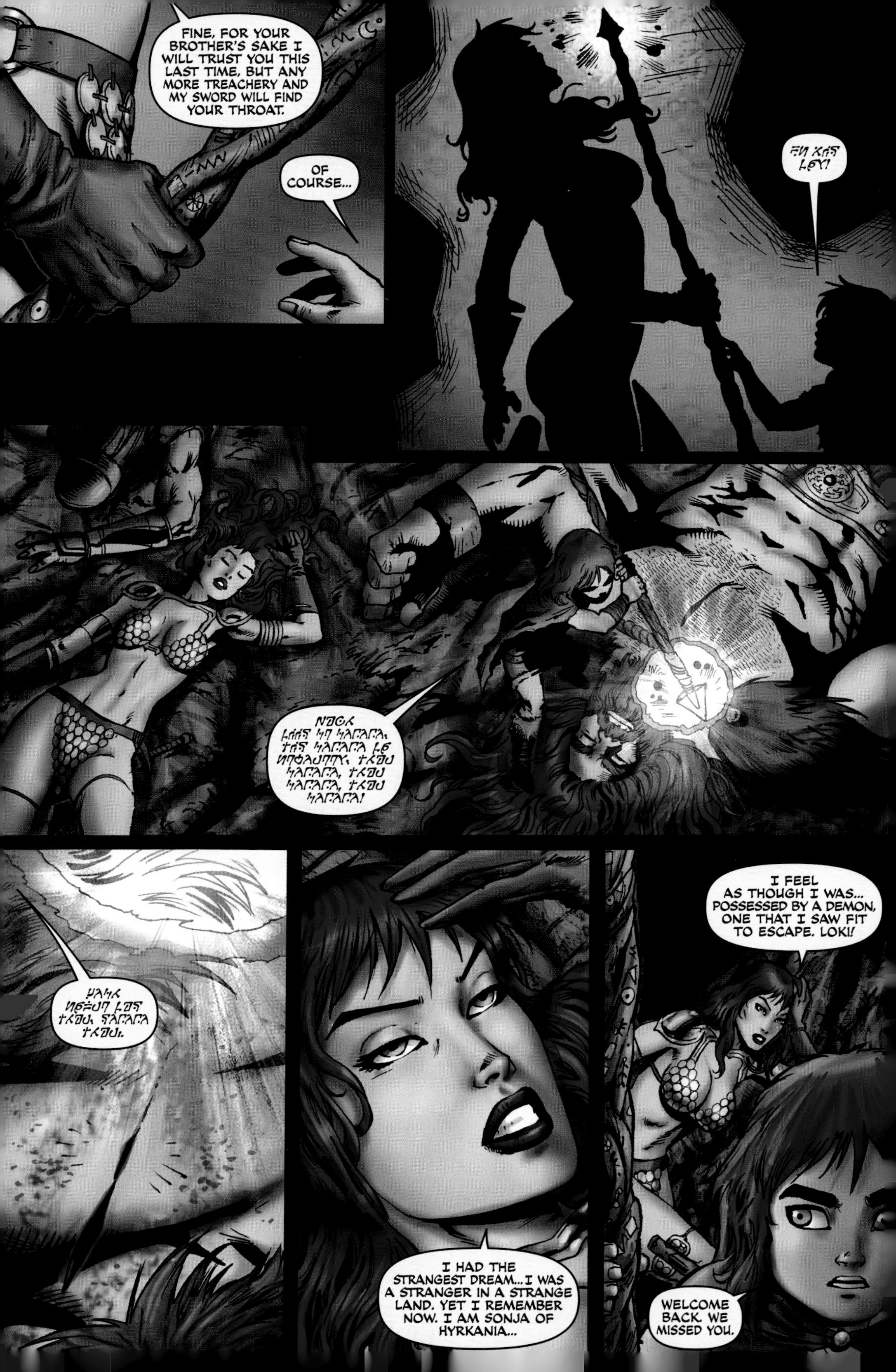
FINE, FOR YOUR BROTHER'S SAKE I WILL TRUST YOU THIS LAST TIME, BUT ANY MORE TREACHERY AND MY SWORD WILL FIND YOUR THROAT.
OF COURSE...
I HAD THE STRANGEST DREAM... I WAS A STRANGER IN A STRANGE LAND. YET I REMEMBER NOW. I AM SONJA OF HYRKANIA...
I FEEL AS THOUGH I WAS... POSSESSED BY A DEMON, ONE THAT I SAW FIT TO ESCAPE. LOKI!
WELCOME BACK. WE MISSED YOU.

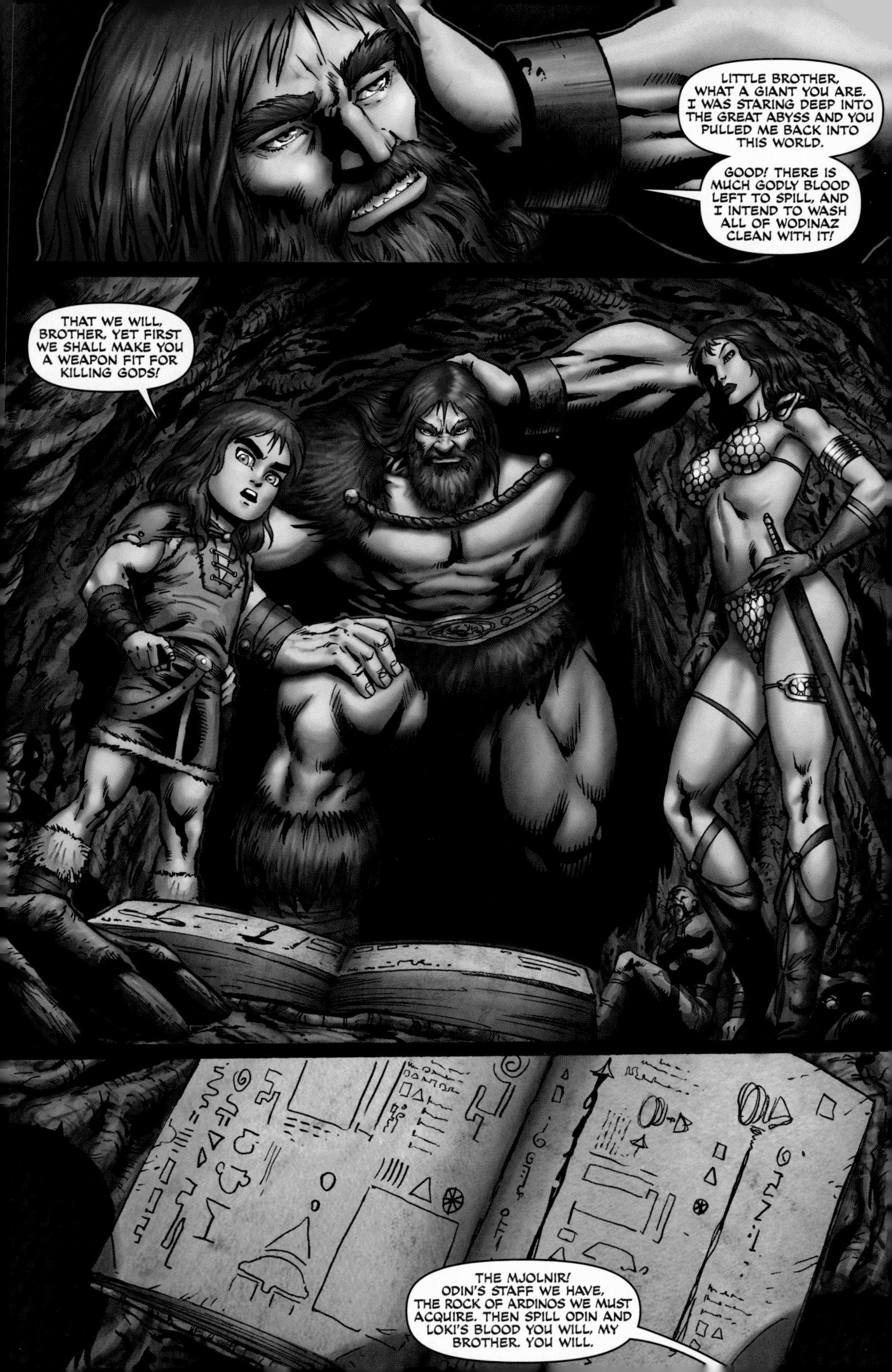
LITTLE BROTHER, WHAT A GIANT YOU ARE. I WAS STARING DEEP INTO THE GREAT ABYSS AND YOU PULLED ME BACK INTO THIS WORLD.
GOOD! THERE IS MUCH GODLY BLOOD LEFT TO SPILL, AND I INTEND TO WASH ALL OF WODINAZ CLEAN WITH IT!
THAT WE WILL, BROTHER, YET FIRST WE SHALL MAKE YOU A WEAPON FIT FOR KILLING GODS!
THE MJOLNIR! ODIN'S STAFF WE HAVE, THE ROCK OF ARDINOS WE MUST ACQUIRE. THEN SPILL ODIN AND LOKI'S BLOOD YOU WILL, MY BROTHER. YOU WILL.

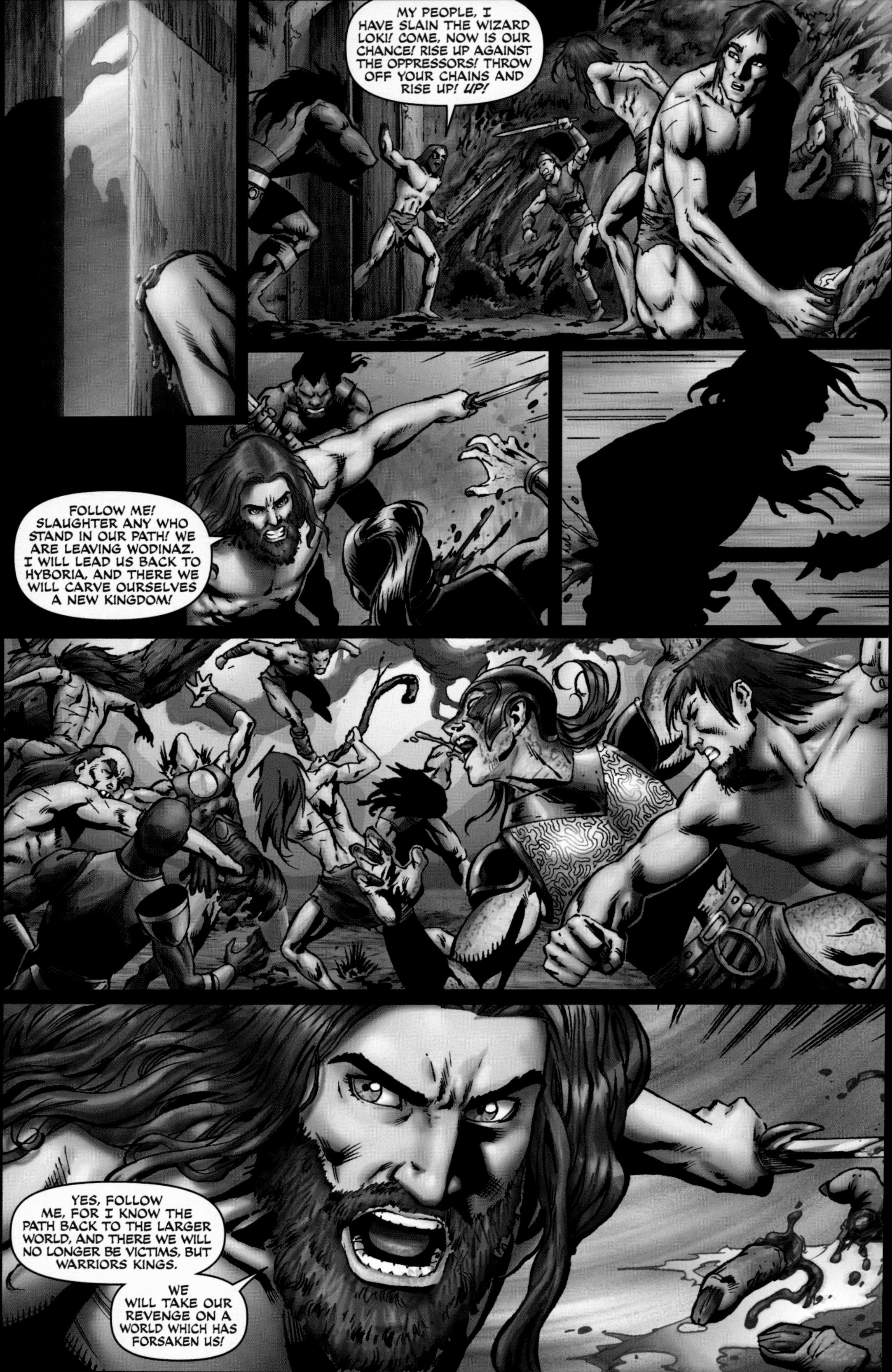
MY PEOPLE, I HAVE SLAIN THE WIZARD LOKI! COME, NOW IS OUR CHANCE! RISE UP AGAINST THE OPPRESSORS! THROW OFF YOUR CHAINS AND RISE UP! UP!
FOLLOW ME! SLAUGHTER ANY WHO STAND IN OUR PATH! WE ARE LEAVING WODINAZ. I WILL LEAD US BACK TO HYBORIA, AND THERE WE WILL CARVE OURSELVES A NEW KINGDOM!
YES, FOLLOW ME, FOR I KNOW THE PATH BACK TO THE LARGER WORLD, AND THERE WE WILL NO LONGER BE VICTIMS, BUT WARRIORS KINGS.
WE WILL TAKE OUR REVENGE ON A WORLD WHICH HAS FORSAKEN US!

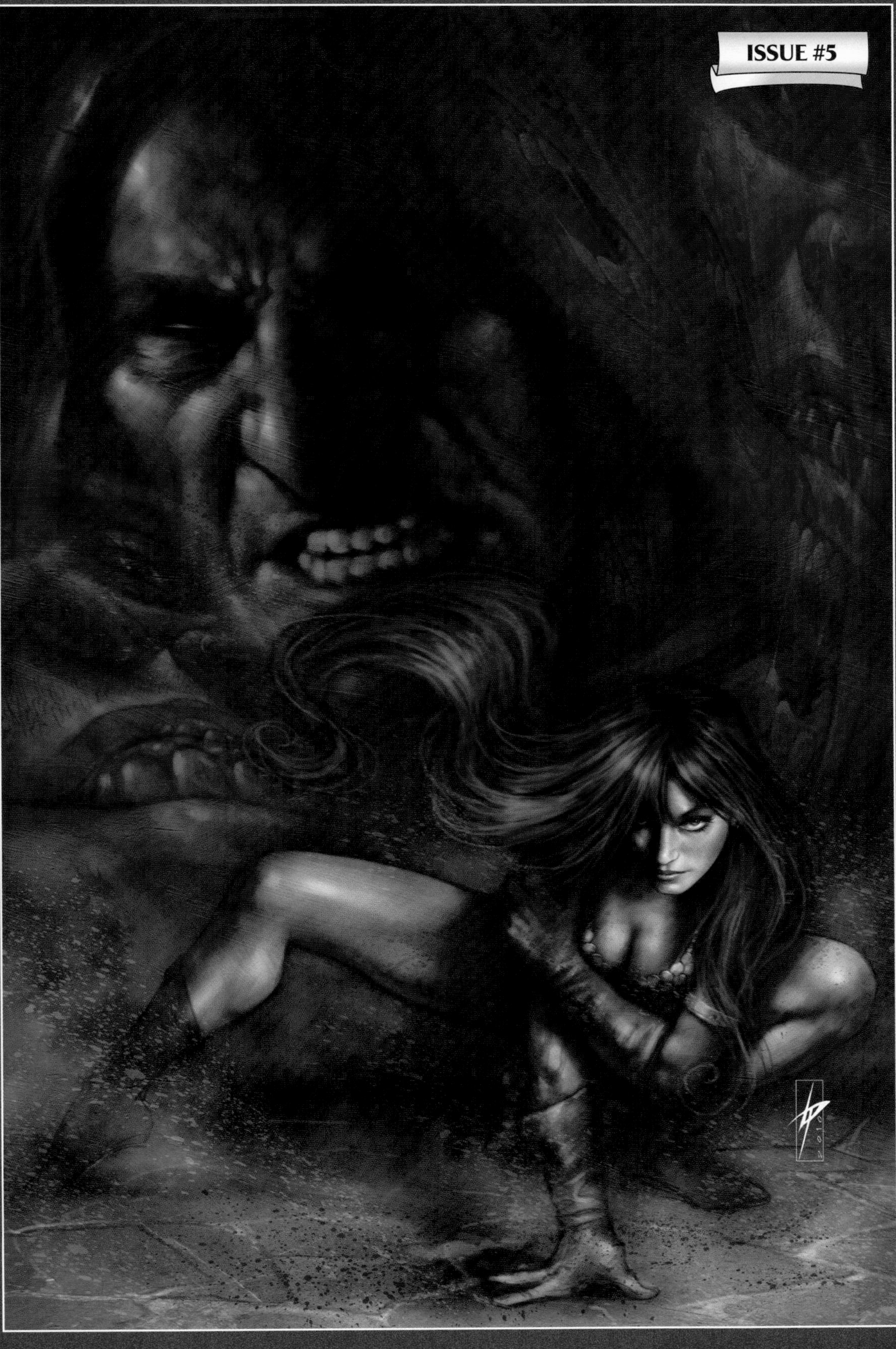
ISSUE #5

ISSUE #5 COVER BY LUCIO PARRILLO

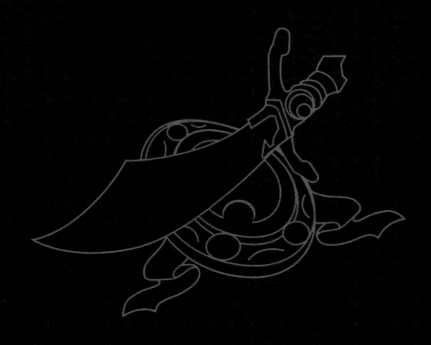

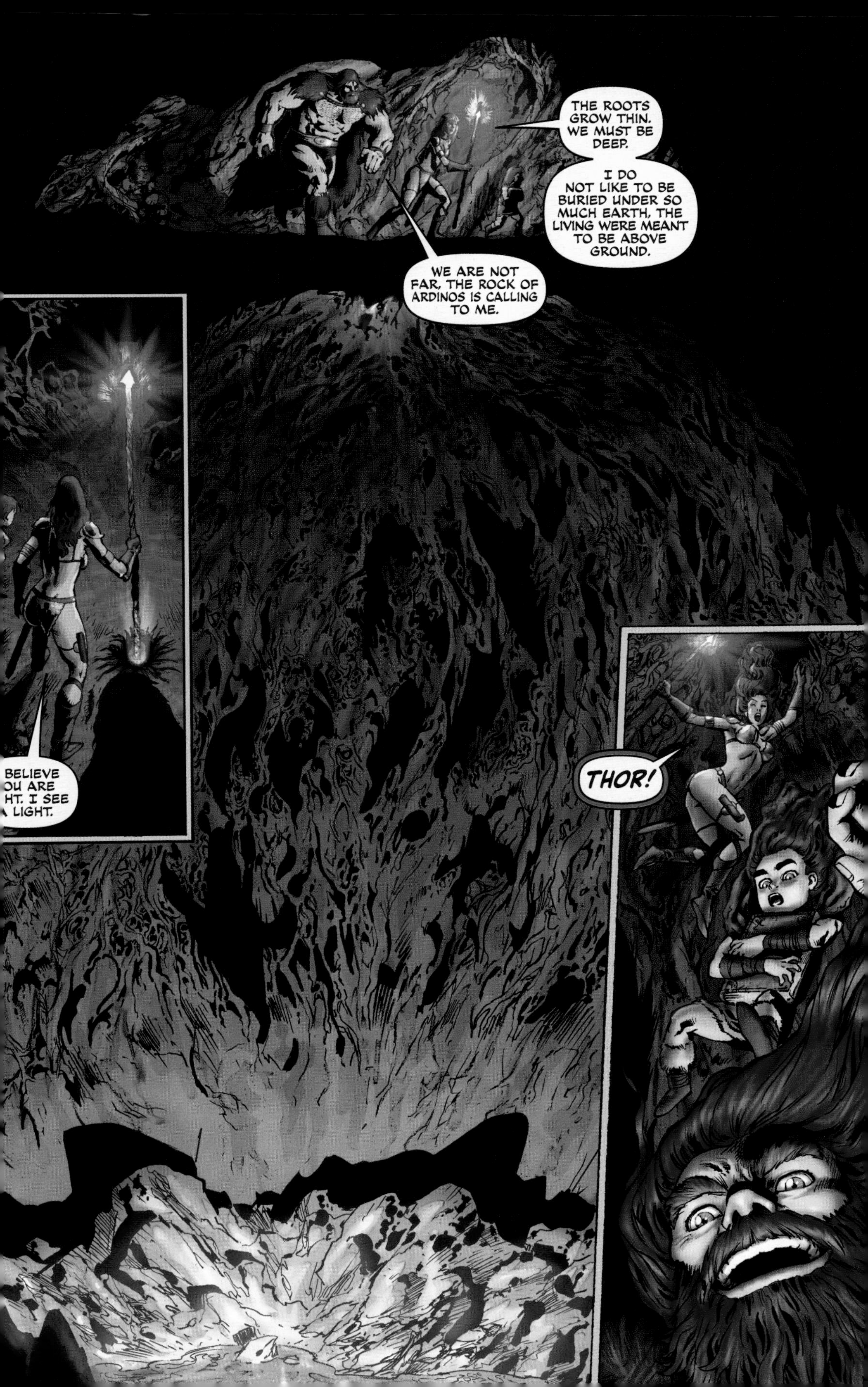
THE ROOTS GROW THIN. WE MUST BE DEEP.
I DO NOT LIKE TO BE BURIED UNDER SO MUCH EARTH, THE LIVING WERE MEANT TO BE ABOVE GROUND.
WE ARE NOT FAR, THE ROCK OF ARDINOS IS CALLING TO ME.
BELIEVE OU ARE HT. I SEE LIGHT.
THOR!

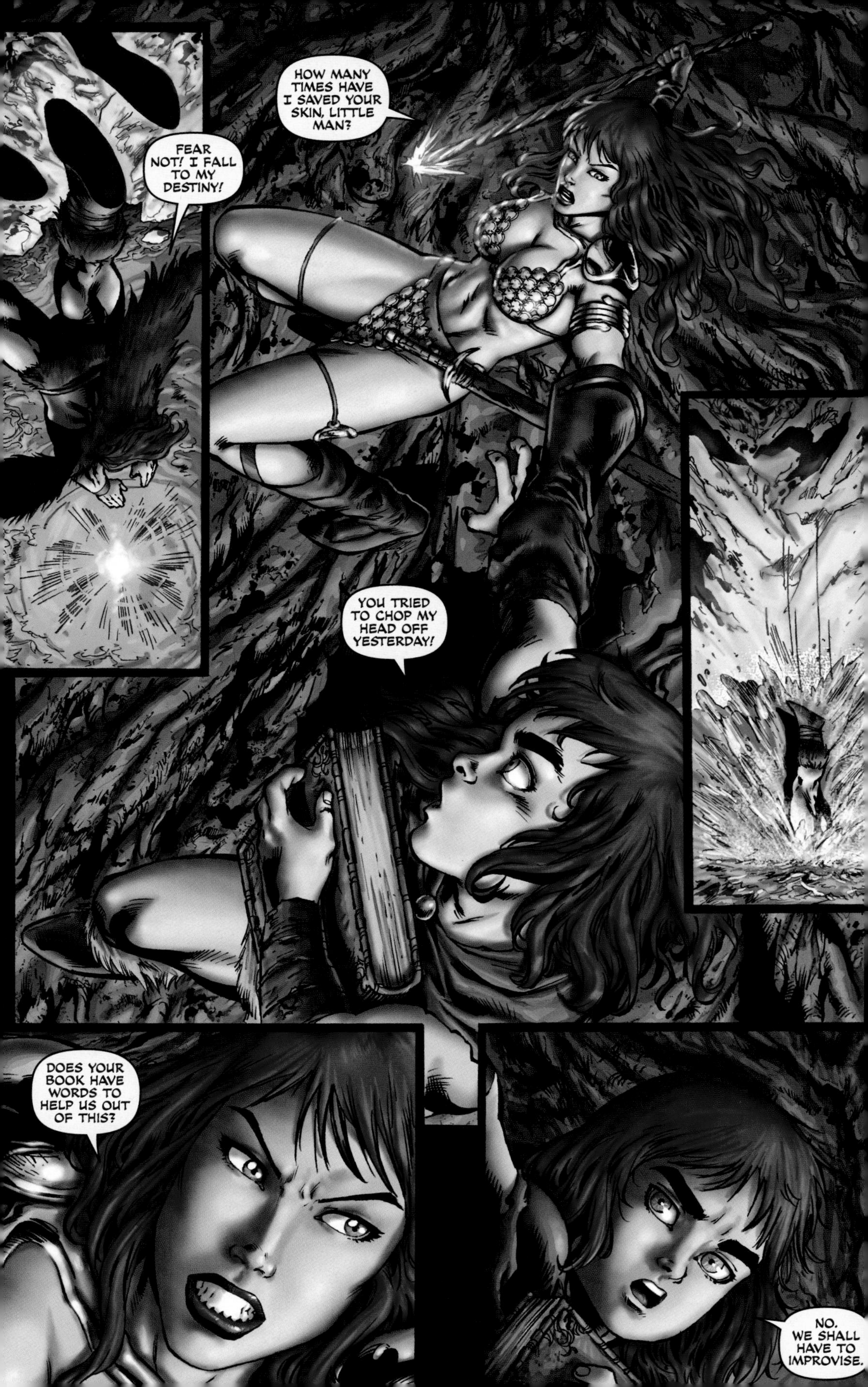
FEAR NOT! I FALL TO MY DESTINY!
HOW MANY TIMES HAVE I SAVED YOUR SKIN, LITTLE MAN?
YOU TRIED TO CHOP MY HEAD OFF YESTERDAY!
DOES YOUR BOOK HAVE WORDS TO HELP US OUT OF THIS?
NO. WE SHALL HAVE TO IMPROVISE.

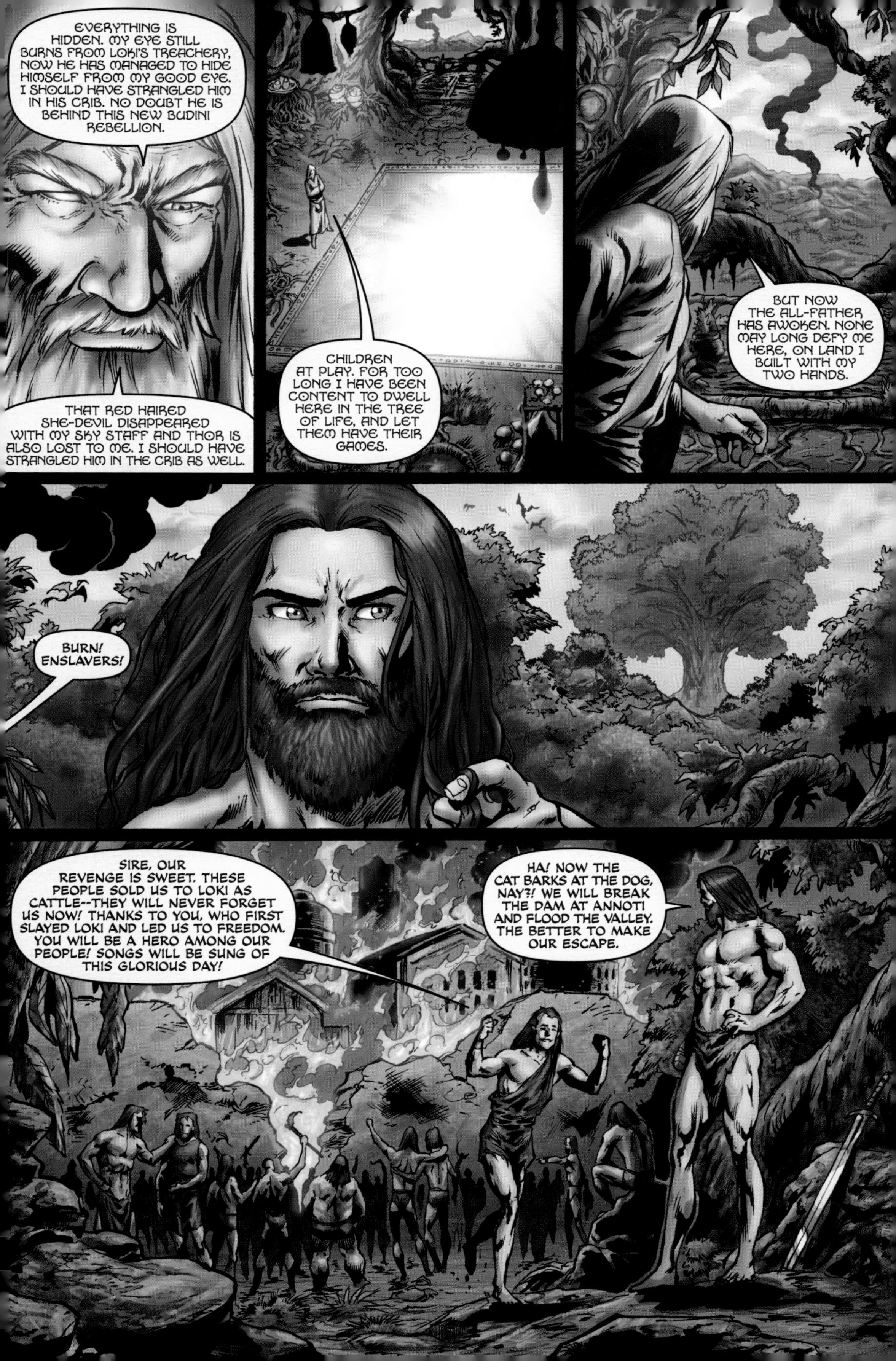
EVERYTHING IS HIDDEN. MY EYE STILL BURNS FROM LOKI'S TREACHERY, NOW HE HAS MANAGED TO HIDE HIMSELF FROM MY GOOD EYE. I SHOULD HAVE STRANGLED HIM IN HIS CRIB. NO DOUBT HE IS BEHIND THIS NEW BUDINI REBELLION.
THAT RED HAIRED SHE-DEVIL DISAPPEARED WITH MY SKY STAFF AND THOR IS ALSO LOST TO ME. I SHOULD HAVE STRANGLED HIM IN THE CRIB AS WELL.
CHILDREN AT PLAY. FOR TOO LONG I HAVE BEEN CONTENT TO DWELL HERE IN THE TREE OF LIFE, AND LET THEM HAVE THEIR GAMES.
BUT NOW THE ALL-FATHER HAS AWOKEN. NONE MAY LONG DEFY ME HERE, ON LAND I BUILT WITH MY TWO HANDS.
BURN! ENSLAVERS!
SIRE, OUR REVENGE IS SWEET. THESE PEOPLE SOLD US TO LOKI AS CATTLE--THEY WILL NEVER FORGET US NOW! THANKS TO YOU, WHO FIRST SLAYED LOKI AND LED US TO FREEDOM. YOU WILL BE A HERO AMONG OUR PEOPLE! SONGS WILL BE SUNG OF THIS GLORIOUS DAY!
HA! NOW THE CAT BARKS AT THE DOG, NAY?! WE WILL BREAK THE DAM AT ANNOTI AND FLOOD THE VALLEY. THE BETTER TO MAKE OUR ESCAPE.

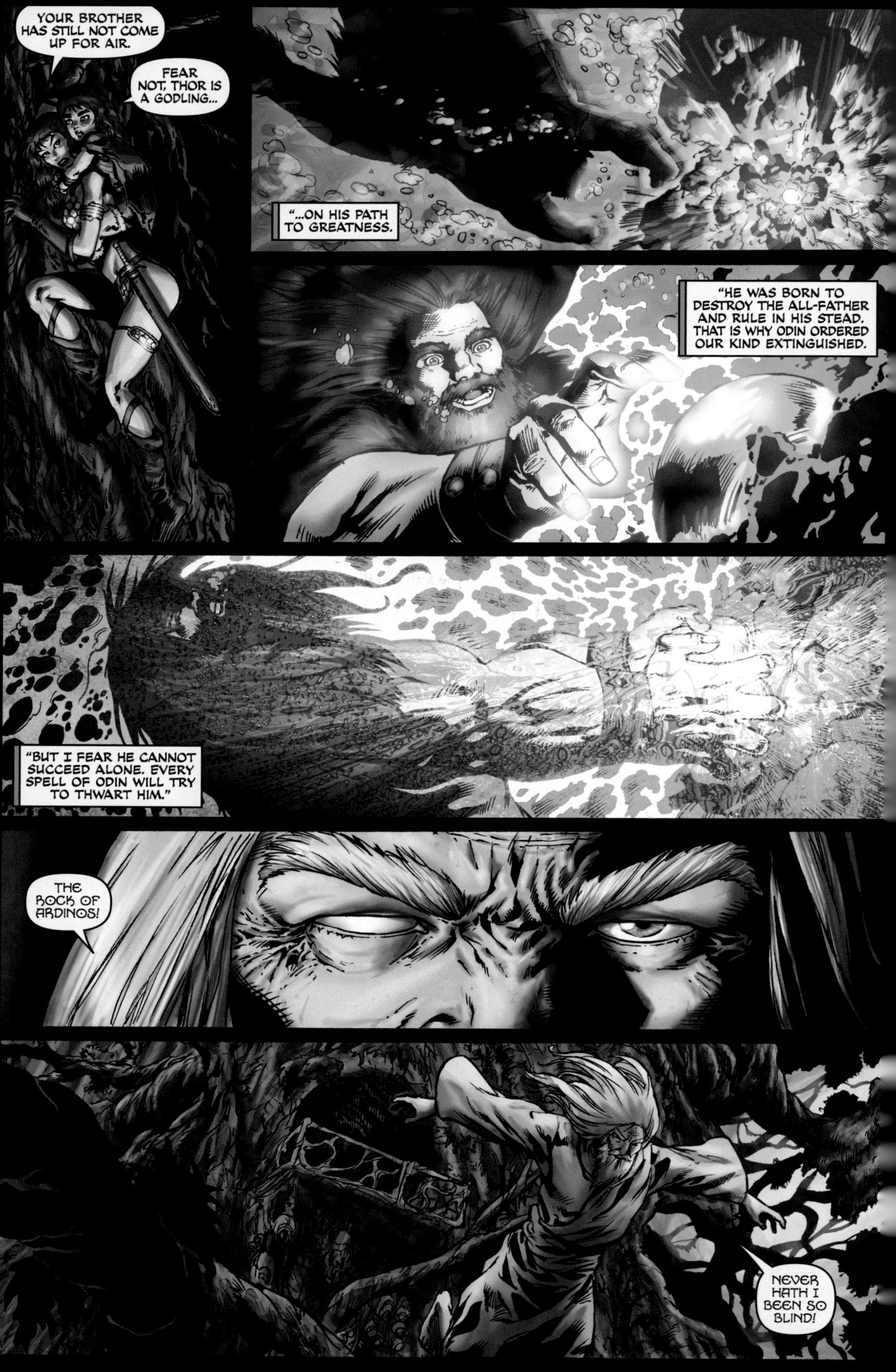
YOUR BROTHER HAS STILL NOT COME UP FOR AIR.
FEAR NOT, THOR IS A GODLING...
"...ON HIS PATH TO GREATNESS.
"HE WAS BORN TO DESTROY THE ALL-FATHER AND RULE IN HIS STEAD. THAT IS WHY ODIN ORDERED OUR KIND EXTINGUISHED.
"BUT I FEAR HE CANNOT SUCCEED ALONE. EVERY SPELL OF ODIN WILL TRY TO THWART HIM."
THE ROCK OF ARDINOS!
NEVER HATH I BEEN SO BLIND!

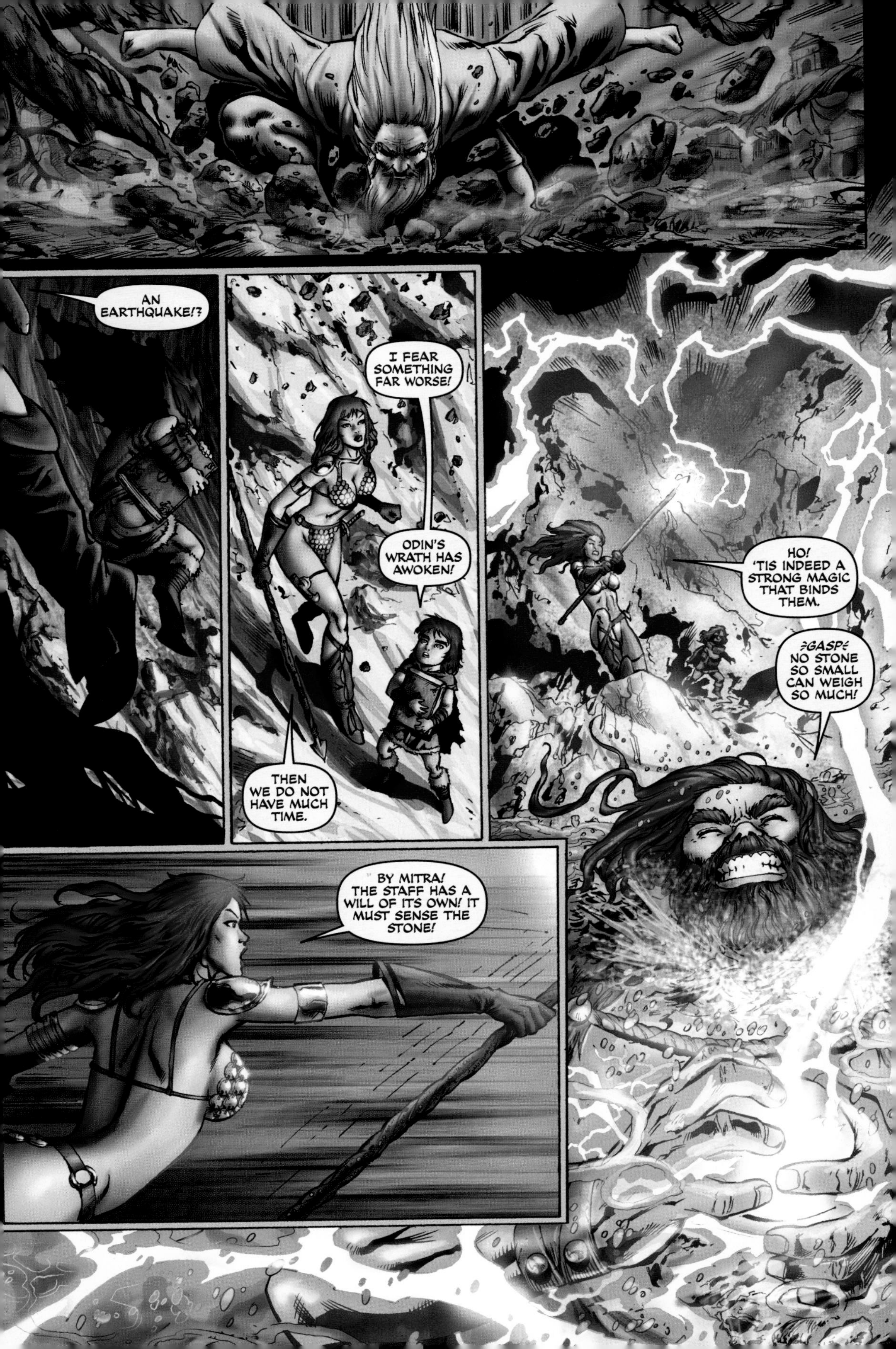
AN EARTHQUAKE!?
I FEAR SOMETHING FAR WORSE!
ODIN'S WRATH HAS AWOKEN!
THEN WE DO NOT HAVE MUCH TIME.
HO! 'TIS INDEED A STRONG MAGIC THAT BINDS THEM.
GASP
NO STONE SO SMALL CAN WEIGH SO MUCH!
BY MITRA! THE STAFF HAS A WILL OF ITS OWN! IT MUST SENSE THE STONE!

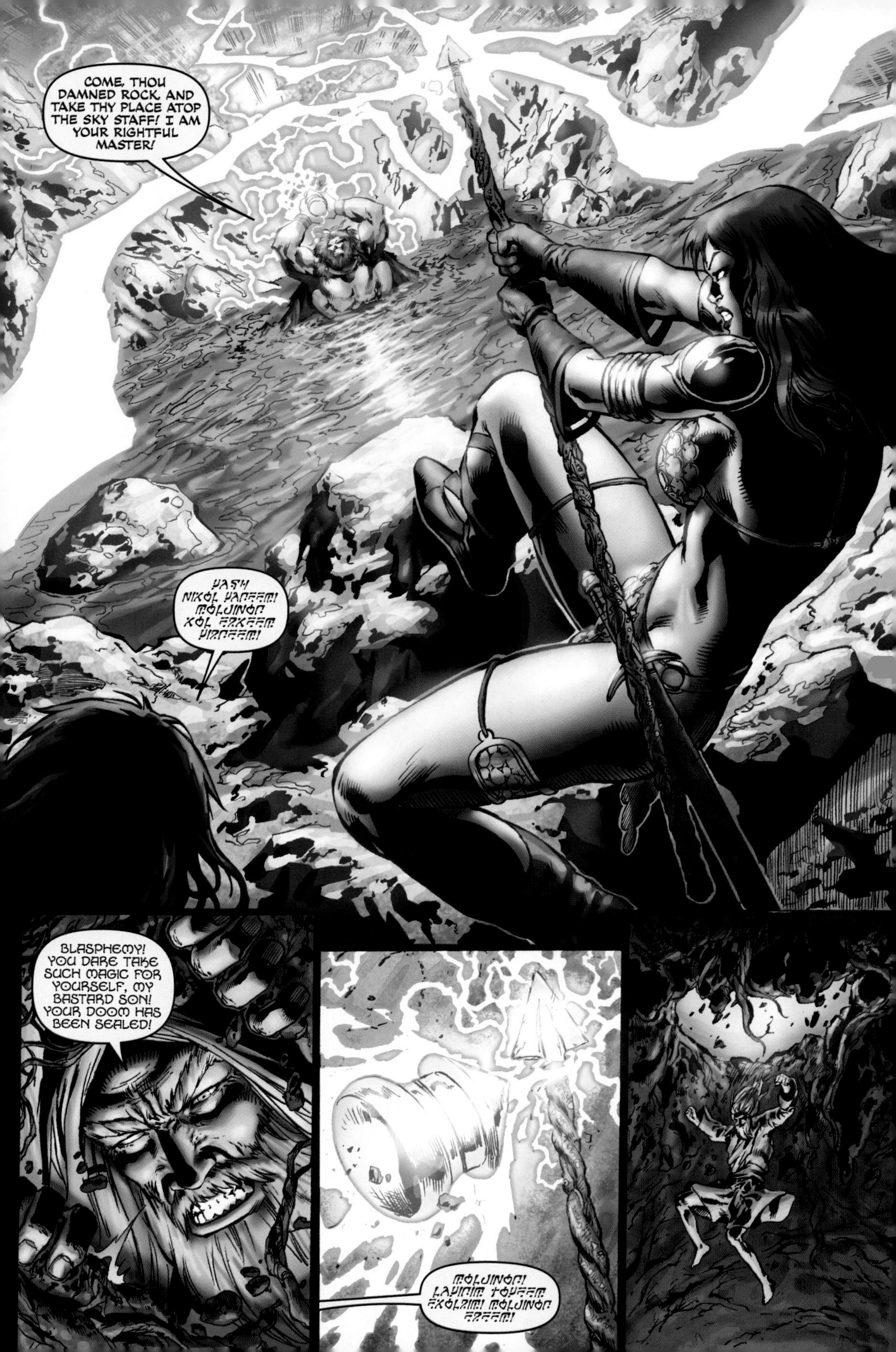

COME, THOU DAMNED ROCK, AND TAKE THY PLACE ATOP THE SKY STAFF! I AM YOUR RIGHTFUL MASTER!
BLASPHEMY! YOU DARE TAKE SUCH MAGIC FOR YOURSELF, MY BASTARD SON! YOUR DOOM HAS BEEN SEALED!

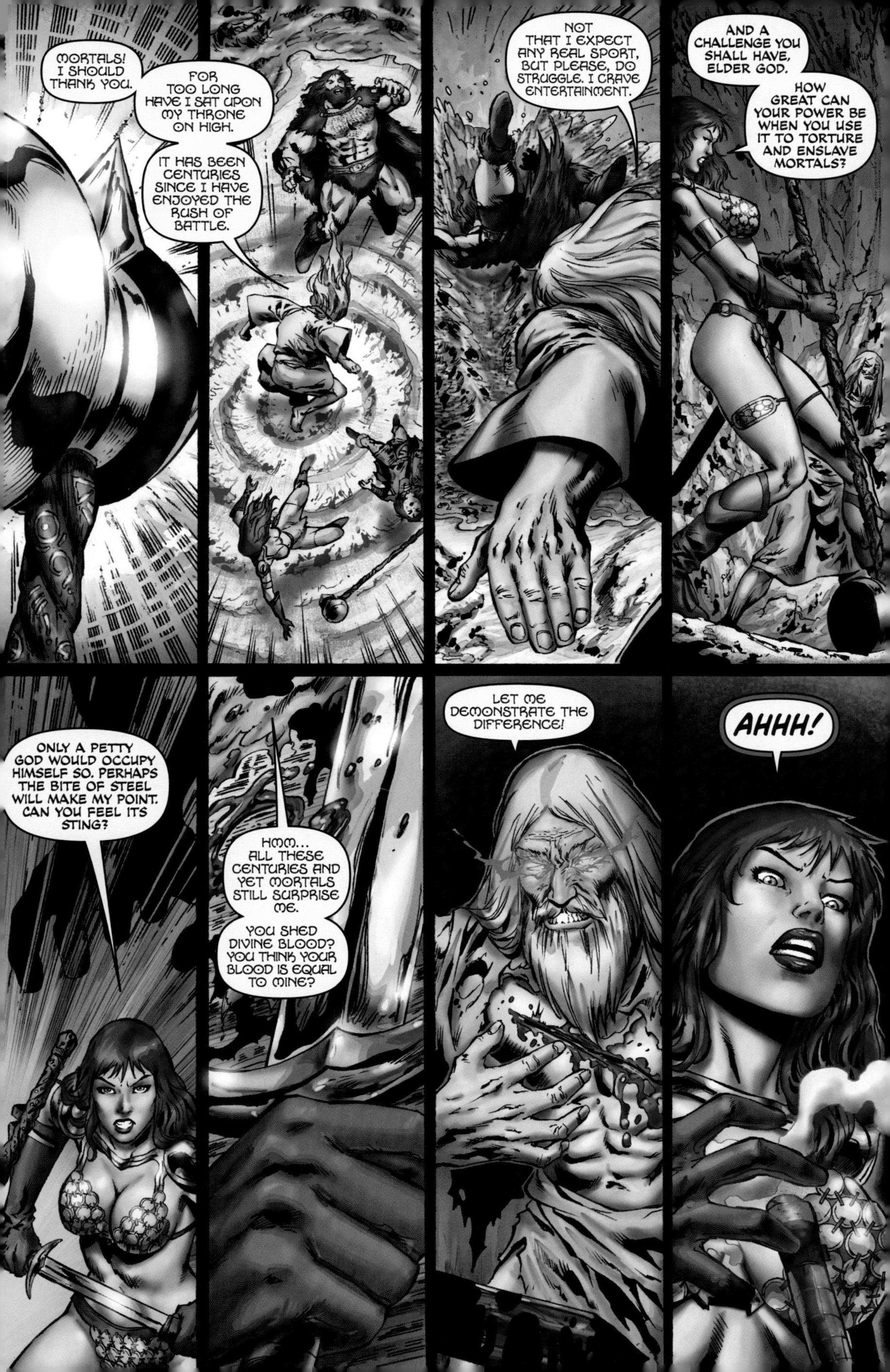

MORTALS! I SHOULD THANK YOU.
FOR TOO LONG HAVE I SAT UPON MY THRONE ON HIGH.
IT HAS BEEN CENTURIES SINCE I HAVE ENJOYED THE RUSH OF BATTLE.
NOT THAT I EXPECT ANY REAL SPORT, BUT PLEASE, DO STRUGGLE. I CRAVE ENTERTAINMENT.
AND A CHALLENGE YOU SHALL HAVE, ELDER GOD.
HOW GREAT CAN YOUR POWER BE WHEN YOU USE IT TO TORTURE AND ENSLAVE MORTALS?
ONLY A PETTY GOD WOULD OCCUPY HIMSELF SO. PERHAPS THE BITE OF STEEL WILL MAKE MY POINT. CAN YOU FEEL ITS STING?
HMM... ALL THESE CENTURIES AND YET MORTALS STILL SURPRISE ME.
YOU SHED DIVINE BLOOD? YOU THINK YOUR BLOOD IS EQUAL TO MINE?
LET ME DEMONSTRATE THE DIFFERENCE!
AHHH!

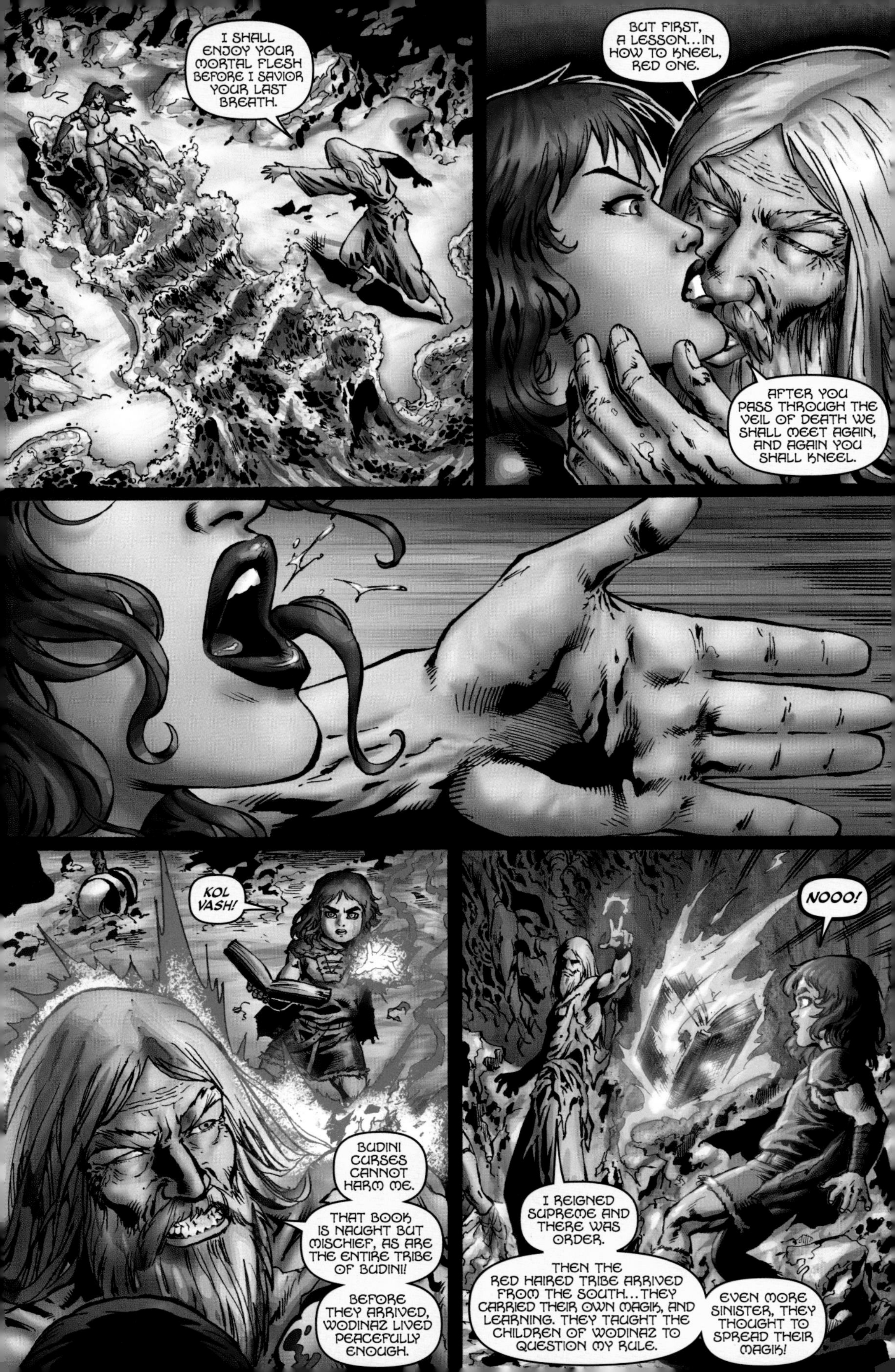
I SHALL ENJOY YOUR MORTAL FLESH BEFORE I SAVIOR YOUR LAST BREATH.
BUT FIRST, A LESSON...IN HOW TO KNEEL, RED ONE.
AFTER YOU PASS THROUGH THE VEIL OF DEATH WE SHALL MEET AGAIN, AND AGAIN YOU SHALL KNEEL.
KOL VASH!
BUDINI CURSES CANNOT HARM ME.
THAT BOOK IS NAUGHT BUT MISCHIEF, AS ARE THE ENTIRE TRIBE OF BUDINI!
BEFORE THEY ARRIVED, WODINAZ LIVED PEACEFULLY ENOUGH.
NOOO!
I REIGNED SUPREME AND THERE WAS ORDER.
THEN THE RED HAIRED TRIBE ARRIVED FROM THE SOUTH...THEY CARRIED THEIR OWN MAGIK, AND LEARNING. THEY TAUGHT THE CHILDREN OF WODINAZ TO QUESTION MY RULE.
EVEN MORE SINISTER, THEY THOUGHT TO SPREAD THEIR MAGIK!

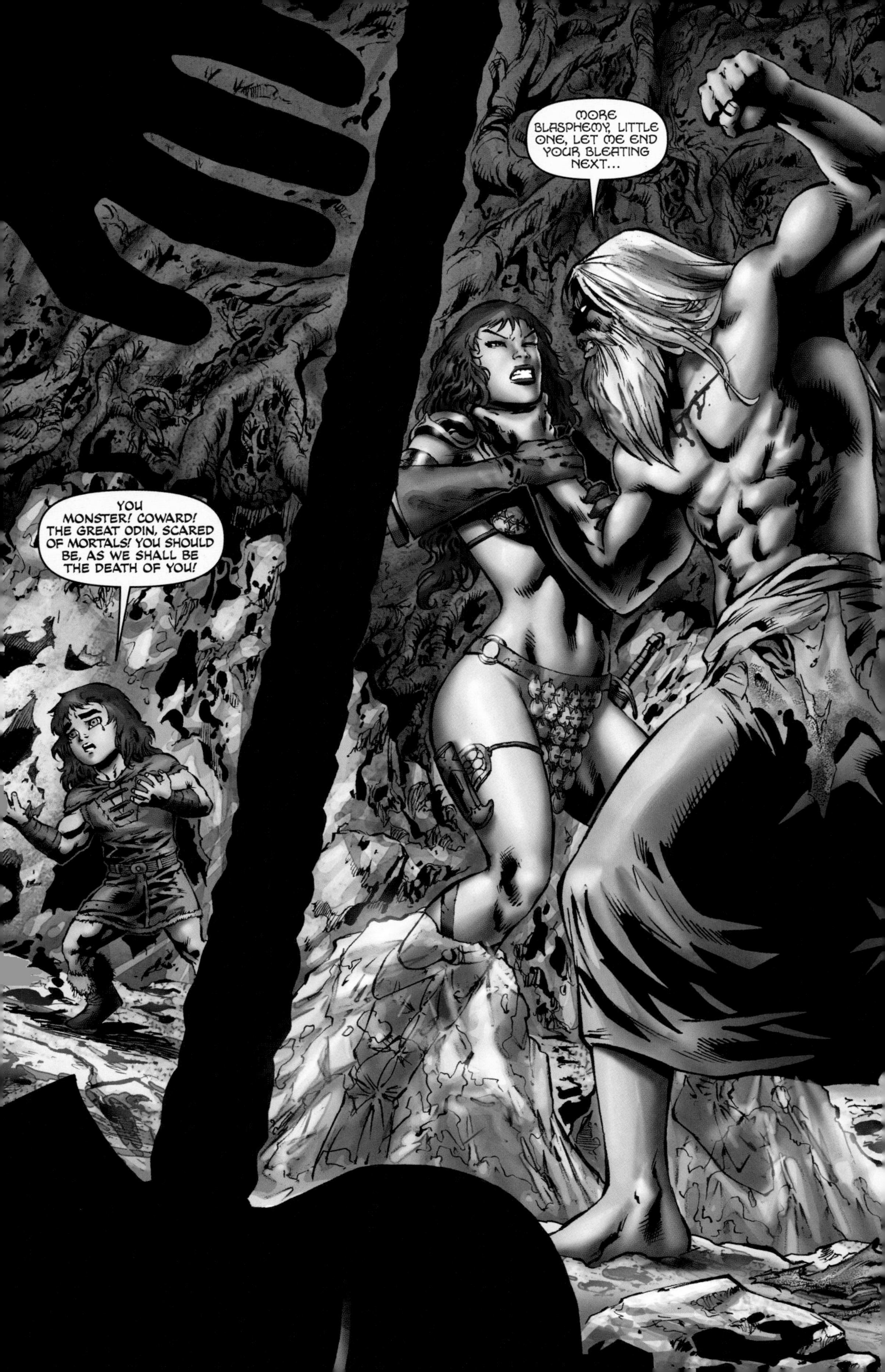
YOU MONSTER! COWARD! THE GREAT ODIN, SCARED OF MORTALS! YOU SHOULD BE, AS WE SHALL BE THE DEATH OF YOU!
MORE BLASPHEMY, LITTLE ONE, LET ME END YOUR BLEATING NEXT...

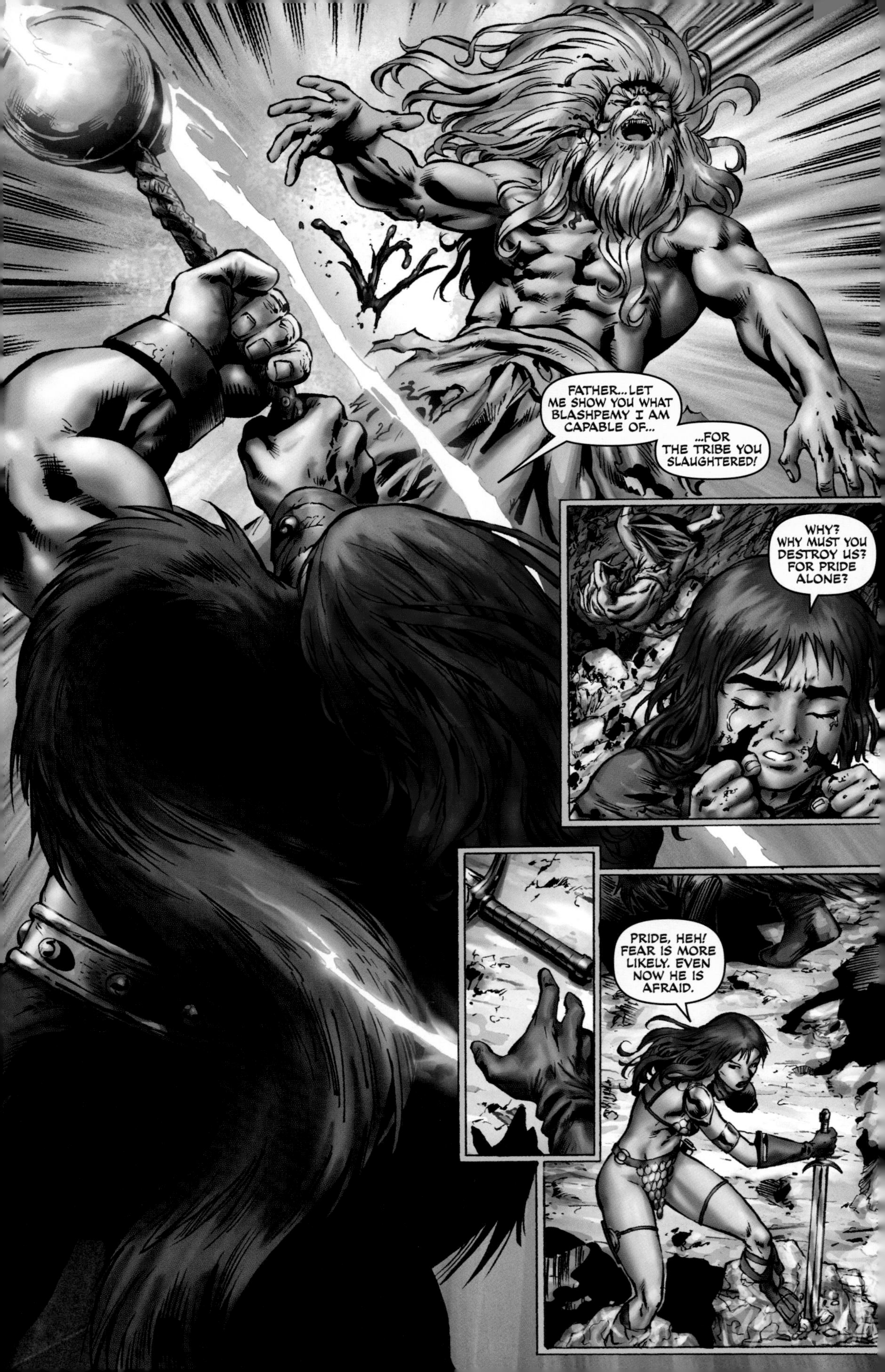
FATHER...LET ME SHOW YOU WHAT BLASHPEMY I AM CAPABLE OF...
...FOR THE TRIBE YOU SLAUGHTERED!
WHY? WHY MUST YOU DESTROY US? FOR PRIDE ALONE?
PRIDE, HEH! FEAR IS MORE LIKELY. EVEN NOW HE IS AFRAID.

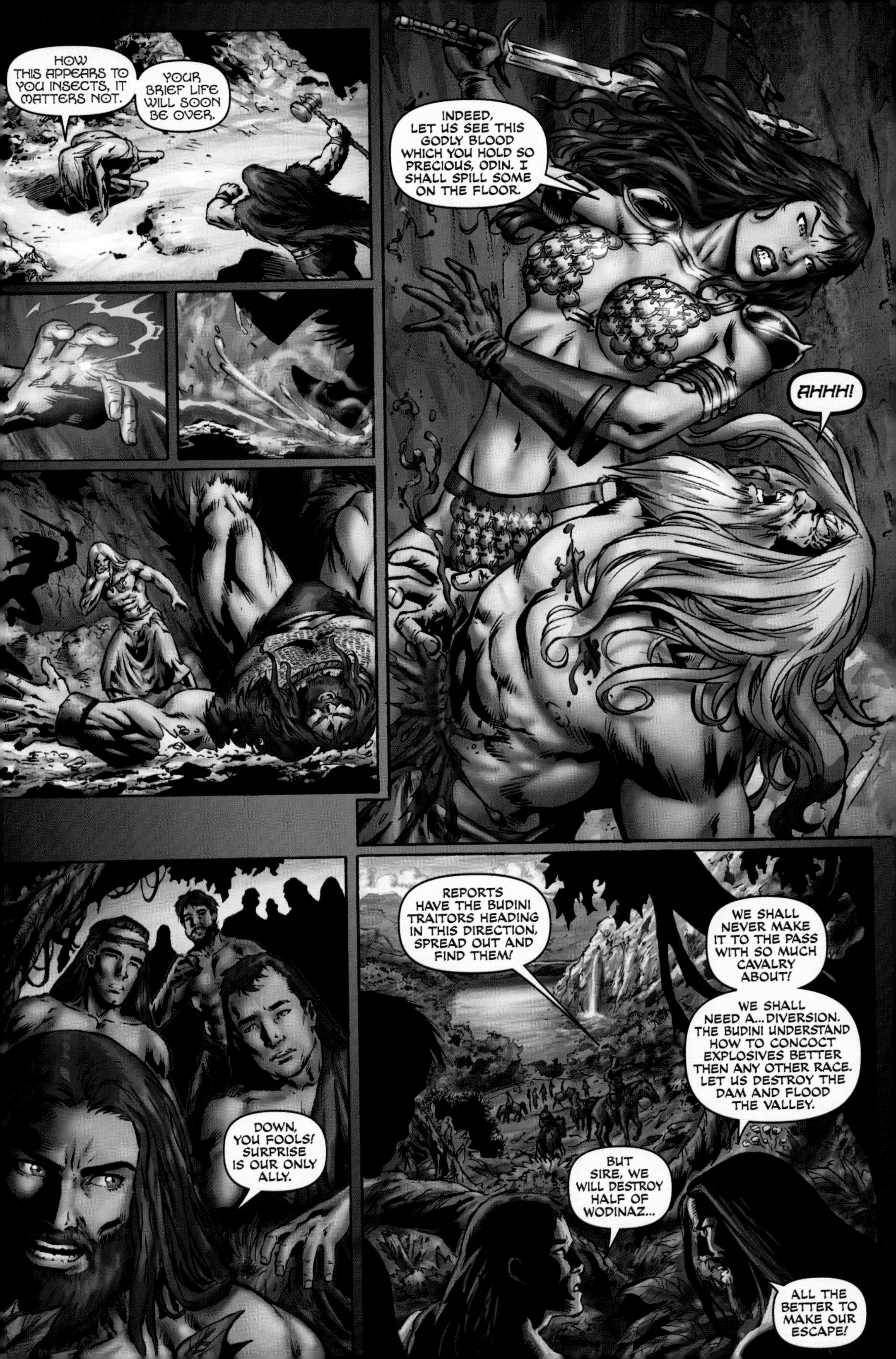
HOW THIS APPEARS TO YOU INSECTS, IT MATTERS NOT.
YOUR BRIEF LIFE WILL SOON BE OVER.
INDEED, LET US SEE THIS GODLY BLOOD WHICH YOU HOLD SO PRECIOUS, ODIN. I SHALL SPILL SOME ON THE FLOOR.
AHHH!
DOWN, YOU FOOLS! SURPRISE IS OUR ONLY ALLY.
REPORTS HAVE THE BUDINI TRAITORS HEADING IN THIS DIRECTION, SPREAD OUT AND FIND THEM!
WE SHALL NEVER MAKE IT TO THE PASS WITH SO MUCH CAVALRY ABOUT!
WE SHALL NEED A...DIVERSION. THE BUDINI UNDERSTAND HOW TO CONCOCT EXPLOSIVES BETTER THEN ANY OTHER RACE. LET US DESTROY THE DAM AND FLOOD THE VALLEY.
BUT SIRE, WE WILL DESTROY HALF OF WODINAZ...
ALL THE BETTER TO MAKE OUR ESCAPE!

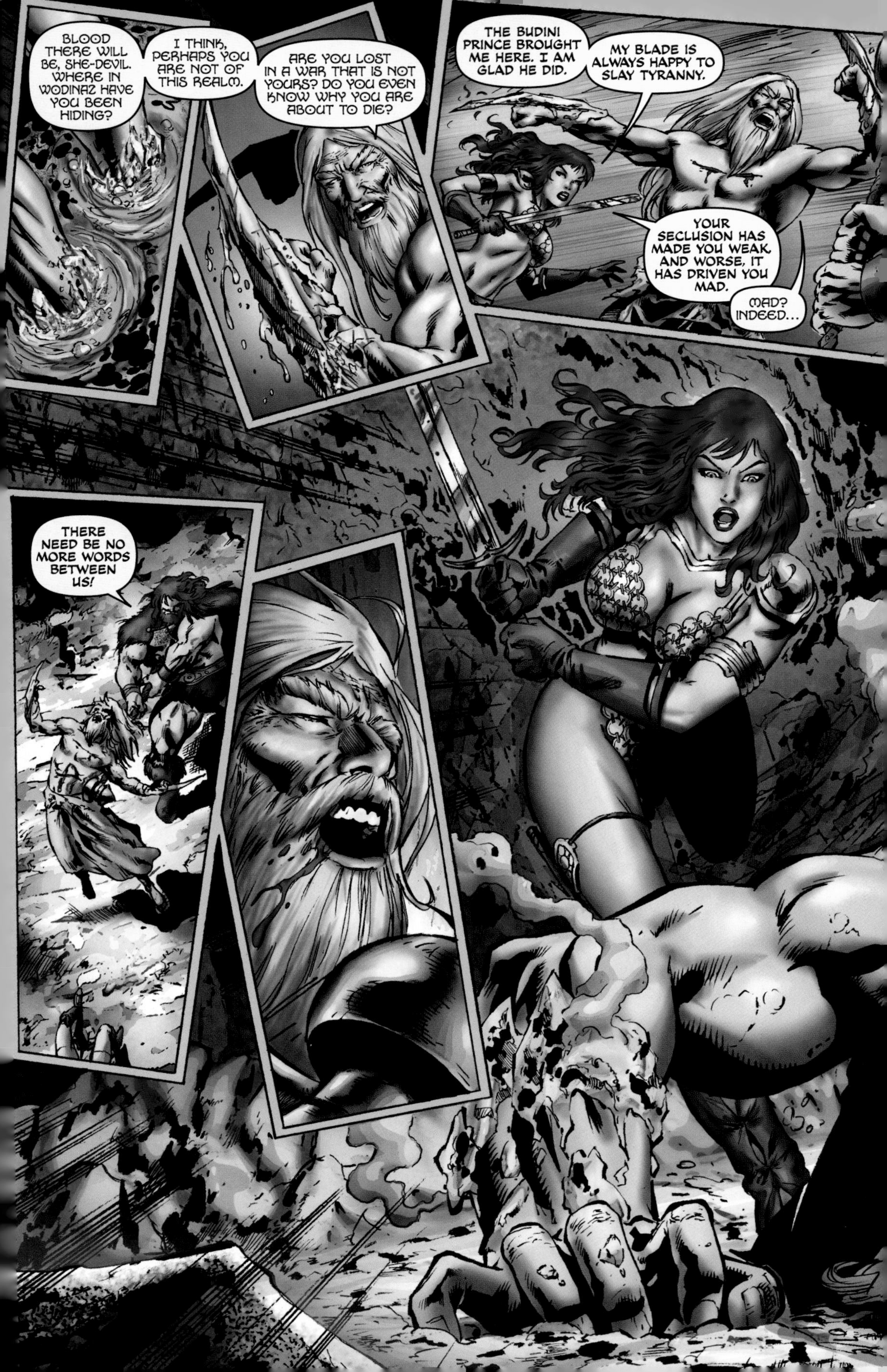

BLOOD THERE WILL BE, SHE-DEVIL. WHERE IN WODINAZ HAVE YOU BEEN HIDING?
I THINK, PERHAPS YOU ARE NOT OF THIS REALM.
ARE YOU LOST IN A WAR THAT IS NOT YOURS? DO YOU EVEN KNOW WHY YOU ARE ABOUT TO DIE?
THE BUDINI PRINCE BROUGHT ME HERE. I AM GLAD HE DID.
MY BLADE IS ALWAYS HAPPY TO SLAY TYRANNY.
YOUR SECLUSION HAS MADE YOU WEAK, AND WORSE, IT HAS DRIVEN YOU MAD.
MAD? INDEED...
THERE NEED BE NO MORE WORDS BETWEEN US!

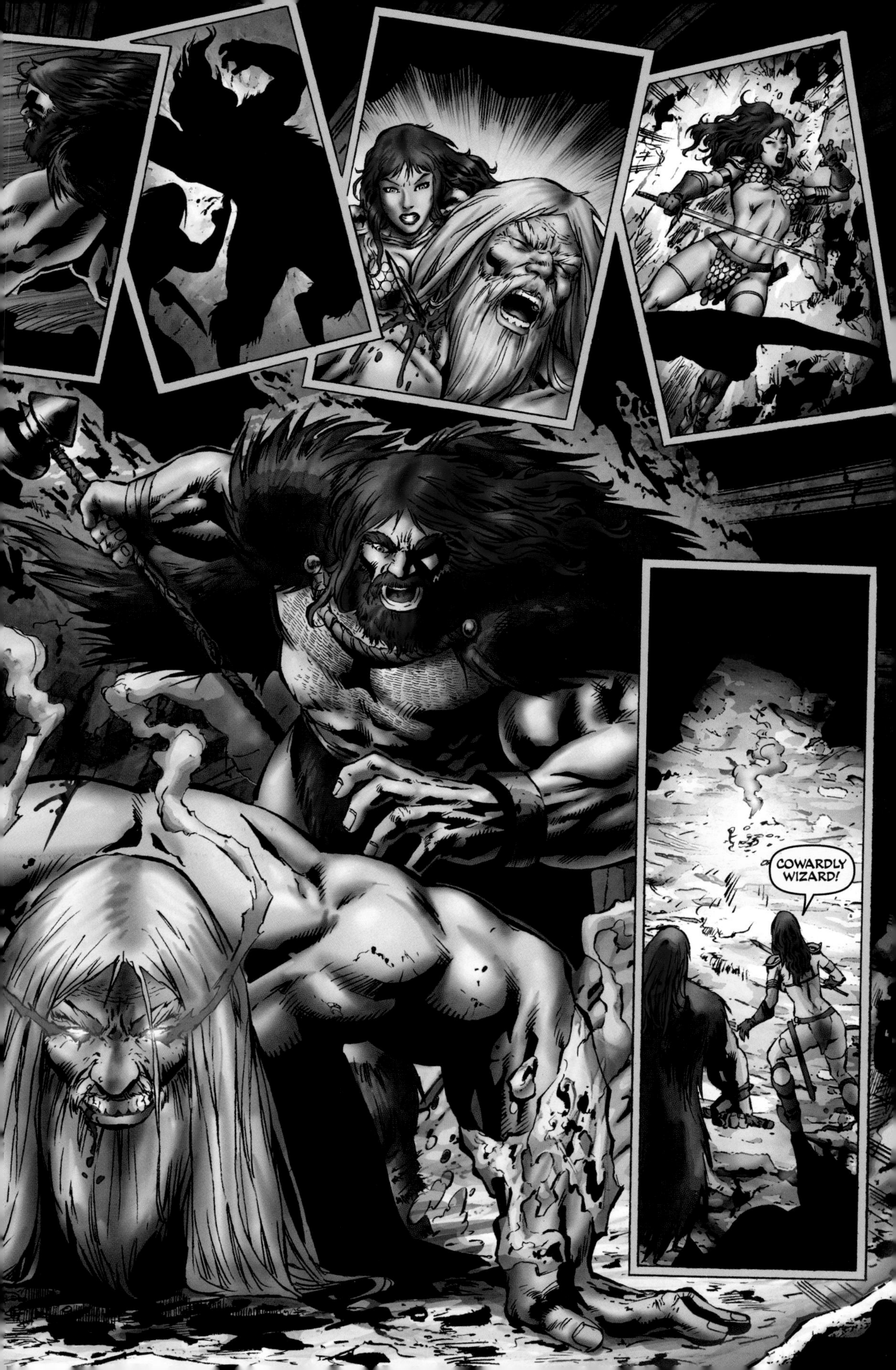
COWARDLY WIZARD!

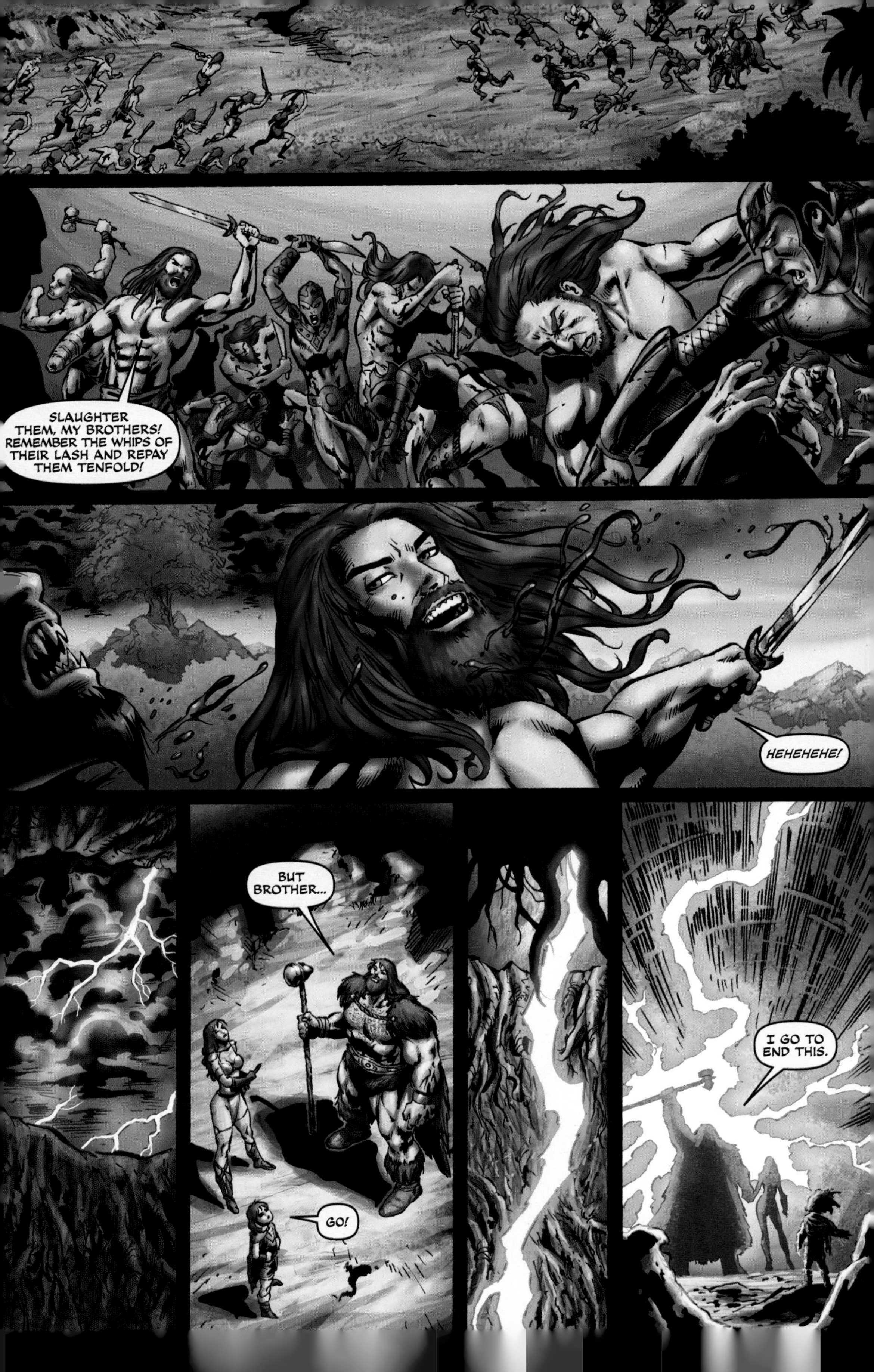
SLAUGHTER THEM, MY BROTHERS! REMEMBER THE WHIPS OF THEIR LASH AND REPAY THEM TENFOLD!
HEHEHEHE!
BUT BROTHER...
GO!
I GO TO END THIS.

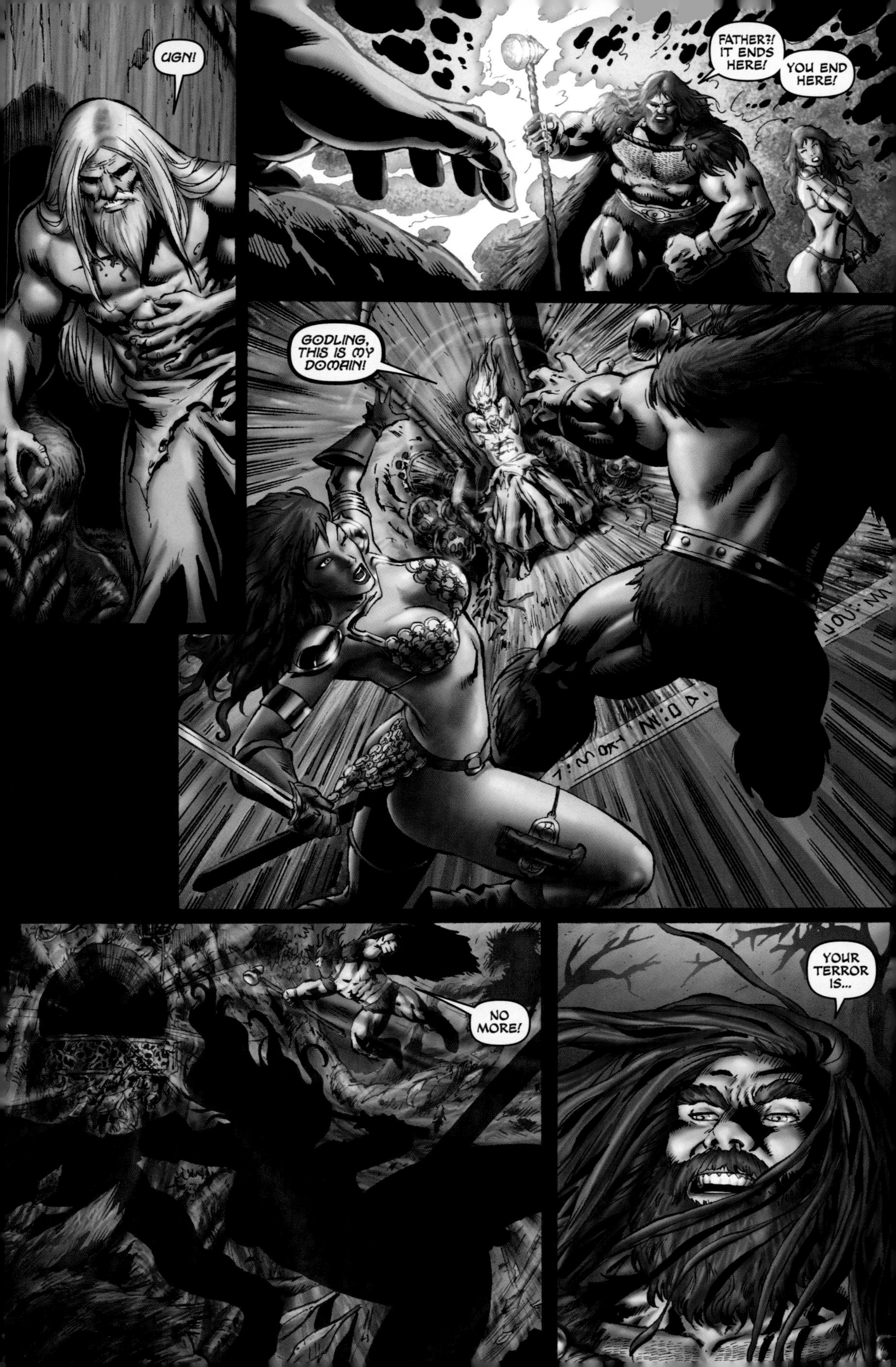
UGN!
FATHER?! IT ENDS HERE!
YOU END HERE!
GODLING, THIS IS MY DOMAIN!
NO MORE!
YOUR TERROR IS...

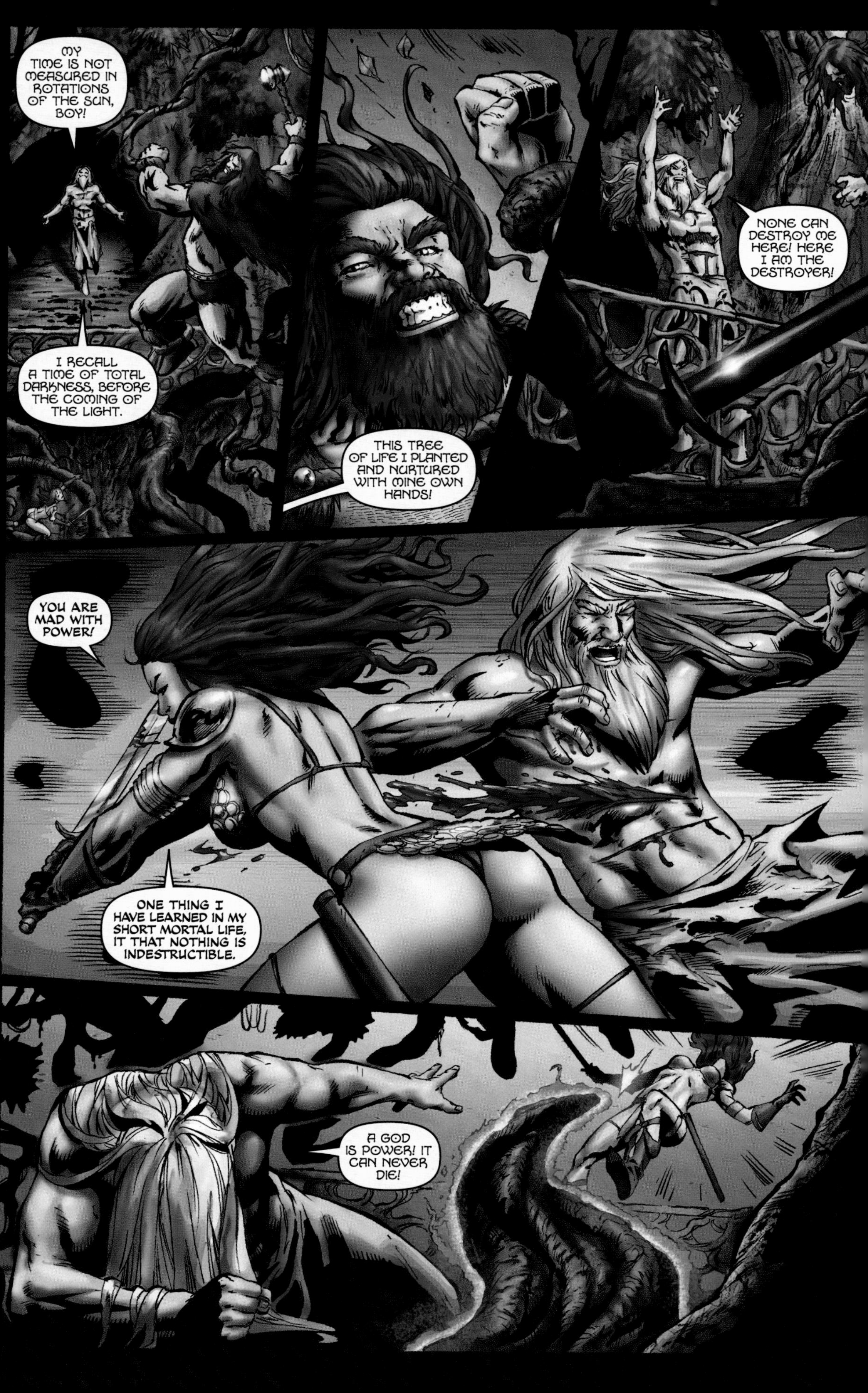
MY TIME IS NOT MEASURED IN ROTATIONS OF THE SUN, BOY!
I RECALL A TIME OF TOTAL DARKNESS, BEFORE THE COMING OF THE LIGHT.
THIS TREE OF LIFE I PLANTED AND NURTURED WITH MINE OWN HANDS!
NONE CAN DESTROY ME HERE! HERE I AM THE DESTROYER!
YOU ARE MAD WITH POWER!
ONE THING I HAVE LEARNED IN MY SHORT MORTAL LIFE, IT THAT NOTHING IS INDESTRUCTIBLE.
A GOD IS POWER! IT CAN NEVER DIE!

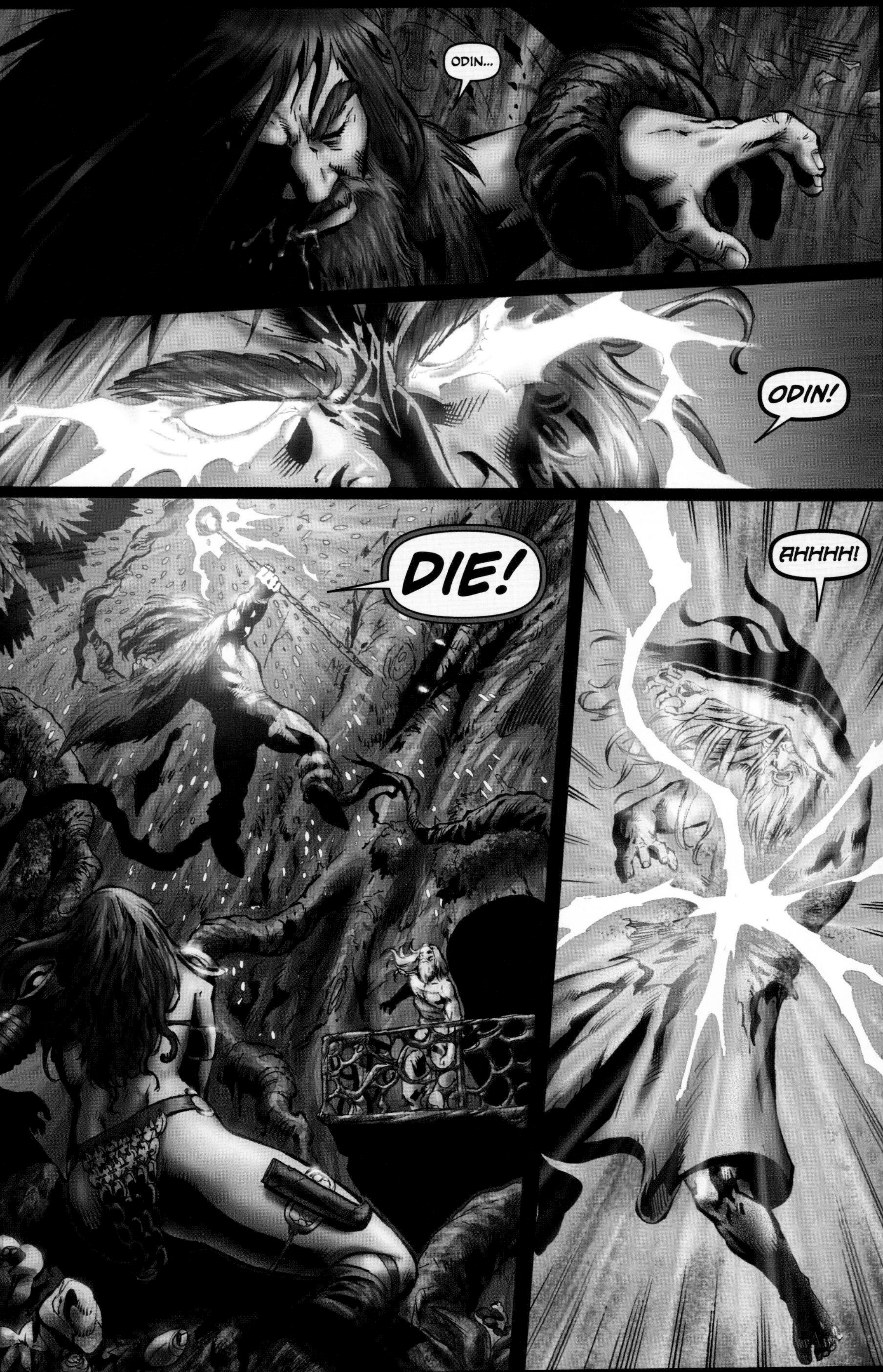

ODIN...
ODIN!
DIE!
AHHHH!

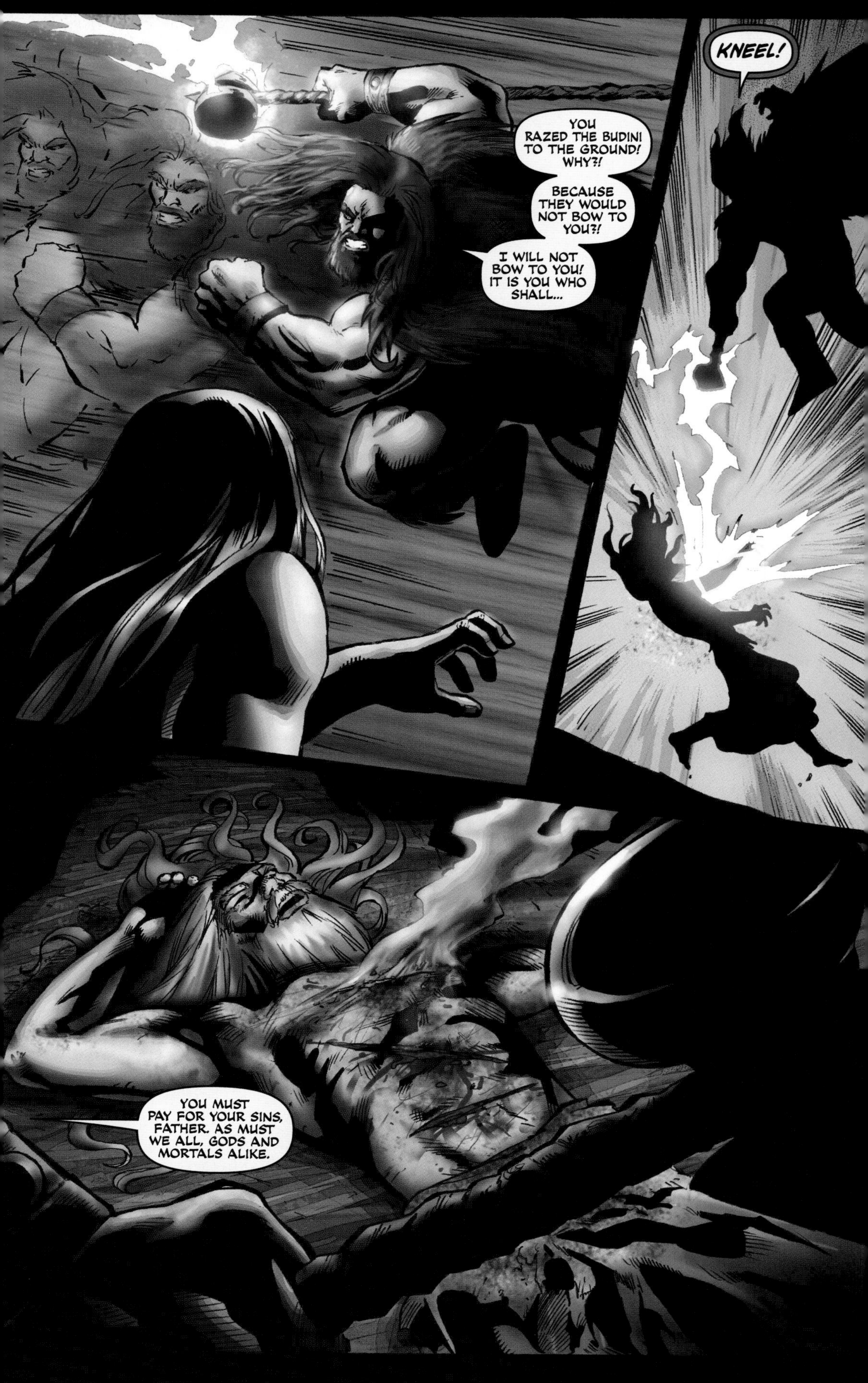
YOU RAZED THE BUDINI TO THE GROUND! WHY?!
BECAUSE THEY WOULD NOT BOW TO YOU?!
I WILL NOT BOW TO YOU! IT IS YOU WHO SHALL...
KNEEL!
YOU MUST PAY FOR YOUR SINS, FATHER. AS MUST WE ALL, GODS AND MORTALS ALIKE.

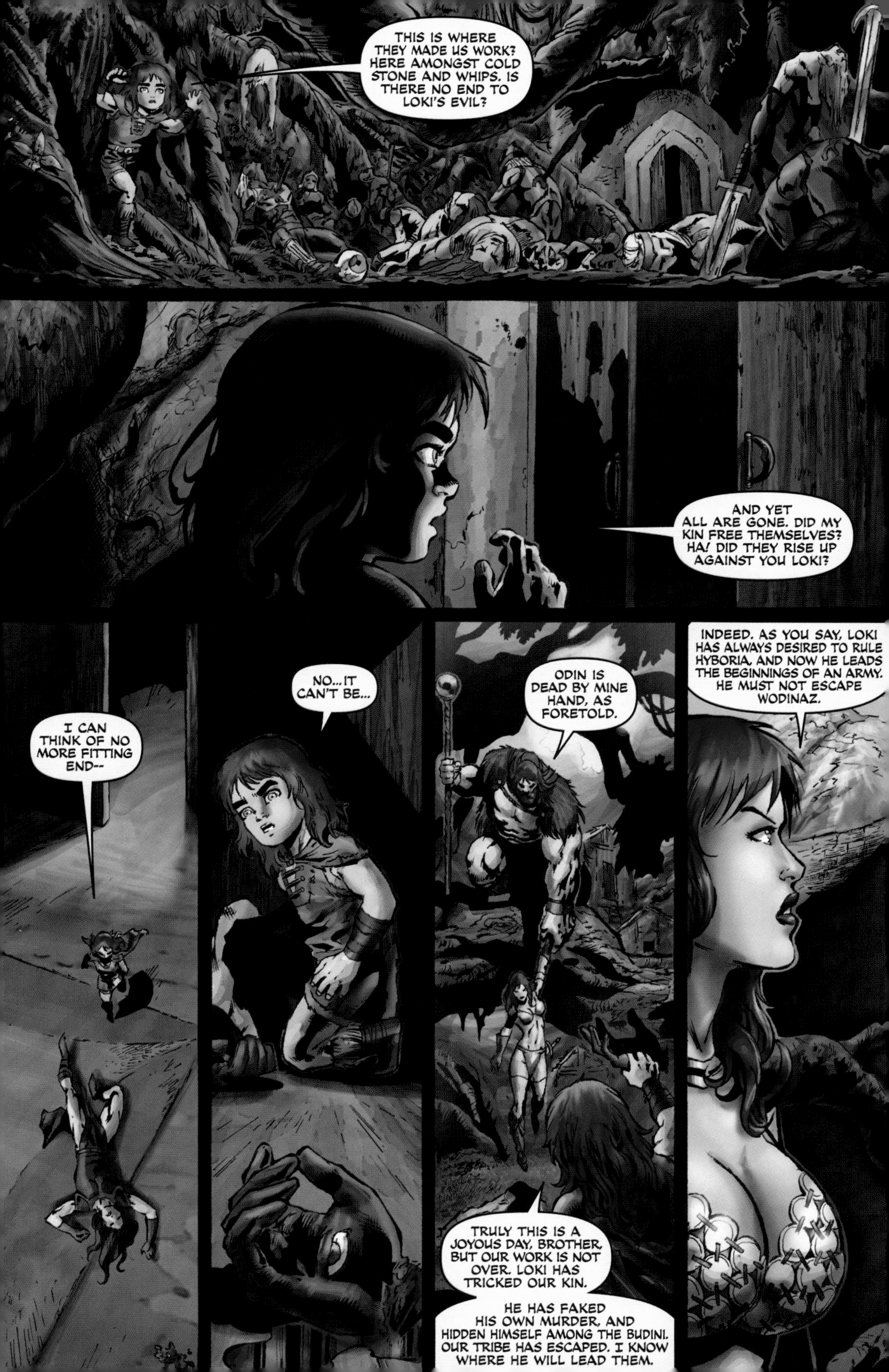
THIS IS WHERE THEY MADE US WORK? HERE AMONGST COLD STONE AND WHIPS. IS THERE NO END TO LOKI'S EVIL?
AND YET ALL ARE GONE. DID MY KIN FREE THEMSELVES? HA! DID THEY RISE UP AGAINST YOU LOKI?
I CAN THINK OF NO MORE FITTING END--
NO... IT CAN'T BE...
ODIN IS DEAD BY MINE HAND, AS FORETOLD.
TRULY THIS IS A JOYOUS DAY, BROTHER, BUT OUR WORK IS NOT OVER. LOKI HAS TRICKED OUR KIN.
HE HAS FAKED HIS OWN MURDER, AND HIDDEN HIMSELF AMONG THE BUDINI. OUR TRIBE HAS ESCAPED. I KNOW WHERE HE WILL LEAD THEM.
INDEED. AS YOU SAY, LOKI HAS ALWAYS DESIRED TO RULE HYBORIA, AND NOW HE LEADS THE BEGINNINGS OF AN ARMY. HE MUST NOT ESCAPE WODINAZ.

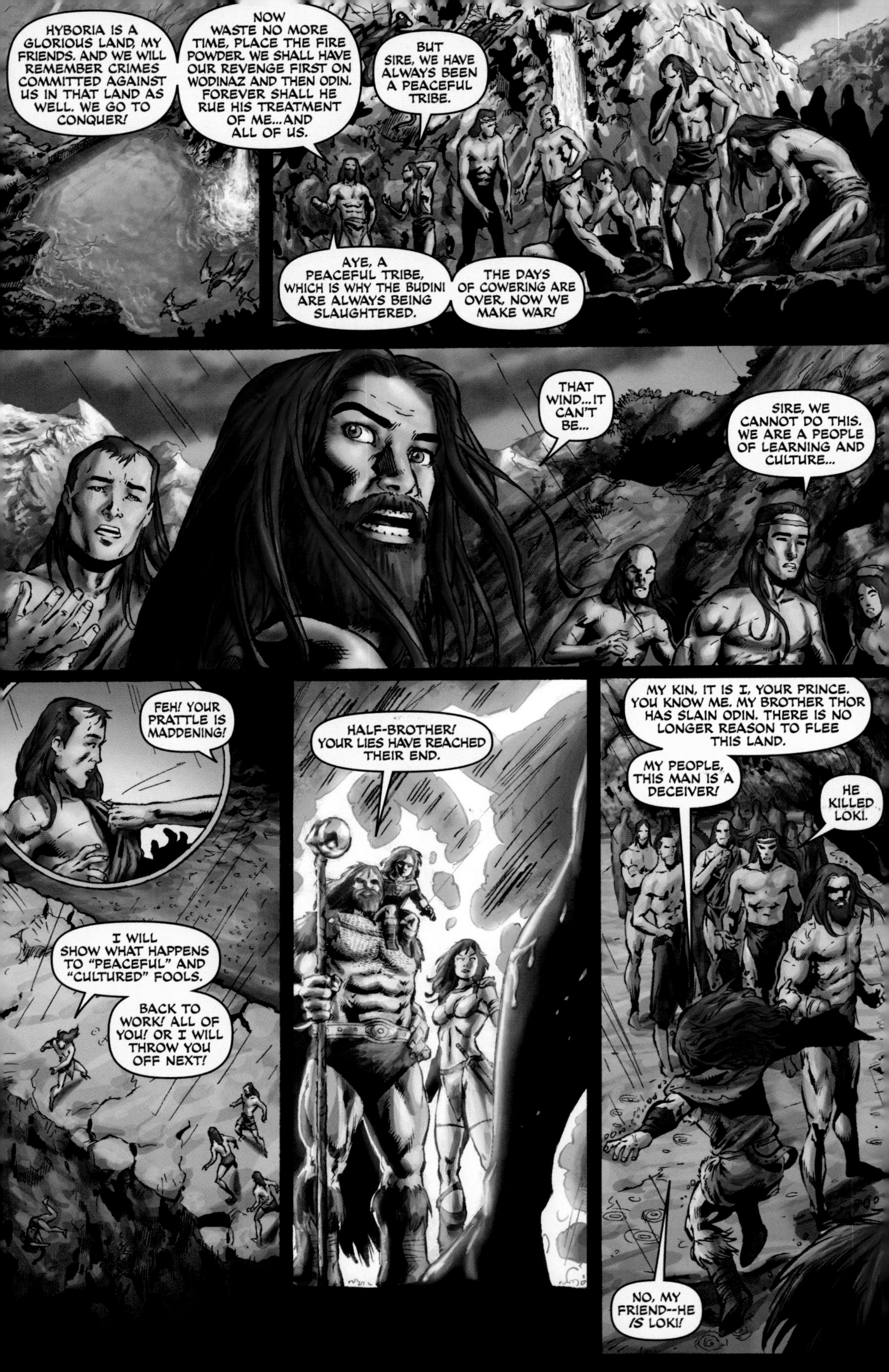
HYBORIA IS A GLORIOUS LAND, MY FRIENDS. AND WE WILL REMEMBER CRIMES COMMITTED AGAINST US IN THAT LAND AS WELL. WE GO TO CONQUER!
NOW WASTE NO MORE TIME, PLACE THE FIRE POWDER. WE SHALL HAVE OUR REVENGE FIRST ON WODINAZ AND THEN ODIN. FOREVER SHALL HE RUE HIS TREATMENT OF ME...AND ALL OF US.
BUT SIRE, WE HAVE ALWAYS BEEN A PEACEFUL TRIBE.
AYE, A PEACEFUL TRIBE, WHICH IS WHY THE BUDINI ARE ALWAYS BEING SLAUGHTERED.
THE DAYS OF COWERING ARE OVER, NOW WE MAKE WAR!
THAT WIND...IT CAN'T BE...
SIRE, WE CANNOT DO THIS. WE ARE A PEOPLE OF LEARNING AND CULTURE...
FEH! YOUR PRATTLE IS MADDENING!
I WILL SHOW WHAT HAPPENS TO "PEACEFUL" AND "CULTURED" FOOLS.
BACK TO WORK! ALL OF YOU! OR I WILL THROW YOU OFF NEXT!
HALF-BROTHER! YOUR LIES HAVE REACHED THEIR END.
MY KIN, IT IS I, YOUR PRINCE. YOU KNOW ME. MY BROTHER THOR HAS SLAIN ODIN. THERE IS NO LONGER REASON TO FLEE THIS LAND.
MY PEOPLE, THIS MAN IS A DECEIVER!
HE KILLED LOKI.
NO, MY FRIEND--HE *IS* LOKI!

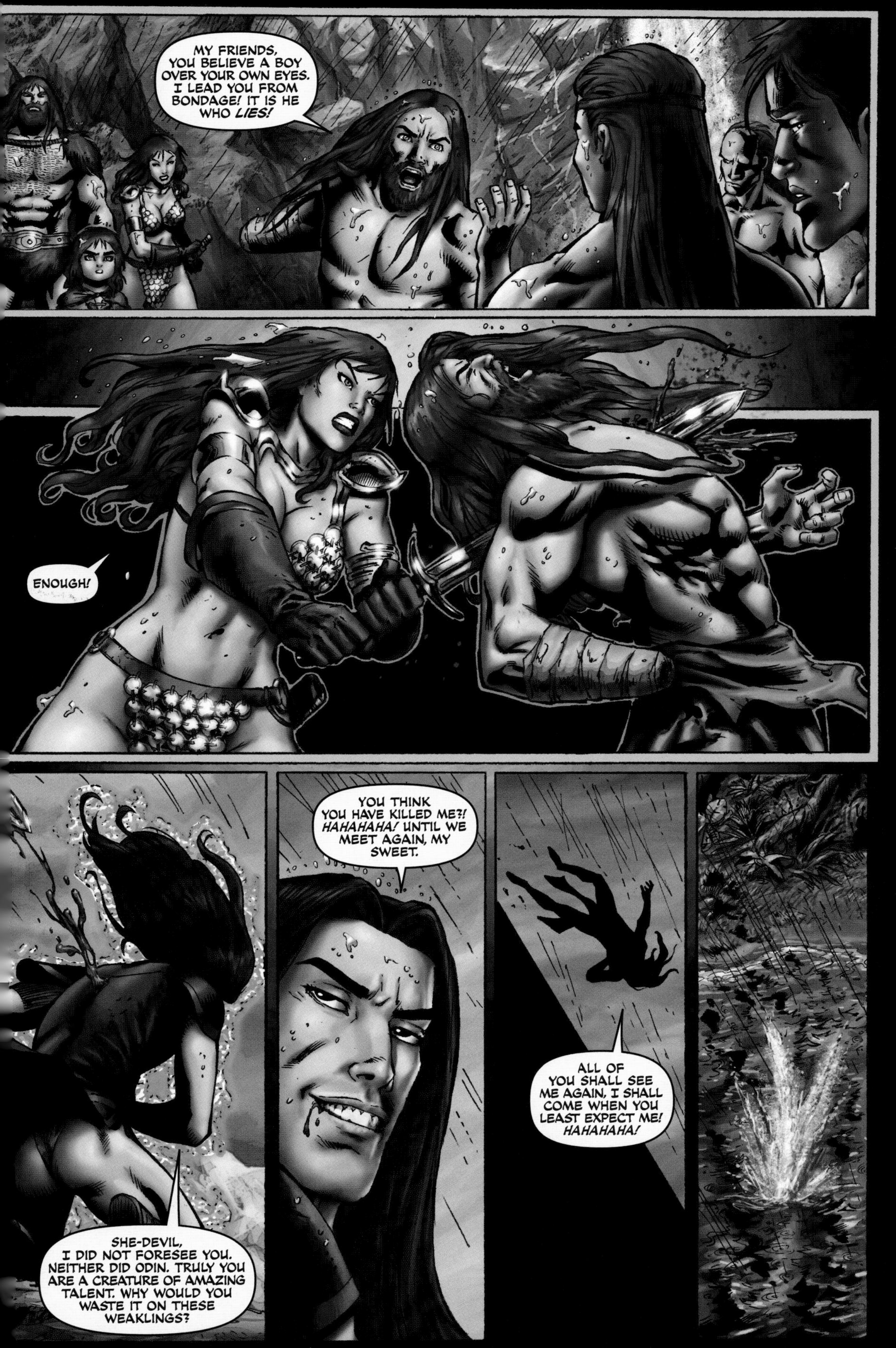
MY FRIENDS, YOU BELIEVE A BOY OVER YOUR OWN EYES. I LEAD YOU FROM BONDAGE! IT IS HE WHO *LIES!*
ENOUGH!
SHE-DEVIL, I DID NOT FORESEE YOU. NEITHER DID ODIN. TRULY YOU ARE A CREATURE OF AMAZING TALENT. WHY WOULD YOU WASTE IT ON THESE WEAKLINGS?
YOU THINK YOU HAVE KILLED ME?! *HAHAHAHA!* UNTIL WE MEET AGAIN, MY SWEET.
ALL OF YOU SHALL SEE ME AGAIN, I SHALL COME WHEN YOU LEAST EXPECT ME! *HAHAHAHA!*

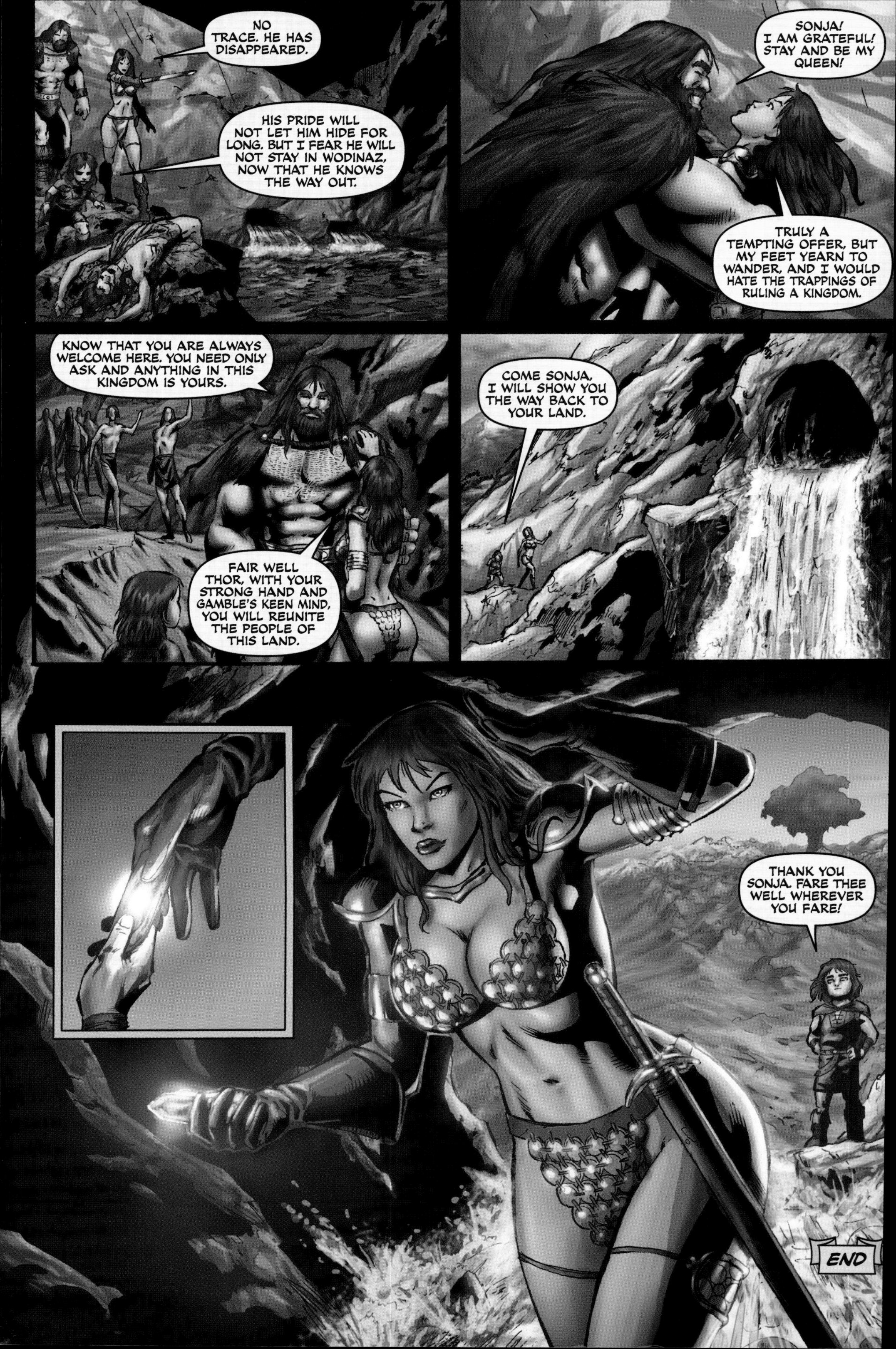
NO TRACE. HE HAS DISAPPEARED.
HIS PRIDE WILL NOT LET HIM HIDE FOR LONG. BUT I FEAR HE WILL NOT STAY IN WODINAZ, NOW THAT HE KNOWS THE WAY OUT.
SONJA! I AM GRATEFUL! STAY AND BE MY QUEEN!
TRULY A TEMPTING OFFER, BUT MY FEET YEARN TO WANDER, AND I WOULD HATE THE TRAPPINGS OF RULING A KINGDOM.
KNOW THAT YOU ARE ALWAYS WELCOME HERE. YOU NEED ONLY ASK AND ANYTHING IN THIS KINGDOM IS YOURS.
FAIR WELL THOR, WITH YOUR STRONG HAND AND GAMBLE'S KEEN MIND, YOU WILL REUNITE THE PEOPLE OF THIS LAND.
COME SONJA, I WILL SHOW YOU THE WAY BACK TO YOUR LAND.
THANK YOU SONJA. FARE THEE WELL WHEREVER YOU FARE!
END

CHARACTER DESIGNS BY WALTER GEOVANI

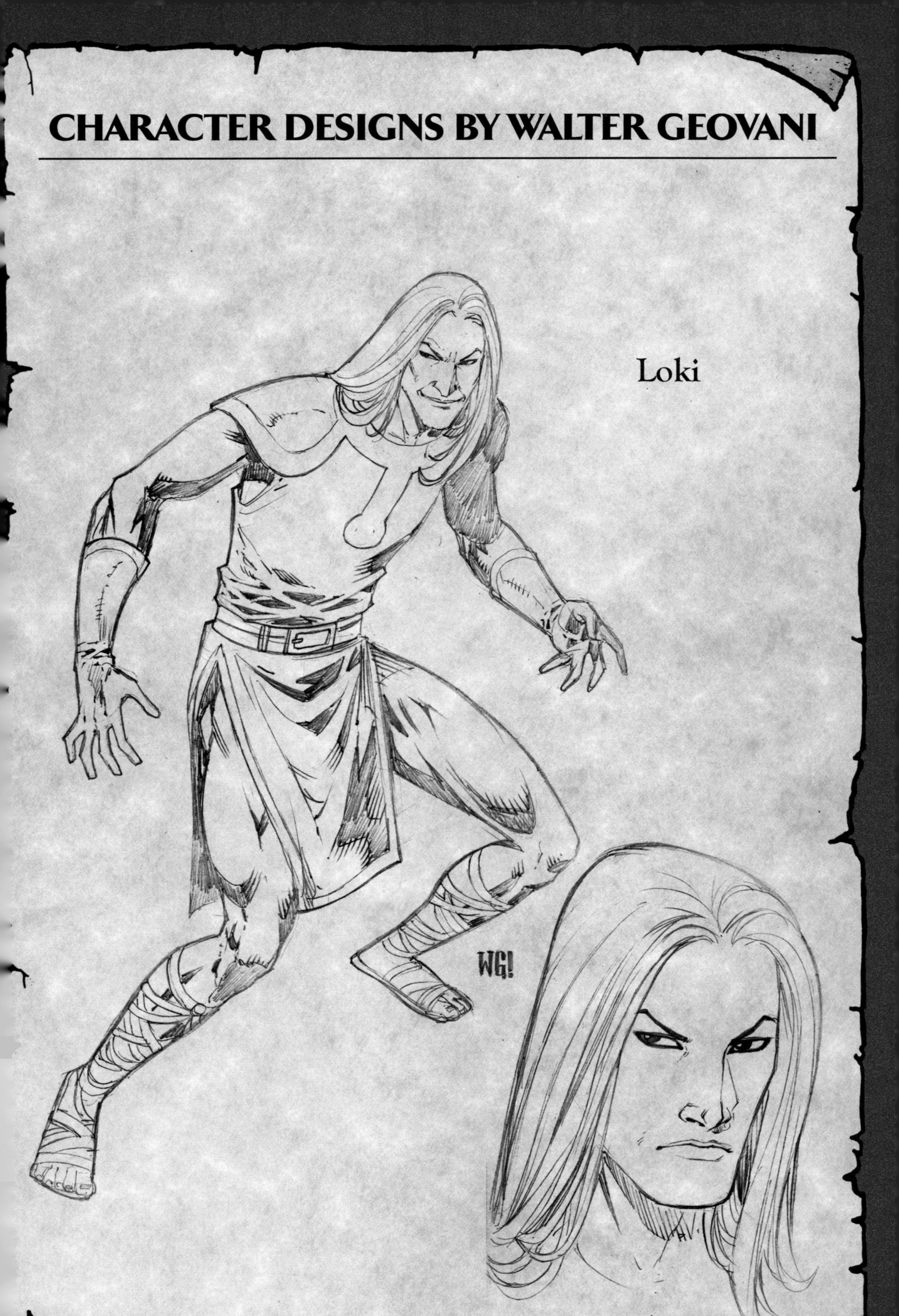
WG!

Loki

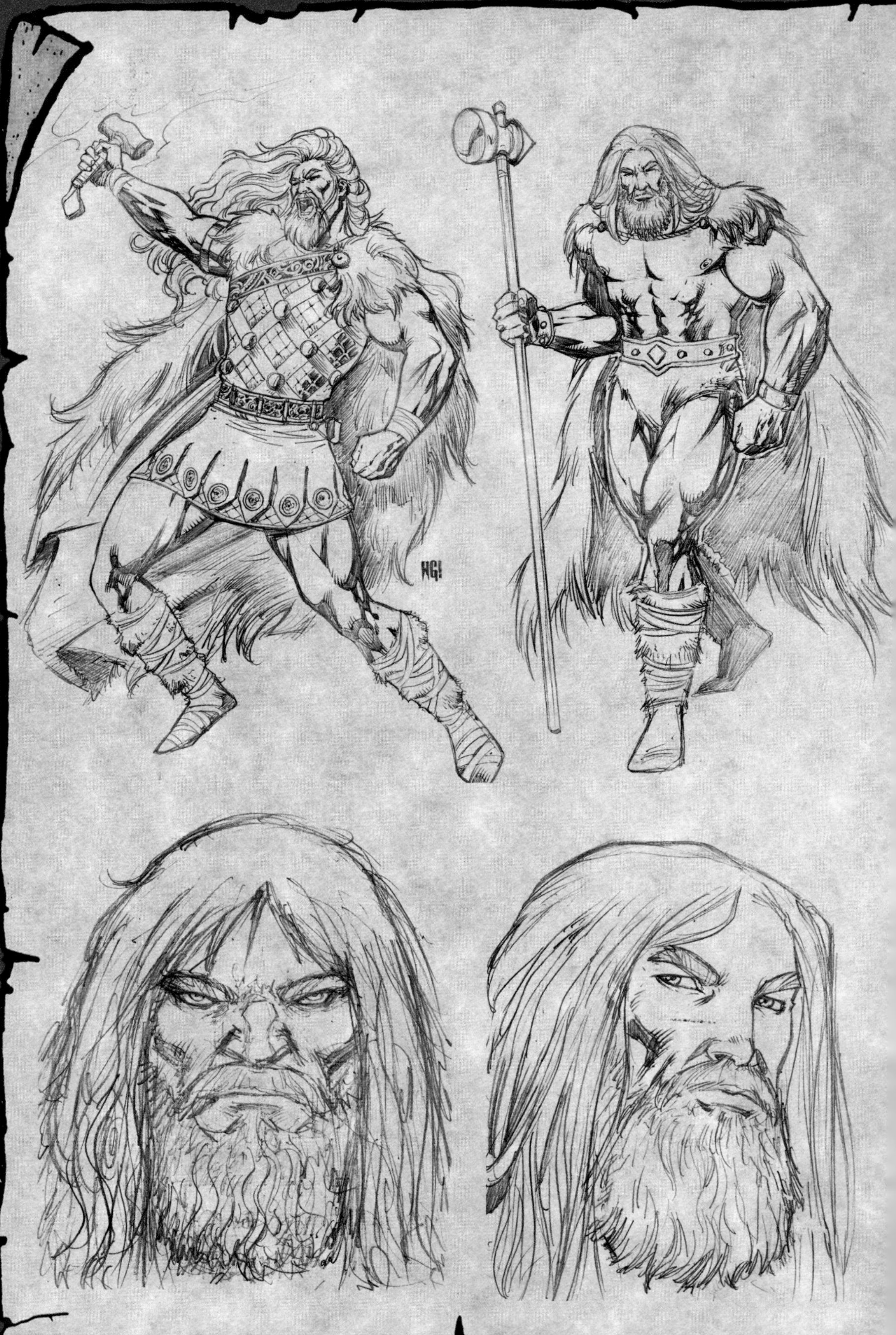

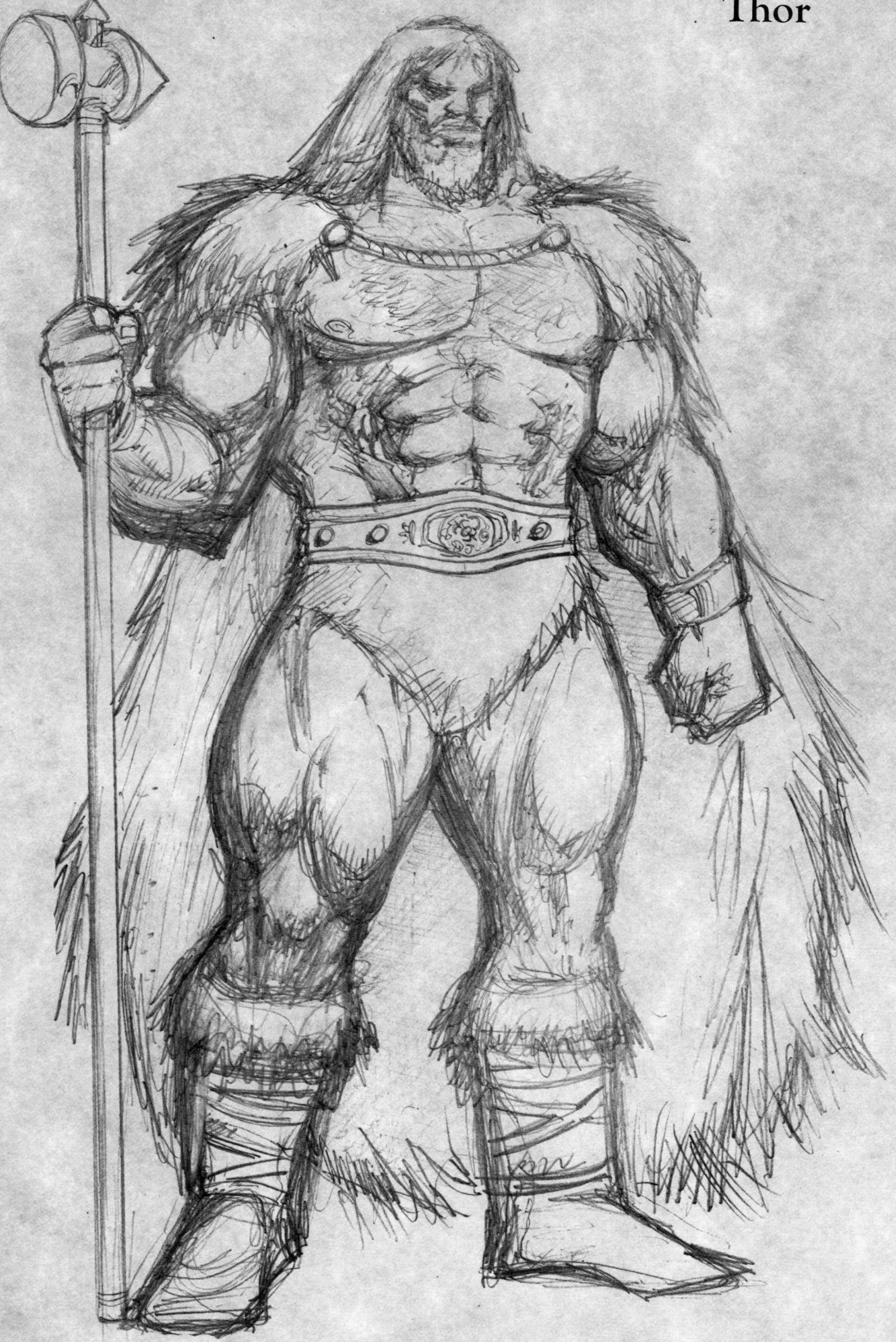
Thor

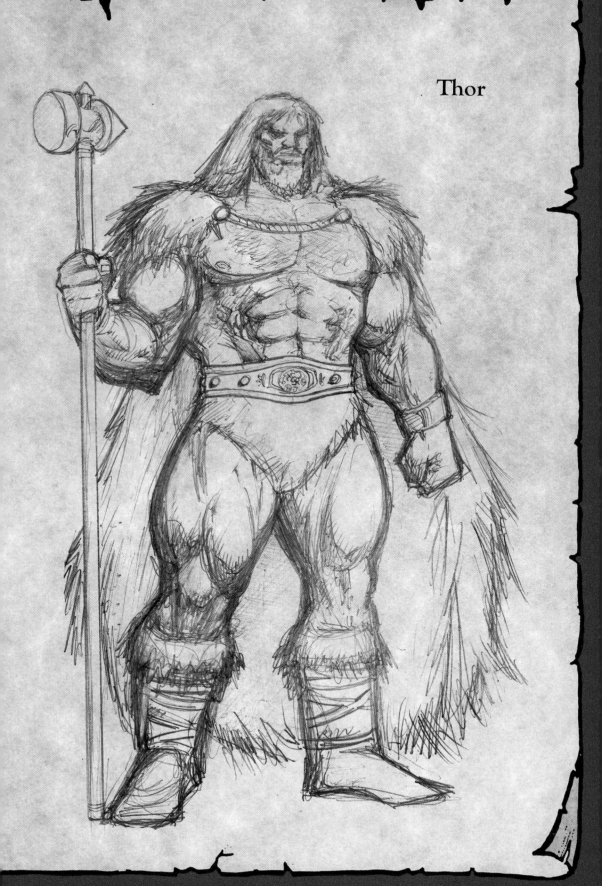

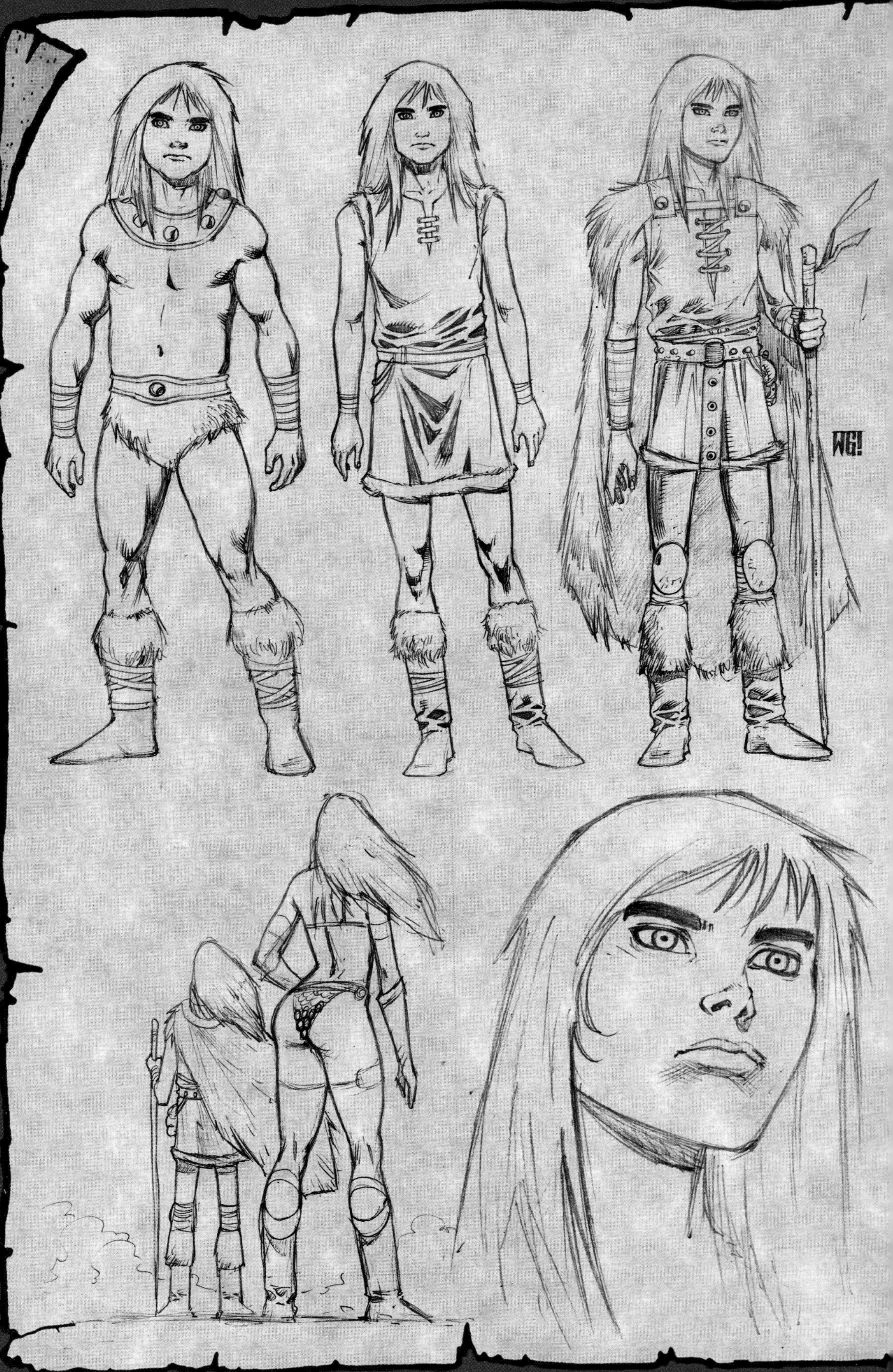
WG!

Gamble

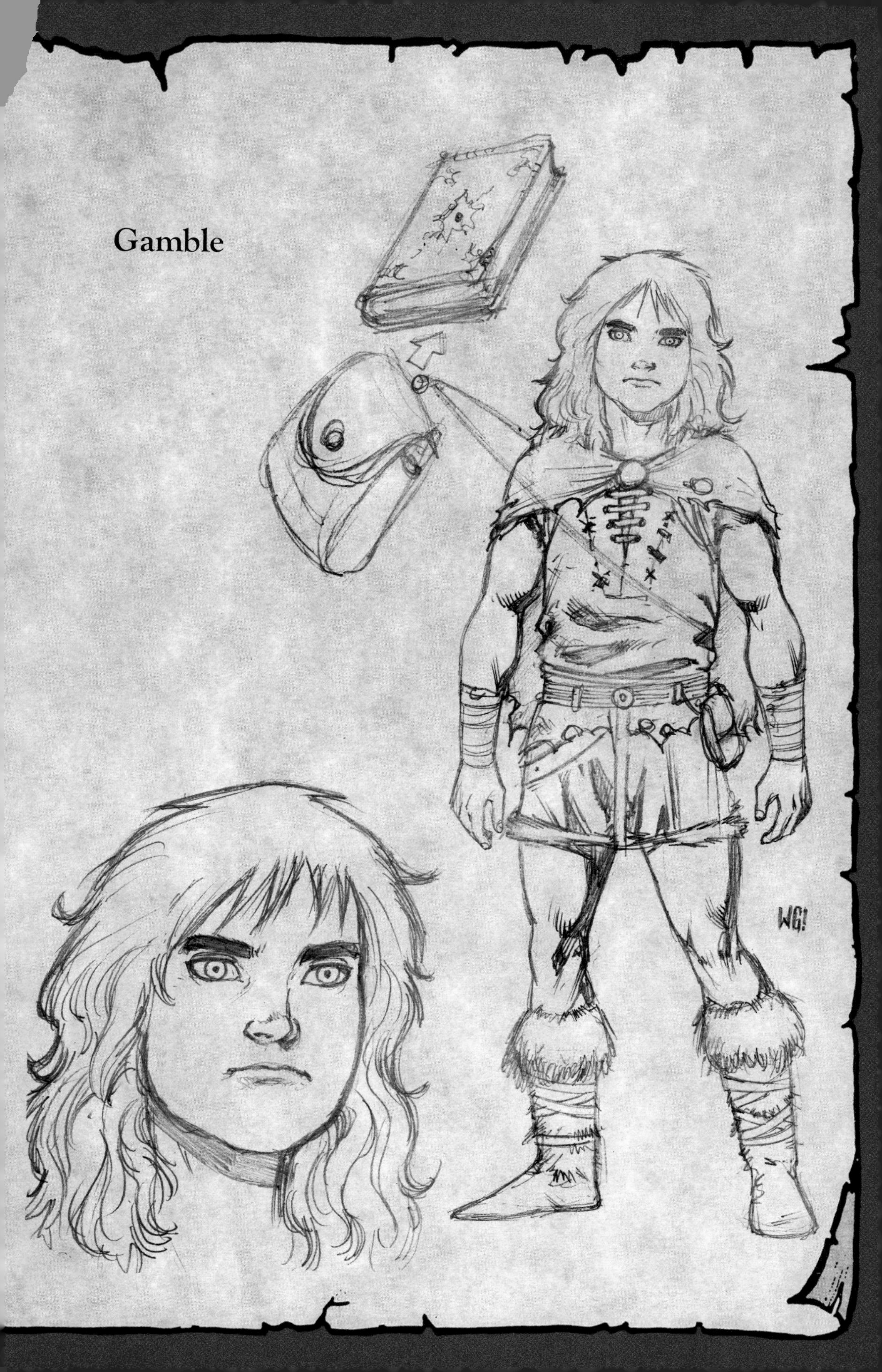
WG!

Odin

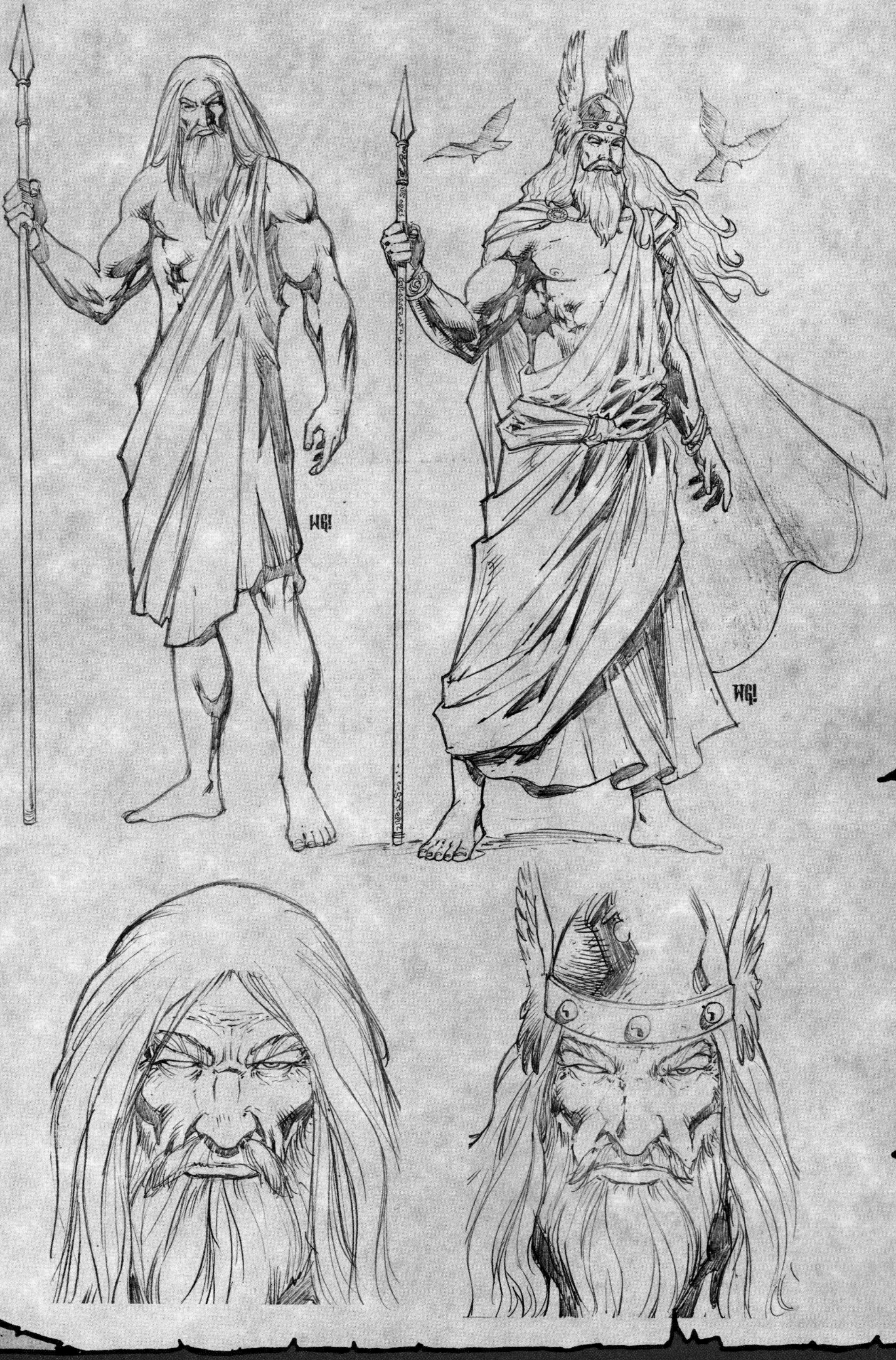

WG!
WG!